SEXUAL FLUIDITY

SEXUAL FLUIDITY

Understanding Women's
Love and Desire

LISA M. DIAMOND

Harvard University Press
Cambridge, Massachusetts
London, England
2008

Library of Congress Cataloging-in-Publication Data

Diamond, Lisa M. (Lisa Michelle)
Sexual fluidity : understanding women's
love and desire / Lisa M. Diamond.
p.   cm.
Includes bibliographical references and index.
ISBN-13: 978-0-674-02624-7 (alk. paper)
ISBN-10: 0-674-02624-1 (alk. paper)
1. Women—Sexual behavior.   2. Bisexuality.   I. Title.
HQ29.D523   2008
306.76′5082—dc22   2007027806

*This book is dedicated to
the 100 women who have so
generously shared their
stories with me.*

Contents

SEXUAL FLUIDITY

Will the Real Lesbians
Please Stand Up?

In 1997, the actress Anne Heche began a widely publicized romantic relationship with the openly lesbian comedian Ellen DeGeneres after having had no prior same-sex attractions or relationships. The relationship with DeGeneres ended after two years, and Heche went on to marry a man. The actress Cynthia Nixon of the HBO series *Sex and the City* developed a serious relationship with a woman in 2004 after ending a fifteen-year relationship with a man. Julie Cypher left a heterosexual marriage for the musician Melissa Etheridge in 1988. After twelve years together, the pair separated and Cypher—like Heche—has returned to heterosexual relationships. In other cases, longtime lesbians have unexpectedly initiated relationships with men, sometimes after decades of exclusively same-sex ties (examples include the feminist folk singer Holly Near, the activist and writer Jan Clausen, and Deborah Sundahl, a founding editor of the lesbian magazine *On Our Backs*). What's going on? Are these women confused? Were they just going through a phase before, or are they in one now?

Consider, too, the growing number of popular terms that have been coined to describe women with changing patterns of same-sex and other-sex behavior, such as "heteroflexibility," "has-bian," and "LUG—lesbian until graduation."[1] This new lexicon has been matched by increasing media depictions of women who pursue sexual contact that runs counter to their avowed sexual orientation, ranging from the much-ballyhooed kiss between Madonna and Britney Spears at the MTV Video Music Awards to films such as *Kissing Jessica Stein* and *Chasing Amy*, which depicts a lesbian becoming involved with a man, contrary to the more widespread depictions of heterosexual women becoming involved in same-sex relationships.

The reason such cases are so perplexing is that they flatly contradict prevailing assumptions about sexual orientation. These assumptions hold that an individual's sexual predisposition for the same sex or the other sex is an early-developing and stable trait that has a consistent effect on that person's attractions, fantasies, and romantic feelings over the lifespan. What few people realize, however, is that these assumptions are based primarily on men's experiences because most research on sexual orientation has been conducted on men.[2] Although this model of sexual orientation describes men fairly accurately, it does not always apply so well to women.

Historically, women who deviated from this model by reporting shifts in their sexuality over time—heterosexual women falling in love with female friends, lesbian women periodically dating men— were presumed few in number and exceptional in nature. In other words, they were just inconvenient noise cluttering up the real data on sexual orientation. Yet as research on female sexuality has increased over the years, these "exceptional" cases now appear to be more common than previously thought. In short, the current conventional wisdom about the nature and development of sexual orientation provides an incomplete picture of women's experiences. Researchers now openly acknowledge that despite significant advances in the science of sexuality over the past twenty years, "female sexual orientation is, for the time being, poorly understood."[3]

This situation is now changing. As scientists have begun investigating female and male sexual orientation as distinct phenomena instead of two sides of the same coin, consensus is gradually building on why women appear so different from men. Specifically, we have found that one of the fundamental, defining features of female sexual orientation is its *fluidity*. We are now on the brink of a revolutionary new understanding of female sexuality that has profound scientific and social implications.

A Brief History of Fluidity

Sexual fluidity, quite simply, means situation-dependent flexibility in women's sexual responsiveness. This flexibility makes it possible for some women to experience desires for either men or women under certain circumstances, regardless of their overall sexual orientation. In other words, though women—like men—appear to be born with distinct sexual orientations, these orientations do not provide the last word on their sexual attractions and experiences. Instead, women of all orientations may experience variation in their erotic and affectional feelings as they encounter different situations, relationships, and life stages. This is why a woman like Anne Heche can suddenly find herself falling madly in love with Ellen DeGeneres after an exclusively heterosexual past, and why a longtime lesbian can experience her very first other-sex attractions in her late forties.

The notion of sexual fluidity is not a new one. Rather, evidence for this phenomenon has circulated in the scientific literature for decades, though it has tended to be "submerged in the data rather than explicitly theorized."[4] Some of the earliest discussions of flexible, changeable patterns of sexuality came from sex researchers who kept finding perplexing cases of same-sex sexuality "in some unexpected places and among some apparently heterosexual people."[5] For example, in 1977 the psychologists Erich Goode and Lynn Haber published a study analyzing "experimental" same-sex behavior pursued by college women who identified themselves as heterosexual.[6] They concluded that though some of these women appeared to be headed toward lesbianism, others simply seemed to be adventurous and open-minded about their sexuality. Similarly, in the late 1970s the sociologists Philip Blumstein and Pepper Schwartz conducted a groundbreaking study of more than 150 men and women with bisexual patterns of sexual behavior. They found that though some of their respondents had experienced same-sex desires for many years, others appeared to have undergone major changes in their sexual attractions.[7] They concluded that early childhood influences on sexuality (whatever they may be) were not immutable, and that most individuals were unaware of their own capacity for change in sexuality over time.

In interviews with fourteen nonheterosexual women, the psychologist Joan Sophie found that many of the women experienced unexpected transitions in their self-identification and sexual expression over time. Sophie concluded that conventional identity models, with their emphasis on fixed selves, needed to be revised to account for such changes.[8] Fritz Klein, Barry Sepekoff, and Timothy Wolf eventually took up the call and developed a new approach to measuring sexual orientation (the Klein Sexual Orientation Grid, or KSOG), which for the first time considered the element of time.[9] Individuals rated their current, past, and "ideal" patterns of attraction, behavior, and identity, making explicit the existence of prior and perhaps future change. However, this time-sensitive approach did not take hold, and researchers generally continued assessing only current attractions, identities, and behaviors.

Around the same time, other academic fields began giving greater consideration to sexual fluidity. In 1984 the anthropologist Gilbert Herdt published a now-famous account of ritualized homosexuality among adolescent boys in Melanesia.[10] What was notable about this practice was its developmental specificity. Unmarried men pursued only same-sex encounters during their adolescent years out of a belief that this practice was necessary for them to reach full maturity as men. Once they were adults, same-sex activity ceased (with a few exceptions); they then married and pursued only other-sex activity. Herdt's account of such an abrupt developmental transition from same-sex to other-sex sexuality showed that our Western notion of fixed sexual "orientations" was culturally specific. We might view homosexuality as an inborn predisposition, but other cultures expected and even arranged for drastic changes in same-sex and other-sex desires and practices over the life course.

The anthropologist Evelyn Blackwood made the same observation in her extensive review of female same-sex sexuality across non-Western cultures, underscoring the limitations of the Western notion of fixed sexual orientations. These perspectives were consistent with a broad class of social constructionist models of sexuality (discussed in more detail in the next chapter), which posited that sexual identities did not exist as fixed types but were created and given meaning through social interactions and cultural ideologies.[11] Most of the scholars advocating this perspective were not specifically interested in sexual fluidity, but they highlighted the evidence for it in order to challenge conventional, biologically determinist views of sexuality.

The poet Adrienne Rich was one of the first people to discuss fluidity's specific relevance to female sexuality, and she took one of the broadest and most explicitly political perspectives on the issue.[12] Rich argued that women throughout history and across a variety of different cultures had always managed to form intimate, emotionally primary ties to other women, despite the persistent efforts of male-dominated societies to rigidly channel them into heterosexual reproduction. Rich argued that all intense bonds between women, even if they were not explicitly sexual, occupied a "lesbian continuum" that ranged from purely emotional relationships to sexual liaisons. This model suggested that regardless of whether a woman currently experienced clear-cut same-sex desires, she maintained a capacity for diverse forms of same-sex intimacy and eroticism.

In the 1980s, the empirical evidence for sexual fluidity and its disproportionate prevalence in women increased. For example, in their study of gay, lesbian, bisexual, and heterosexual people living in San Francisco in the 1980s, Martin Weinberg, Colin Williams, and Douglas Pryor found that many of their participants—but especially the women—recalled experiencing both minor and major changes over time in their sexual attractions. This finding led the researchers to conclude that "sexual preference is not always a fixed phenomenon." Although gay, lesbian, and heterosexual people reported smaller and less frequent changes than did bisexuals, Weinberg and his colleagues attributed this difference to the anchoring effects of claiming a gay, lesbian, or heterosexual identity, since such identities have "definable boundaries that can restrict the ability or desire to explore change."[13] They came to the conclusion that some degree of fluidity was a general property of sexuality, a view that already had a steady group of adherents at that time, and which continues to be influential.[14] Although Weinberg, Williams, and Pryor observed more sizable and frequent changes among their female respondents, they did not advance an explanation for this difference, except to speculate that it might have to do with the women's involvement with lesbian and feminist groups, which often encouraged women to question their sexual identities.

The psychologist Carla Golden provided some of the most compelling discussions to date of diversity and variability in female sexuality in her interview study of heterosexual, bisexual, and lesbian women in their twenties, thirties, and forties.[15] She specifically analyzed the contexts that elicited sexual transitions, for example, political organizations and women's studies classes. Golden argued against the notion that such experiences simply prompted women to "discover" long-suppressed same-sex orientations. Rather, she argued that in some cases, same-sex sexuality "may have started as an idea but it did not remain purely in the cognitive realm." In other words, women were capable of real change occurring in real time.[16]

As for the causes underlying such changes, the psychologists Celia Kitzinger and Sue Wilkinson emphasized sociocultural influences and opportunities. They interviewed women who undertook abrupt transitions from heterosexuality to lesbianism in mid- to late adulthood, and concluded that such women "are no more driven by biology or subconscious urges than they are when, for instance, they change jobs; such choices could be viewed as influenced by a mixture of personal reevaluation, practical necessity, political values, chance, and opportunity."[17] The sociologist Paula Rust also emphasized complex interactions between personal and cultural factors that led some women to adopt different sexual identities and different practices at different times of life, depending on their circumstances.[18]

The role of intimate emotional relationships as a catalyst for change in women's sexuality was also gaining attention. The psychologist Rebecca Shuster, for example, noted that "often women fall in love with someone of an unexpected gender, and the power of that relationship pulls them to re-evaluate their identity." She argued that such experiences "uncover a range of sexual and emotional attraction and closeness of infinite variety" and pose an inevitable challenge to the notion of fixed sexual identities.[19] The psychologist Vivian Cass made similar observations, noting that same-sex emotional ties were particularly influential for women: "It is not uncommon to see a woman who in mid-life 'falls in love' with another woman for the first time in her life. This experience may not necessarily include sexual responses, although the quality of the emotional experience is similar to other love relationships she may have had with men. Where a sexual component does become present, this may occur after a period of time or after the emotional responses have been reciprocated."[20] Other researchers had begun to wrestle with these apparent gender differences. The sociologist Vera Whisman conducted a comparison of lesbians' and gay men's personal understandings of the causes of their same-sex sexuality. She found that men were significantly more likely to view their sexuality as fixed and innate, whereas women more often acknowledged a role for specific relationships, choice, change, and circumstance.[21]

Current Perspectives

The psychologist Roy Baumeister was the first researcher to synthesize these accumulating strands of evidence into a comprehensive argument for female sexual variability.[22] Several years ago he published a review of the extensive psychological, historical, and sociological evidence suggesting that women's sexuality is more "plastic" than men's. His notion of "plasticity" includes not just same-sex and other-sex sexuality but also overall sex drive, desired partner characteristics, preferred sexual practices, and consistency between attitudes and behaviors. His work provides critical support for the notion of a robust gender difference in women's capacity for sexual variability. Note that I use the term "sexual fluidity" to distinguish flexibility in same-sex and other-sex sexuality, which is the topic of this book, from the broader forms of variability in sexual attitudes and practices discussed by Baumeister.

New research has provided even more support for the notion of gender differences. One study (described in detail in Chapter 4) found that both lesbian and heterosexual women became physically aroused by visual images of both men and women. In contrast, men's responses fell in line with their self-described sexual orientations.[23] That said, genital responses should not be considered more accurate measures of desire than individuals' own subjective experiences (in fact, interpretation of genital arousal in such studies has long been controversial). But such findings certainly dovetail with the extensive evidence suggesting a pervasive gender difference in erotic variability and flexibility.

Not all sex researchers agree with this view. Some have argued strongly against the notion of a gender difference in fluidity, maintaining that women's apparently greater sexual variability might be due to social and cultural factors.[24] Blumstein and Schwartz, for example, echoing a widely held view, argued that "there are few absolute differences between male and female sexuality. What differences we observed are primarily the result of the different social organization of women's and men's lives in various cultural contexts."[25] Other researchers have similarly argued that the appearance of a distinctively female capacity for fluidity might simply be an artifact of female sexual socialization. For example, the social and cultural forces that have long controlled and suppressed female sexuality[26] may have left women with blunted awareness of their own sexual feelings and identities and few opportunities to express and experiment with those feelings.[27] In this case, women's sexual variability might simply be a manifestation of sexual repression; apparent changes in sexual feelings and behaviors might simply stem from changes in women's awareness of their "true" sexual nature.

Cultural assumptions and expectations about female versus male sexuality certainly contribute to gender differences in fluidity. However, such differences are not wholly cultural; nor is women's variability largely an artifact of denial and sexual repression. Although this is certainly the case for some women, it is unlikely to account for the full range of findings reviewed above. It is also inconsistent with many first-person accounts from women undergoing sexual transformation, including the accounts of the young women in this book.[28]

Something more is going on. The hypothesis that female sexuality is fundamentally fluid provides the most robust, comprehensive, and scientifically supported explanation for the research data. Yet this notion has not yet entered popular consciousness. Despite the increased visibility of incidents like the Madonna-Britney kiss, most people continue to view such cases as exceptional, and to hold fairly rigid views about the nature of sexuality and sexual orientation more generally. I hope to change this thinking.

This book is based on findings from my longitudinal research study on female sexuality. For the past ten years, I have been following a group of nearly one hundred young women whom I have interviewed every two years, as they have moved through different patterns of attraction, behavior, and sexual identification from adolescence to adulthood.[29] My study is the first to follow young women's sexual transitions over an extended period of time, and thus it provides an unprecedented glimpse into how women experience the changes brought about by sexual fluidity while such changes are under way, and not as they are sketchily remembered years later. These women's experiences, recounted in their own words throughout this book, provide powerful testimony to the potentially transforming effect of sexual fluidity on women's lives.

I am well aware that the notion of sexual fluidity is potentially controversial and susceptible to politically motivated distortions.[30] For that reason, I would like to address some of the most common misconceptions at the outset:

Does fluidity mean that all women are bisexual? No. Just as women have different sexual orientations, they have different degrees of sexual fluidity. Some women will experience relatively stable patterns of love and desire throughout their lives, while others will not. Currently, we simply do not know how many women fall into each group because a number of different factors determine whether a woman's capacity for sexual fluidity will actually manifest itself.

Does fluidity mean that there is no such thing as sexual orientation? No. Fluidity can be thought of as an additional component of a woman's sexuality that operates in concert with sexual orientation to influence how her attractions, fantasies, behaviors, and affections are experienced and expressed over the life course. Fluidity implies not that women's desires are *endlessly* variable but that some women are capable of a wider variety of erotic feelings and experiences than would be predicted on the basis of their self-described sexual orientation alone.

Does sexual fluidity mean that sexual orientation can be

changed? No. It simply means that a woman's sexual orientation is not the only factor determining her attractions. A predominantly heterosexual woman might, at some point in time, become attracted to a woman, just as a predominantly lesbian woman might at some point become attracted to a man. Despite these experiences, the women's overall orientation remains the same.

Does fluidity mean that sexual orientation is a matter of choice? No. Even when women undergo significant shifts in their patterns of erotic response, they typically report that such changes are unexpected and beyond their control. In some cases they actively resist these changes, to no avail. This finding is consistent with the extensive evidence (reviewed in Chapter 8) showing that efforts to change sexual orientation through "reparative therapy" simply do not work.[31]

Does fluidity mean that sexual orientation is due to "nurture" instead of "nature"? No. In fact, sexual fluidity sheds no light on this question, since it deals with the expression of same-sex and other-sex attractions rather than with their causes. Questions of causation typically receive the most debate and attention, but questions about expression are equally important. Nonetheless, fluidity raises important questions about how we think about biological versus cultural influences on sexuality, and it highlights the need for more integrative models.

Couldn't all individuals be characterized as fluid? Perhaps, though women appear to be more fluid than men. Certainly, few researchers would argue that sexual orientation is the sole factor determining each and every instance of sexual desire and behavior. Human sexual responses have been shown to be somewhat flexible, and thus *any* individual should be capable of experiencing desires that run counter to his or her overall sexual orientation.[32] For example, many men from different cultures and times have been shown to periodically pursue sexual behaviors that are atypical of their overall pattern of desire.[33] But in general, the degree of fluidity in women appears substantially greater than in men, though we do not yet have enough data to fully evaluate this possibility. More rigorous investigation of fluidity in male sexuality is beyond the scope of this book, but it has begun to receive some attention and will likely be a fascinating area of future research.[34]

Key Terms and Concepts

In this book I use the term "sexual orientation" to mean a consistent, enduring pattern of sexual desire for individuals of the same sex, the other sex, or both sexes, regardless of whether this pattern of desire is manifested in sexual behavior. A woman can have a lesbian orientation but never have a same-sex relationship, just as she can have a heterosexual orientation and still pursue multiple same-sex affairs. Most scientists consider desire, not behavior, the marker of sexual orientation. "Sexual identity" refers to a culturally organized conception of the self, usually "lesbian/gay," "bisexual," or "heterosexual." As with sexual orientation, we cannot presume that these identities correspond to particular patterns of behavior. Nor can we presume that they correspond to particular patterns of desire. Because sexual identities represent self-concepts, they depend on individuals' own notions about the most important aspects of their sexual selves. These notions, as we will see, can vary quite a bit from individual to individual. Moreover, some people—particularly women—reject conventional lesbian/gay/bisexual identity labels in favor of alternative labels such as "queer," "questioning," or "pansexual." Others reject all identity labels in order to make room for a broad range of sexual possibilities, as well as to acknowledge the fact that all labels are somewhat arbitrary.[35] I devote substantial attention to this issue later in the book, as it is directly related to the phenomenon of fluidity.

Global terms like "homosexuality" or "lesbianism" imply that same-sex desires, behaviors, and identities cluster together as part of an overall syndrome. But again, this is not always true. For this reason I find such terms to be potentially misleading. Instead, I use the term "same-sex sexuality" to refer to all experiences of same-sex desire, romantic affection, fantasy, or behavior. A person might experience one and only one form of same-sex sexuality (like same-sex attractions), or perhaps several (such as same-sex attraction and a lesbian identity), but I do not assume that any of these experiences necessarily cluster together. Correspondingly, I use the term "other-sex sexuality" to refer to all aspects of other-sex desire, romantic affection, fantasy, or behavior (readers will be more familiar with the phrase "opposite-sex," but researchers have increasingly gravitated toward "other-sex" because it is more scientifically accurate. The two sexes are certainly different from each other, but they are by no means opposites).

Terms like "lesbian" and "bisexual" are also problematic. Do they refer to an individual's sexual orientation, sexual identity, or sexual behavior? To avoid confusion, I always pair these terms with the words "orientation" and "identity." Hence a "lesbian sexual orientation" can be taken to mean a pattern of near-exclusive desire for the same sex, even if a woman does not call herself a lesbian. A "lesbian sexual identity," in contrast, refers to a woman's self-description and self-presentation. Thus she might have a bisexual orientation but a lesbian identity (or vice versa).

When referring to desires and behavior, I use the descriptors "same-sex" and "other-sex." I refer to attractions and behaviors pursued with both sexes (either concurrently or sequentially) as "nonexclusive." If being 100 percent attracted to one sex means that you are *exclusively* attracted, then all other patterns of attraction are *nonexclusive*. I use this term rather than "bisexual," which has a wide range of different definitions across cultures and communities, making it potentially confusing. Of course, "nonexclusive" comes with its own problems. Because the term "exclusive" is often used to describe monogamous sexual relationships, "nonexclusivity" could be misinterpreted as sexual infidelity. This is *not* what I mean! I use "nonexclusive" simply to refer to the capacity to experience both same-sex and other-sex desires and behaviors, though not necessarily at the same point in time. Someone with nonexclusive attractions might have experienced only other-sex attractions up until adolescence, and then only same-sex attractions thereafter. Someone else might experience desires for both women and men concurrently. All that matters is that for that person, both types of desire are possible, in contrast to someone who has always been exclusively attracted to one sex or the other.

Finally, when speaking in the most general sense about individuals who have any experience with same-sex sexuality, at the level of orientation, desire, behavior, or identity, I use the term "sexual-minority." This term captures the fact that regardless of a person's identity or orientation, any experience with same-sex sexuality—from fantasy to unrequited love to sexual behavior—violates societal norms prescribing exclusive heterosexuality, thereby making that person a sexual minority.

Why It Matters

The writer Minnie Bruce Pratt, reflecting on the confusion she experienced when she first discovered her capacity for same-sex sexuality, recalled being aware that such an abrupt change seemed impossible and incongruous:

> I didn't feel "different," but was I? (From whom?) Had I changed? (From what?) Was I heterosexual in adolescence only to become lesbian in my late twenties? Was I lesbian always but coerced into heterosexuality? Was I a less authentic lesbian than my friends who had "always known" that they were sexually and affectionally attracted to other women? What kind of woman was a lesbian woman?[36]

Pratt perfectly captures the conundrum created by sexual fluidity. Because our culture believes that all individuals are, unequivocally, one sexual type or the other (such that a lesbian must have "always known" of her essential lesbian nature), women with more complex and variable patterns of sexual experience are inherently suspect. No wonder Pratt felt "inauthentic" when comparing herself with the cultural prototype of lesbianism as uniformly stable, early-developing, and exclusive.

Yet it is this rigid prototype that is inauthentic, not experiences like Pratt's. Greater appreciation and awareness of sexual fluidity are critical not only for building more accurate models of sexuality but also for communicating to women—young and old, lesbian and heterosexual, married and single—that flexible, changing patterns of sexual response are normal rather than deviant, and that they can occur in any woman at any stage of life. This information needs to be integrated into the numerous educational and therapeutic programs aimed at providing support and acceptance for individuals coming to grips with their same-sex desires. If such programs cling to rigid models of sexual orientation that inadequately represent the enormous variability in female sexuality, women may end up feeling doubly deviant, their experiences reflecting neither mainstream societal expectations nor perceived norms of "typical" gay experience. We must refashion science and public outreach to better represent women's experiences.

But this brings its own challenges. Almost every time I present my research publicly, someone raises their hand and asks, "Isn't the idea of fluidity dangerous? Couldn't it feed right into antigay arguments that sexual orientation can—and should—be changed?" Let me be clear: fluidity does *not*, in fact, imply that sexual orientation can be intentionally changed. But I know from experience that some people will nonetheless manipulate and misuse the concept of fluidity, despite my best efforts to debunk such distortions. Yet the solution to this danger is not to brush fluidity under the rug and stick to outdated, overly simplistic models of sexuality. Such an approach offers no real protection against political distortion: the truth is that any scientific data on sexual orientation can be—and pretty much have been—appropriated to advance particular world-views. If scientists discovered tomorrow that same-sex sexuality was 100 percent genetically determined, some people would say, "Aha, this proves that homosexuality is normal, natural, and deserving of social acceptance and full legal status!" Others would say, "Aha, this proves that homosexuality is a dangerous genetic disorder that can be screened for, corrected, and eliminated!" In short, there are no "safe" scientific findings—all models of sexuality are dangerous in the present political climate. The only way to guard against the misuse of scientific findings is to present them as accurately and completely as possible, making explicit the conclusions that they do and do not support. This is my goal in this book.

The well-being of all women will be improved through a more accurate, comprehensive understanding of female sexuality in all its diverse and fluid manifestations. In short, women like Anne Heche, Cynthia Nixon, Julie Cypher, and Holly Near are not "noise in the data" on sexual orientation. Rather, they *are* the data with something important to tell us about the nature of female sexuality. Any model of female sexual orientation that fails to account for their experiences is no model at all.

CHAPTER 2

Gender Differences in Same-Sex Sexuality

Scientific inquiry into the nature and development of same-sex sexuality continues to be one of the most fascinating areas of sexuality research.[1] It is also one of the most controversial. Popular discussions in newspapers, books, magazines, and television shows typically frame the issue around the classic "nature versus nurture" question; that is, is sexual orientation preordained at birth, or is it acquired through social-environmental influences (take your pick: poor family relationships, social permissiveness, exposure to same-sex sexuality in the media)? Is it fixed, or can it change? Is it beyond an individual's control, or is it consciously chosen?

These questions are compelling, but they vastly oversimplify the issue. Sexual thought, behavior, and development are governed by a range of interactions between biological and social processes that can be exceedingly hard to disentangle.[2] Neither sensationalized news stories nor activists making political arguments about the social, moral, or legal status of sexual minorities do justice to this complexity.[3]

Gender is another complicated facet of the nature-nurture debate. Arguments about whether "homosexuals" are born versus made do not usually distinguish between women and men, implicitly presuming that the same cause operates for both sexes. Yet this does not appear to be the case. Although scientists continue to disagree about various biological influences on same-sex sexuality, they do agree on one thing: the developmental pathways that operate for men are probably different from those that operate for women.

The psychologist Brian Mustanski and his colleagues went so far as to proclaim that "the male model of sexual orientation has been rejected in women" and that "the challenge of defining sexual orientation in women and understanding how biological influences function in women remains to be adequately addressed."[4] Janet Hyde, a psychologist known for her pioneering investigations of gender differences, concluded in her review of genetic research on sexual orientation that female same-sex sexuality was "undertheorized" and probably required an altogether separate explanatory model. The same conclusion has been reached by numerous other researchers considering the basic nature of same-sex sexuality.[5]

Why are we so far behind in understanding women? Part of the problem is a lack of research. For example, one recent review found that since 1990, roughly twice as many articles have appeared on male sexual orientation as on female sexual orientation.[6] It is interesting to note, however, that early studies investigating biological causes of sexual orientation included both men and women. Over time, it appears, researchers shifted their emphasis to men because the findings for men were so much more consistent and promising than the findings for both sexes considered together.

In this chapter I review the most up-to-date research on the potential origins and development of same-sex sexuality, with an emphasis on gender differences. In the past, discussions of sexual fluidity have been interpreted as "antibiological," as if same-sex sexuality had to be either biological and fixed or nonbiological and fluid. This is a false choice. Fluidity does not necessarily disprove biological influences on sexual orientation; rather, it helps to explain why the biological data regarding women are so inconsistent.

To provide some context for the discussion, I begin by reviewing some of the key philosophical and methodological issues involved in studying the causes and development of sexual orientation: Why are we so preoccupied with these questions? What is at stake? How exactly are such studies conducted, and which individuals do or do not get included? I then review the two most promising areas of biological research on sexual orientation—behavioral genetics and prenatal neuroendocrinology—highlighting the evidence for gender differences. Finally, I conclude by addressing gender differences in psychological and behavioral aspects of the development of same-sex sexuality.

Readers will notice that all the research findings I review in this chapter are mixed. This area of study has yielded no cut-and-dried answers. My hope is that readers end this chapter, not with a clear sense of exactly what sexual orientation is, what causes it, and how it normally develops, but with an awareness that these processes are fundamentally different for women than for men.

Origin Stories: Essentialism versus Social Constructionism

One reason that questions about the origin of sexual orientation are so controversial is that they highlight larger philosophical divides between people with an essentialist perspective on sexuality and those with a social constructionist perspective. Briefly, essentialists view sexual orientation (and sexuality more generally) as based in internal, intrinsic, biological processes. Social constructionists, in contrast, maintain that sexuality and sexual orientation are culturally constructed, meaning that they are determined by social norms, culture, and systemic political forces. For essentialists, sexual orientation is a part of basic human nature. For social constructionists, the very concept of human nature is suspect; they would maintain that so far as some individuals might feel that they possess an essential sexual orientation, it is only because our culture leads us to interpret sexual thoughts and feelings in this way.[7] After all, in many other cultures and historical eras, same-sex feelings and behaviors have been interpreted not as signs of an essential same-sex orientation but as fully compatible with heterosexual marriage and identification.[8] The very notion of "homosexual" as a category of personhood is a recent phenomenon.[9] Essentialists acknowledge such cultural variation, but they do not think it implies that sexual orientation is a wholly cultural construct. They would simply argue that though same-sex sexual orientations have always existed, different cultures develop vastly different interpretations of them and different rules governing their expression.[10]

Advocates of these two different perspectives (which I admittedly present in extreme form for the sake of clarity) use different types of theories to explain human sexuality. Essentialists typically emphasize evolutionary theory, arguing that various features of human sexuality and gender differences are "coded in our genes" because over the course of human history they promoted survival and reproduction. For example, consider gender differences in sex drive. Social scientific studies have found that on average, women in our culture and many others report less frequent and less intense desires for sexual activity than do men.[11] Some evolutionary theorists view this disparity as the legacy of evolved gender differences in reproductive strategies. They argue that because women need to invest so much time and energy in every baby they bear (nine months of gestation followed by several years of intensive care and feeding), they ought to be fairly reticent and "choosy" about sexual activity, mating only with high-quality men who have lots of resources to invest in the resulting child.[12] In theory, a low sex drive would facilitate this reticence. This is not the only possible evolutionary model of female sexuality, however; a number of recent theories have shown that promiscuous sexual behavior might actually have proven adaptive for females under certain circumstances.[13] The main point is that despite their differences, all evolutionary models view human sexuality as governed by evolved, biologically based "programs."

Social constructionists, by contrast, emphasize cultural factors. They maintain that despite the biological architecture of human sexual organs and functions, men's and women's experiences of their sexuality are constituted entirely by social and cultural influences, ranging from large-scale cultural ideologies to specific socialization practices. Feminist social constructionists have called particular attention to the political context of our experiences of sexuality.[14] Specifically, they argue that social forces collectively define and reproduce certain notions of female sexuality—for example, the idea that females are "naturally" sexually passive or uninterested in sex—which serve the interests of male authority and power. Over the course of history, societies have consistently constrained and controlled female sexuality by restricting not only women's sexual behaviors but also their thoughts and feelings.[15] Thus when interpreting the finding that women report less interest in sex than men, we must take into account the powerful cultural norms telling women that a lack of interest in sex is normal and natural. Girls learn from an early age that only "slutty" women want a lot of sex, whereas "good" girls are supposed to serve as gatekeepers for men's uncontrollable desires. Such messages inevitably shape girls' understanding of their sexuality and lead them to discount their own experiences of sexual arousal.[16] This might be why adult women are often totally unaware of changes in their own physiological states of sexual arousal, and why low sexual desire is the single most common form of sexual dysfunction in American women.[17] Girls internalize cultural and social factors, which then shape their experiences of sexuality at a deep level.

Taken alone, neither essentialism nor social constructionism adequately explains women's sexuality. Pure essentialism, for example, is blind to the powerful sociocultural forces that mold individuals'—especially women's—sexual desires over the lifespan. There is simply no way to identify, measure, or even conceptualize sexual desires outside of their situational and sociocultural contexts. Hence, investigations of love and sexuality must always consider the multiple social and cultural factors that make some types of affection and eroticism acceptable for women, whereas other types are suppressed, punished, or never even imagined.[18]

But pure social constructionism is also deeply problematic. As a feminist, I champion its emphasis on the social, political, and cultural factors that structure women's experiences. Yet as a psychologist interested in the links between mind and body, I am frustrated by the fact that pure social constructionism discounts the role of bodies and biological processes in sexual experience and rejects the very concept of sexual orientation.[19] Pure social constructionism fails to consider how sociocultural factors interact with real bodies in real time to generate different forms of erotic experience.

In the end I count myself among the growing number of social scientists who view sexual feelings and experiences as simultaneously embedded in both physical-biological and sociocultural contexts that require integrated biosocial research strategies.[20] This is the perspective I take on sexual fluidity. This view fits squarely within those of feminists like the philosopher Elizabeth Grosz, who has argued that though biological processes provide the raw material of human sexuality, these building blocks are altogether powerless to shape human experience until cultural meaning systems organize them into conscious, intelligible, embodied drives and desires.[21] This integrative perspective helps us avoid misinterpreting fluidity as the antithesis of biologically based approaches to sexual orientation just because it emphasizes culturally and situationally influenced changes.

The notion that evolutionary theories and culturally based theories of human sexuality must be viewed as opposing perspectives reflects faulty assumptions about how both biology and culture operate to shape variability in sexuality. Most notably, such a view presumes that anything biological or essential is fixed over time, whereas anything culturally, environmentally, or situationally influenced is fundamentally variable. This is not the case. The psychologist John Money used the example of language to demonstrate the misguided nature of such assumptions.[22] You were not born with your native language, and nothing in your "nature" predisposed you to learn English rather than Swahili. Nor did you "choose" English over Swahili. Rather, language was determined by your native culture. Yet our brains are innately predisposed to assimilate a native language, whatever that language turns out to be. Once acquired, it cannot be unacquired—it is as firmly fixed as if we were born with it. Some people have contended that certain environmental influences on sexuality operate in similar ways. As Anne Fausto-Sterling has argued, "bodily experiences are brought into being by our development in particular cultures and historical periods. . . . As we grow and develop, we literally, not just 'discursively' (that is, through language and cultural practices), construct our bodies, incorporating experience into our very flesh."[23]

Research on alcohol use provides a good example of how traits can be biologically influenced and flexible. There is solid evidence that some individuals have a genetic predisposition to excessive alcohol use.[24] Yet genetic influences on complex behaviors are rarely rigid and deterministic, and so situational and environmental variation can modify the expression of such a trait despite its essential components. The psychologists Brian Mustanski and J. Michael Bailey called attention to one notable study showing that the heritability of adolescent alcohol use (that is, the degree to which variation in this behavior was due to genetic versus environmental factors) actually changed as a function of the amount of migration and social mobility in a community.[25] The investigators found that communities with more social mobility and less social control tended to foster the expression of youths' genetic predispositions to alcohol use. In contrast, communities with more stable social structures and more social control over adolescent behavior had the effect of constraining the expression of young people's genetic predispositions to drinking. As a result, adolescent drinking was less "genetically determined" in one community than in another. This finding clearly shows not only that genetically influenced traits show significant variation in expression but that the very *balance* of genetic versus environmental influences is also variable.

How do these examples relate to the case of sexual fluidity? As I argued earlier, sexual fluidity can be seen as a component of female sexuality that operates in concert with sexual orientation to shape women's sexual desires. Thus the notion of female sexual fluidity suggests not that women possess no generalized sexual predispositions but that these predispositions will prove less of a constraint on their desires and behaviors than is the case for men. As a result, it might be impossible to determine whether, in a particular instance, a woman's desires or behaviors are more attributable to dispositional or situational factors.

Because sexual fluidity should strengthen situationally influenced pathways to female same-sex sexuality, it should correspondingly dilute—but not completely cancel out—the overall evidence for biological contributions to female sexuality. The evidence for biological contributions to male same-sex sexuality, in contrast, should be stronger and more consistent. This effect is, in fact, supported by the biological data. Yet before I review this evidence, let us consider how such research is conducted and which individuals are included.

Who Gets Studied?

Scientific research is a fundamentally social practice that relies on the same cultural preconceptions that govern general society. This has been particularly problematic with respect to research on sexual orientation. Historically, sexual orientation has been considered a phenomenon with only two forms: exclusive same-sex sexuality (traditionally called "homosexuality") and exclusive other-sex sexuality ("heterosexuality"). This rigid dichotomy has its roots in the historical view of homosexuality as a form of pathology with an associated cluster of signs and symptoms.[26] Quite simply, homosexuality was an illness that you either had or did not have.

Alfred Kinsey famously challenged this dichotomy. He argued that "the world is not to be divided into sheep and goats," meaning that distinctions between "homosexuals" and "heterosexuals" were matters of degree rather than of kind.[27] In other words, you could be somewhat attracted to the same sex without being 100 percent "homosexual." To represent such possibilities, he developed a tool known as the Kinsey Scale. Individuals would rate their sexual behavior on a scale ranging from 0 (representing exclusive other-sex behavior) to 6 (representing exclusive same-sex behavior). In later applications of the scale, individuals rated different aspects of their sexuality, typically their attractions, fantasies, behavior, and identity. Thus instead of simply proclaiming someone either homosexual or heterosexual, researchers could instead characterize him or her as a "0" for identity, a "1" for behavior, and a "3" for both fantasy and attraction.

The Kinsey Scale provides a more nuanced picture of the complexity of sexual experience than did simple either-or characterizations. Yet such complexity is difficult to accommodate at the level of basic empirical research. If the ratings differ, which one is most important? To avoid having to resolve such questions, many researchers average participants' ratings on different dimensions, which washes away the very complexity that Kinsey sought to reveal.[28] Moreover, many researchers turn their participants' Kinsey ratings back into rigid categories by designating certain ratings "heterosexual" (0–1), "bisexual" (2–4), or "lesbian/gay" (5–6).[29] Clearly, the "sheep versus goat" model of sexuality is alive and kicking.

This tendency toward rigid categorization is also reflected in the way researchers recruit participants for studies of sexual orientation. Even today, researchers recruit samples of "homosexual" or gay/lesbian/bisexual individuals on the basis of self-identification;

in other words, they look for individuals who call themselves gay/lesbian/bisexual and are willing to take part in a research study on that basis. Yet because individuals (including the social scientists themselves) have diverse definitions of "lesbian," "gay," "homosexual," and "sexual orientation," different studies end up with very different subject populations. One study might include men who openly identify themselves as gay, another might also include bisexuals, another might include men who have sex with men, regardless of identity, another might include men with same-sex attractions, regardless of sexual behavior, and so on.[30] This ambiguity makes it extremely difficult to interpret and compare research findings.

For example, consider the following cases: a teenage girl falls in love with her female best friend but does not experience any other same-sex attractions; a thirty-year-old man had sex with other males throughout his adolescent years but currently desires only women; a woman experiences her first same-sex attractions at age forty. None of these cases fits the conventional prototype of a lesbian or gay person, that is, someone who has been *consistently and exclusively* drawn to the same sex from early adolescence onward. Should a researcher studying sexual orientation include these ambiguous cases? What if some of them are not "really" gay or lesbian? Wouldn't including them introduce significant error into the study? If they are included, how should they be categorized? Does any experience of same-sex sexuality automatically land you in the "homosexual" category, or must your interest in same-sex partners be long-standing? Alternatively, does one same-sex relationship disqualify you as "heterosexual," even if it was many years ago? Should we put all ambiguous cases into a catch-all "bisexual" category?

If you are uncertain, you are in good company. No scientific or popular consensus currently exists on the precise cluster of experiences that qualify an individual as lesbian, gay, or bisexual instead of just curious, confused, or experimenting. Faced with this ambiguity, researchers seeking the most interpretable data have traditionally tended to exclude individuals whose mixed patterns of attraction or behavior make them difficult to classify.[31]

We now realize that it was a mistake not to include individuals whose experiences and desires did not fit into neat categories. People with nonexclusive (or "bisexual") attractions provide perhaps the most salient example. Early on, many scientists as well as lay people doubted whether bisexuality even existed, and consequently it received virtually no attention. Between 1975 and 1985, for example, only 3 percent of the journal articles on same-sex sexuality included discussions of bisexuality in the title, abstract, or subject headings. Between 1985 and 1995, this figure increased to 16 percent, reflecting the growing acknowledgment of bisexuality as a legitimate sexual identity. In the past ten years, however, that percentage has climbed only 3 more points, demonstrating that bisexuality continues to be systematically understudied.

Yet we now know from research using representative samples that individuals with bisexual attractions actually outnumber individuals with exclusive same-sex attractions, especially among women. Combined with the fact that most individuals with same-sex attractions do not publicly identify themselves as lesbian/gay/bisexual, this means that studies of self-identified lesbians and gays actually focus on a very small and unrepresentative subset of all sexual minorities.[32]

This weakness is widely acknowledged among sexuality researchers, and many studies have attempted to correct it by recruiting research populations on the basis of same-sex behavior rather than lesbian/gay identification. Accordingly, many researchers now speak of "WSW" (women-who-have-sex-with-women) and "MSM" (men-who-have-sex-with-men) instead of lesbian/gay/bisexual men and women.[33] This approach is especially useful when sampling ethnic-minority populations that may reject lesbian/gay/

bisexual identities as largely white constructs. Yet focusing exclusively on same-sex behavior still underrepresents individuals who experience same-sex attractions but never act on them. Consider, for example, the following survey item which appeared in the national representative sample administered by the sociologist Edward Laumann and colleagues in the early 1990s: "I find the idea of sex with the same sex appealing."[34] Surprisingly, this was the single most widely endorsed measure of same-sex sexuality among women. In other words, more women agreed with this statement than reported experiencing same-sex attractions or behavior. Yet because only a minority of these women identified as lesbian or bisexual, it is safe to say that they have been entirely absent from previous research on same-sex sexuality.

We do not know how much this omission has distorted research findings. Excluding such individuals would not be a significant problem if researchers were confident that there was only one causal developmental pathway that produced all possible forms of same-sex sexuality. Yet this is not the case. Rather, researchers view same-sex sexuality as the product of multiple, interacting processes involving a range of biological factors in combination with a range of environmental factors. Furthermore, not everyone experiences the same mix of influences, and so two women might end up lesbian through entirely different routes.[35] Because previous studies have sampled only a subset of individuals who have experienced some degree of same-sex sexuality, they leave us with only a partial picture of the nature and development of sexual orientation.

Genetic Influences

No area of research generates more nature-nurture debate about sexual orientation than genetic research. These debates reached a peak in July 1993, when the geneticist Dean Hamer published an article in *Science* identifying a potential genetic marker for homosexuality.[36] Immediately, some activists seized on the findings to argue that same-sex sexuality was equivalent to height or eye color and therefore merited acceptance and tolerance. Others worried that the finding might reinvigorate the old pathology model of same-sex sexuality and inspire homophobic physicians to screen for and "cure" homosexuality.

Nearly fifteen years later, the debate continues to rage. Typing "gay gene" into Google yields more than four million hits, ranging from lesbian/gay/bisexual support groups publicizing the latest scientific findings to politically conservative organizations denouncing attempts to make same-sex sexuality seem "natural." Not surprisingly, most of these discussions rely on the kinds of simplistic dichotomies that I critiqued earlier as misleading and inaccurate.

One thing that these debates almost never mention is the existence of gender differences in the genetic data. For example, Hamer's investigation of a potential genetic marker for same-sex sexuality on the X chromosome included only men. A subsequent study by a different research team replicated Hamer's findings for men but found no evidence that lesbians shared this marker.[37] Moreover, a third independent study failed to replicate Hamer's findings, though there were methodological differences between the studies that might explain the discrepancies.[38] More recently, the first full genome scan for sexual orientation was published. The researchers found intriguing evidence for genetic transmission on three different chromosomes, but (sound familiar yet?) they studied only men.[39]

Most researchers believe that if sexual orientation is biologically based, it is probably influenced by multiple genes rather than by just one (this is called "polygenic" influence). If so, then studies focusing on the overall heritability of same-sex sexuality are more likely to be successful than studies looking for a single "gay gene." Many such studies have been conducted with both men and women, and the results consistently suggest greater heritability of same-sex sexuality among men than among women.[40]

To make sense of this finding, it helps to have a firm grasp of heritability and how it is measured. Heritability is defined as the proportion of variation in a trait that is due to genetic factors. Estimates are typically represented as numbers ranging from 0 to 1, with 0 representing no genetic effects and 1 representing complete genetic determination. For the sake of familiarity, these numbers can be thought of as percentages; thus, if a trait has 50 percent heritability, this means that half of the population variability in a trait is due to genetic factors.

Estimates of heritability are typically computed by comparing identical twins (who have 100 percent of their genes in common) and fraternal twins (who have 50 percent of their genes in common) on the trait of interest. If a trait is highly heritable, we would expect to find substantially greater similarity between identical twins than between fraternal twins, and almost no similarity between adopted siblings. In the early 1990s, the psychologist J. Michael Bailey and his colleagues conducted a series of studies making just such comparisons, and the results were reliably consistent with the hypothesis of genetic influence.[41]

Of course, to draw this conclusion we have to assume that identical twins are not treated more similarly by their parents than are fraternal twins. If this were the case, then identical twins' greater similarity in sexual orientation could be attributed to family treatment. Yet this does not appear to be the case. Research suggests not only that identical and fraternal twins have similar childhood experiences but also that similarity of childhood family environments is not significantly associated with twin resemblance on same-sex sexuality.[42]

A more significant problem with interpreting these early studies comes from the fact that the researchers recruited participants by advertising for lesbian/gay individuals who had a twin; it is possible, then, that gay individuals with a gay twin were more likely to volunteer than gay individuals with a nongay twin.[43] Furthermore, these studies sampled only individuals who openly identified as gay and did not typically include bisexuals or other individuals with "partial expression" of same-sex sexuality.[44]

Researchers have rectified these problems by using twin registries, lists of thousands of identical and fraternal twins who have agreed to participate in different studies measuring the effects of genes and environment on human behavior. The participants who register do not know in advance the kinds of studies in which they will take part. The primary advantage of these studies is that they use populations that are not "self-selected," and so they tend to have very large sample sizes. Several registry studies have been published, along with a number of studies using large samples of twins not recruited on the basis of sexual orientation, and all have found significant evidence for the heritability of sexual orientation.[45] In other words, if one member of a twin pair reports some aspect of same-sex sexuality (even if he or she does not actually identify as gay), the other member is likely to report same-sex sexuality as well. Furthermore, just as one would expect, this correspondence is substantially more likely among identical than fraternal twins.

Nonetheless, heritability estimates vary from study to study, and no study provides evidence for complete heritability (in which case you would expect to find that identical twins always have the same sexual orientation). Rather, heritability estimates range between 30 percent and 60 percent. Specific estimates vary from study to study but are typically larger among men than among women.

When considering these heritability estimates, it is useful to compare them to heritability estimates that have been calculated for other complex behavioral traits. For example, twin studies have found that the heritability of smoking (a behavior that most people consider to be under conscious control and yet situationally influenced) is also around 60 percent. Similar estimates have been found for the heritability of marijuana and alcohol use. Even job satisfaction shows significant heritability, most likely because it is strongly related to personality, which yields heritability estimates ranging from 45 to 60 percent.[46] We tend to trumpet biological effects when it comes to homosexuality, but I have yet to see the cover of *Time* or *Newsweek* display a newborn baby with the headline "Born unsatisfied with his job?"

Given that genetic influences are not completely deterministic and operate more strongly in men than in women, how do we account for the rest of the variation, and especially for the gender difference? In the terminology of behavioral genetics, nongenetic factors are linked to "the environment." But what exactly does this mean? What specific environmental factors might contribute to same-sex sexuality?

Family influence seems an unlikely factor, since behavioral genetic studies typically find that most of the nongenetic variance is attributable to nonshared environments, meaning aspects of the environment that are different across twins/siblings. Furthermore, research finds no evidence that childhood rearing influences sexuality, despite early psychoanalytic theories to the contrary.[47] There is also the obvious fact that lesbian/gay/bisexual individuals are almost always raised by heterosexual parents, and usually fairly conventional ones at that. This fact contradicts the notion of a "modeling" effect.[48] Only one study has found any evidence of increased exploration of same-sex sexuality among young adults raised by lesbian parents, but almost all of these individuals identified as heterosexual as adults. Given their home environment, they may have been more open to considering same-sex relationships, but doing so did not "turn" them gay.[49]

Consider, too, the results of several "natural experiments" with gender-reversed rearing that have occurred in different cultures. In the now-famous case of David Reimer, a male infant was raised as a girl after his penis was severely damaged during circumcision. Despite the fact that David received every possible push to behave in a female-typed fashion and to perceive males as sexual objects, he developed sexual desires for women at puberty. When his mother finally confessed to David that he was actually male, he immediately assumed a male gender identity and eventually pursued sexual relationships with women. Similar outcomes have been found in other cases of young boys who were raised as girls owing to genital abnormalities, in our own society as well as in other cultures.[50] We would expect a very different result if early rearing had an appreciable influence on same-sex sexuality. Furthermore, in cultures in which young boys traditionally engage in same-sex sexual behavior during adolescence, they show no enduring preference for such behavior as adults.[51] No cultures with analogous same-sex practices among young girls have been documented.

What about general cultural permissiveness? Can exposure to images of same-sex sexuality in popular culture, combined with the fact that American society has become more accepting of same-sex sexuality, influence sexual orientation? If this were so, then we would expect to find higher rates of same-sex sexuality in more tolerant societies. Yet this is not the case. For example, despite the fact that Denmark, the Philippines, and Thailand are relatively non-homophobic societies, they have low rates of same-sex sexuality.[52]

Another possibility is that environmental influences become relevant only for individuals with an existing predisposition to same-sex sexuality. In other words, same-sex sexuality might be influenced by specific gene-environment interactions. In this case, certain environments might be considered "releasers" for a same-sex predisposition. Yet again, the nature of such releasers is unknown; nor do we know whether certain environmental conditions might be capable of triggering same-sex sexuality in the total absence of any genetic predisposition. If so, such "pure environment" cases would end up reducing heritability estimates.[53] Thus, the fact that lower heritability estimates have been found among women than among men is consistent with the possibility that if there are purely environmental pathways to same-sex sexuality, they are more likely among women.

Additionally, the relative balance of genetic and environmental factors might vary substantially from person to person. To make sense of this, keep in mind that an estimate of, say, 40 percent heritability does not mean that 40 percent of one person's sexuality is attributed to genetics. Rather, it means that within a population, 40 percent of the person-to-person variability in same-sex sexuality can be attributed to genetic versus environmental factors. This explains why estimates of heritability can vary quite a bit when they are computed in different populations.

Knowing about the general range of genetically influenced variability of same-sex sexuality cannot tell us how many individuals— or which ones—were (1) so strongly predisposed toward same-sex sexuality that their environment did not matter; (2) needed some sort of environmental "releaser" for their same-sex sexuality; or (3) needed only the right environment and had no genetic predisposition whatsoever. All three of these "types" probably exist in the overall population, yet the genetic data suggest that the last two profiles might be more common among women than among men.

The Neuroendocrine Theory

Although research on the genetics of sexual orientation gets the most media attention, the neuroendocrine theory of sexual orientation is arguably the "origin story" generating the most contemporary scientific research.[54] Some consider it the most promising explanation for sexual orientation, but there are far too many conflicting findings and unanswered questions to warrant firm conclusions.[55] Moreover, as with genetic factors, it is likely that if neuroendocrine influences matter, it is only for some individuals, and more likely men than women.

The neuroendocrine theory is based on the idea that prenatal hormonal exposure in utero might influence sexual orientation. To understand this theory, keep in mind that certain regions of the mammalian brain are sexually dimorphic, that is, different for males than for females. Examples include the hypothalamus, the septum, the preoptic area, and the amygdala, among others.[56] Of course, the notion of intrinsic differences between female and male brains has a long and troubled history and continues to spark controversy and debate.[57] Most recently, in 2005 Lawrence Summers, then president of Harvard University, was roundly denounced after suggesting that one reason women are consistently underrepresented among high-level scientists may have to do with intrinsic differences between the cognitive abilities of men and women. The resulting firestorm contributed to his eventual resignation. Yet keep in mind that gender differences in brain structure and function say nothing about the implications of such differences.[58] In many cases, all we can reliably say is that men's and women's brains perform the same tasks through slightly different routes. For example, men typically show greater lateralization in brain function than women do, meaning that for many tasks they tend to use one side of their brain or the other, whereas women use both.[59]

Returning to the neuroendocrine theory, extensive animal research has shown that androgens and estrogens secreted by the developing fetal genitals play a fundamental role in sexual differentiation in mammalian brains.[60] Furthermore, alterations in fetal hormone exposure have been associated with alterations in animals' adult sexual behavior. Specifically, male-typed sexual behavior in female animals has been associated with abnormally high levels of prenatal androgen exposure, whereas female-typed sexual behavior in male animals has been associated with abnormally low levels of androgen exposure.[61]

This finding has led researchers to speculate that similar processes might operate for humans, such that same-sex sexual orientations might reflect alterations in brain "masculinization" or "feminization" owing to altered prenatal hormone environments.[62] Yet there are some important hurdles in applying this theory to humans. First, we know much less about the processes that produce gender differences in human brains than in animal brains, and some biologists warn against extrapolating findings regarding hormonal organization of animal mating behavior to complex gender-linked phenomena in humans.[63] With animals, scientists have been able to manipulate hormone levels in utero and directly observe the resulting brain effects. This is impossible in humans; instead, we have to rely on "natural experiments" that arise when babies are born with genetic and endocrine disorders.[64] Studies of such cases suggest that the links among genes, hormones, gender identity, and sexual identity are complex in humans, making straightforward cause-and-effect pathways hard to identify.

Second, the central assumption of neuroendocrine theory—that the brain structures which differ between males and females happen to be those that are involved in sexual orientation—has no direct evidence in humans. In animals, this notion is supported by the fact that animals who have been exposed to sex-atypical hormonal environments in utero show sex-atypical sexual behavior in adulthood.[65] Yet in these animals, sexual behavior is a fairly automatic, hormonally controlled behavioral program. For some species, simple exposure to an animal of the right sex is sufficient to trigger sexual activity. In humans, sexuality is more complex (how is *that* for an understatement?) and is mediated by an array of cognitive, emotional, and environmental factors. Hence, a direct causal connection between brain structure and sexual orientation may be less plausible in humans than in animals. The neuroendocrine theory has also been criticized because it presumes that same-sex sexual orientation is, at heart, a form of sex-atypicality in brain structure. This theory of course harks back to historical models—and contemporary stereotypes—of minority sexual orientations as disorders involving gender reversal and inversion.[66]

I will revisit this issue, and the broader question of links between sexual orientation and gender identity, a little later. For now, I review the existing evidence for the neuroendocrine theory. As noted, because researchers cannot directly manipulate humans' fetal hormone exposure, the available evidence is indirect. It is based on studies of humans who had unusually high or low androgen exposure in utero as a result of congenital abnormalities, maternal stress, or maternal medication, as well as on studies of sexual orientation differences in a variety of psychological, morphological, and neuroanatomical domains known to be influenced by prenatal hormonalization. I focus only on the most notable findings, since comprehensive reviews of this research can be found elsewhere.[67]

Some of the most intriguing evidence for the neurohormonal theory comes from research on girls with congenital adrenal hyperplasia (CAH), a condition in which girls are exposed to abnormally high levels of androgens in utero because the adrenal gland does not produce enough cortisol. Girls with CAH are typically born with partially masculinized genitals, which are usually surgically altered at birth, and they must undergo cortisol-replacement therapy throughout their lives.[68] Girls with CAH provide a natural experiment for the investigation of prenatal androgen effects on a variety of sex-linked phenomena, from sexual orientation to sex-typed play and activity preferences, and the condition is common enough to have received fairly extensive study.

Are girls with CAH more likely to develop same-sex sexuality? Longitudinal studies conducted by the psychologist Sheri Berenbaum and her colleagues suggest that they are, but not uniformly.[69] Overall, girls with the condition generally have higher levels of gender-atypical behavior during childhood and adolescence and higher levels of same-sex attractions in adolescence and adulthood, consistent with the neuroendocrine theory. Other researchers studying CAH have found similar effects.[70] However, as noted, these effects are not uniform: some girls with CAH report same-sex attractions and fantasies, but others do not. More important, these periodic attractions and fantasies are not typically manifested in consistent same-

sex behavior or lesbian/bisexual identification.[71] If prenatal androgen exposure was a key pathway to female same-sex orientation,
we would expect *all* girls with CAH to develop stable, robust, and
consistent lesbian/bisexual orientations.

A common critique of the CAH research is that increased same-
sex sexuality could stem from social rather than hormonal factors.
Specifically, given that girls with CAH are born with masculinized
genitals and undergo hormonal treatment over the course of their
lives, they may be aware of their "differentness" from other girls,
and might also be (consciously or unconsciously) treated as more
masculine by their parents. If such girls consequently come to perceive themselves as less feminine than other girls, this might account for their male-typed play preference in childhood and their
higher rates of same-sex sexuality in adolescence and adulthood.

But we would not expect this alternative explanation to apply to
"DES girls," girls whose mothers took diethylstilbestrol (DES) during pregnancy. This nonsteroidal estrogen was widely prescribed
from the 1940s through the 1960s to reduce the risk of miscarriage,
until it was found to potentially increase women's cancer risks and
to have masculinizing effects on female fetuses, though these effects
were not as extreme as in the case of CAH. Girls exposed to DES
are not born looking different from other girls, as is the case with
CAH, and so they are not treated as different. But do they show increased rates of same-sex sexuality in adulthood? The answer is
somewhat; like girls with CAH, they tend to grow up heterosexual
but report an increased prevalence of same-sex fantasies.[72] Thus
this line of research suggests that prenatal androgen exposure does
not produce lesbian or bisexual women. Rather, it appears to produce heterosexual women with periodic same-sex attractions.

An interesting corollary to the research on excessive prenatal androgen exposure is the research on androgen insensitivity syndrome
(AIS).[73] Children with this syndrome are genetically male, but because of a mutation on the gene for the human androgen receptor,

their bodies are either completely or partially "insensitive" to the masculinizing effects of prenatal androgens. In the case of complete AIS, the fetus has undescended testes but develops female external genitalia and a female-appearing body (but no uterus, fallopian tubes, or ovaries). These children are raised as girls, develop and maintain female gender identities, and grow up attracted to men. Such cases provide powerful evidence that genes alone do not determine either gender identity or sexual orientation. Without the masculinizing effects of prenatal androgen exposure, these genetically male fetuses develop into (heterosexual!) women.

Another line of research on the neuroendocrine theory concerns male children born to mothers who were exposed to extremely high levels of stress during pregnancy. Animal research has found that such experiences can affect sexual differentiation in utero through a delay of the testosterone surge that influences brain masculinization. Although some of this research finds small but significant associations between maternal stress and the eventual sexual orientation of male children, the findings have been inconsistent and the studies have notable methodological shortcomings.[74] As a result, this evidence is not considered conclusive.

More consistent findings have come from studies investigating the surprisingly robust phenomenon that men with same-sex orientations are more likely than heterosexual men to have older brothers, a finding that has been called the "fraternal birth-order effect."[75] Researchers have hypothesized that this effect is due to the fact that pregnant women show an immune response to male fetuses (specifically, immunization to Y-linked minor histocompatibility antigens, called H-Y antigens) that becomes stronger with each successive male pregnancy. Thus boys born after multiple brothers would be exposed to progressively higher prenatal levels of H-Y antigens, which may alter the sexual differentiation of the brain in a more female-typed direction (much like low androgen levels contribute to undermasculinization).

Currently, there is no direct evidence that this particular cascade of prenatal events can lead to male same-sex sexuality, but some research provides indirect evidence. Specifically, studies have found that men with same-sex orientations who have older brothers have lower birth weights than heterosexual men with older brothers, suggesting that a prenatal phenomenon might be responsible for both low birth weight and same-sex sexuality. Yet the maternal immune hypothesis would suggest a more pervasive brain "feminization" in men with same-sex orientations than is typically observed, and its purported effects are not consistent with other phenomena that have been observed among men with same-sex orientations. Notably, no birth-order effects have been detected among lesbian-bisexual women.[76]

Another line of evidence for the neuroendocrine hypothesis concerns sexual orientation differences in brain structures and functions that are affected by prenatal hormone exposure, such as lateralization. Recall that lateralization refers to the fact that men's brain functioning tends to be more specialized in one hemisphere or the other, whereas women's brain functioning is more evenly distributed between the hemispheres. If men with a same-sex orientation have less masculinized brains, we might hypothesize that they should show less lateralization. A comprehensive review of studies investigating this possibility found largely inconsistent results, as have several studies of handedness, which is an indirect index of lateralization.[77] In fact the handedness studies actually show greater support for an association between same-sex orientation and handedness in women (specifically, increased left-handedness in lesbians, which would be consistent with high fetal androgen exposure) than in men (decreased left-handedness in gay men, which would be consistent with low fetal androgen exposure). Given such conflicting findings, researchers have been reluctant to draw strong conclusions from this line of evidence.

As for brain structure, there was much publicity in the early

1990s about a finding by Simon LeVay showing that the third interstitial nucleus of the anterior hypothalamus, which is typically larger in males than in females, was significantly smaller (and in fact comparable in size to that of heterosexual women) in the brains of gay men.[78] Although this study was widely criticized because it included gay men who had died of AIDS, the findings were successfully replicated when the comparison group of heterosexual men was restricted to those who had also died of AIDS. Other studies have found sexual orientation differences in some—but not all— sexually dimorphic structures in the same general brain region, specifically, the medial preoptic anterior hypothalamic region, or mPOA.[79] This region is thought to be involved in the regulation of male sexual behavior, which is consistent with the fact that no sexual orientation effects have been found in these regions among women.[80]

Much publicity also accompanied recent findings suggesting sexual orientation differences in finger-length ratios. Specifically, women typically have index fingers that are comparable in length to the ring finger (this ratio is typically called the 2D:4D ratio), whereas men's index fingers are typically shorter than their ring fingers (meaning that their 2D:4D ratios are smaller). This difference between the sexes is thought to become established as a result of fetal androgen exposure, a theory consistent with research demonstrating that both boys and girls with CAH, who therefore had higher than normal prenatal androgen exposure, show smaller 2D:4D ratios than unaffected children.[81] Thus if male same-sex orientations result from low androgen exposure in utero, we would expect men with same-sex orientations to show larger 2D:4D ratios, similar to those observed among heterosexual women. Conversely, if female same-sex orientations result from excessive androgen exposure, we would expect women with same-sex orientations to show smaller 2D:4D ratios.

Studies testing this hypothesis have yielded mixed results. Some have found sexual orientation differences in the predicted directions, whereas others have found significant differences in the opposite direction or different kinds of effects in different subsamples or different genders in samples collected in Europe as opposed to the United States, or in samples using measurements of real fingers versus photocopies of fingers.[82] Thus though these studies provide some support for the prenatal hormone hypothesis, the discrepancies between findings—and particularly the fact that some of the significant effects are in the wrong direction—pose problems that require future investigation.

Similarly perplexing patterns have emerged from research on two auditory phenomena related to prenatal hormone exposure: "otoacoustic emissions," or CEOAEs, which are click-like noises emitted by the cochlea in response to sounds, and auditory evoked potentials, or AEPs, which are brainwave responses that result when individuals are exposed to sound. Both of these measures show reliable gender differences that show up as early as infancy and have been attributed to the fact that the fetal auditory system develops at approximately the same time as the hormone-induced sexual differentiation of the fetal brain.[83]

Support for the influence of androgen exposure comes from research demonstrating that female twins with male co-twins have lower, or more "male-like," CEOAEs than girls with female twins because they were exposed to higher androgen levels produced by their brothers' bodies. Analogously, studies have found that lesbian/bisexual women had lower CEOAEs than heterosexual women, though gay-bisexual men did not have higher CEOAEs than heterosexual men.[84]

Similar results for women have been found with AEPs, with lesbian/bisexual women showing male-typed patterns.[85] Yet in this case, not only did gay/bisexual men not show "female-typical" patterns, but they actually showed more extreme male-typed patterns than heterosexual men. In other words, they appeared hyper-masculinized, in direct contradiction to the neuroendocrine hypothesis. This finding is similar to some of the "wrong direction" effects noted above with regard to finger-length ratios. One possible interpretation, then, is that either abnormally high or abnormally low levels of prenatal androgen exposure might produce different "types" of male same-sex sexuality. The situation for women is clearly quite different. The CAH and DES findings, in concert with the auditory findings, suggest potential effects of high but not low androgen exposure. Yet as noted, the evidence is certainly not strong enough to suggest that this is a key pathway for women.

Gender and "Inversion"

Before leaving the biological evidence, some reflections on the overall question of gender reversal are warranted. One key source of controversy about biological investigations of same-sex sexuality, particularly the neuroendocrine theory, is the suggestion that gay men are female-like (in their hormone exposure, brain structure, and brain function), whereas lesbian women are male-like. This, of course, is a long-standing stereotype about homosexuality that has its roots in the "inversion" theories of homosexual pathology first proposed in the late nineteenth and early twentieth centuries.[86] The assumption is that because the sexual attractions of gay men parallel those of heterosexual women, then all other biological and psychological features must be similarly female-like or, in scientific terms, gender-atypical.

Although psychologists reject this extreme, global hypothesis of sex inversion, there is in fact evidence for a link between gender atypicality and same-sex sexuality, at least among some individuals. A subset of lesbians, gay men, and bisexuals—more often men than women—report gender-atypical interests or behaviors, sometimes beginning in early childhood.[87] Of course, this might have nothing to do with biology. It is possible that boys and girls with nascent same-sex attractions begin internalizing cultural stereotypes linking gender atypicality to same-sex sexuality and unwittingly conform to these expectations.[88] Alternatively, these stereotypes might make lesbian/gay/bisexual adults more likely than heterosexuals to notice, remember, and report gender atypicality.

Another source of evidence for a link between gender atypicality and same-sex sexuality comes from several well-known longitudinal studies that followed groups of extremely gender-atypical boys from childhood to adulthood; importantly, these boys were outside the normal range of "feminine-masculine" behavior that one might observe on the average playground. In fact, they were so female-typed in behavior and interests that they were referred to gender-identity clinics. Ultimately, the majority of these boys identified as gay in adulthood. Yet as many researchers have pointed out, such studies are not really about gay men, they are about extremely feminine boys, who are much less common in the population than gay/bisexual men.[89] Thus though extremely feminine boys may be disproportionately likely to develop same-sex sexuality, they account for only a small subset of the overall gay/bisexual population. Studies among girls demonstrate that gender atypicality is generally more mild, less stigmatized, and less likely to be treated as an indicator of psychiatric disturbance, and less strongly associated with later sexual orientation, among girls than among boys.[90]

When considering the neuroendocrine theory more generally, we might interpret it as a theory not of same-sex sexuality but of gender-atypicality in which one accompanying outcome is a particular variant of same-sex sexuality. Recall the CAH findings noted above: exposure to prenatal androgens does not appear to "create" lesbian and bisexual women; rather, it may cause a subset of otherwise heterosexual girls to show higher-than-normal male-typical behaviors, interests, and sexual fantasies. Furthermore, neuroendocrine factors do not always operate in a gender-atypical direction: the fact that abnormally high androgen exposure may also be associated with male same-sex sexuality provides an important corrective to simplistic stereotypes about gender reversal. Along the same lines, it is interesting that the tendency for gay men to have a disproportionately high number of older brothers is directly contrary to the long-held stereotype that gay men were exposed to excessive female influence during childhood and became more female-typical as a result.[91]

It bears noting that studies of gay men's and lesbians' attitudes and behaviors regarding sexual and romantic relationships have found much more evidence of gender typicality than of gender atypicality. For example, both gay and heterosexual men place more emphasis on sex in relationships than do lesbian and heterosexual women (who, comparatively, place more emphasis on emotional intimacy).[92] Of course, this may reflect straightforward socialization effects. The point is that global associations between same-sex sexuality and gender atypicality are unsupportable. Even when such associations are detected, they appear to characterize only a subset of sexual minorities, more typically male than female.

The difficult next step for this line of research, then, is to document systematically the many possible pathways to adult same-sex sexuality, how they interact with one another and with multiple environmental factors, and whether certain pathways are more influential for some individuals than for others. Little of this work has been done, though there are some intriguing examples. The psychologist Ray Blanchard and his colleagues have attempted to estimate the proportion of men whose same-sex sexuality might be due to the maternal immune pathway. They concluded that it might account for the same-sex sexuality of approximately one in seven gay men.[93] Whether or not this figure turns out to be accurate, it underscores the message that same-sex sexuality has different causes for different individuals.

A related question relevant to female sexual fluidity is whether certain pathways produce more stable or consistent forms of same-sex sexuality than do others. Recall my criticism of the common misconception that if sexual orientation is biologically based, it should be stable and impervious to environmental influence. It should now be clear why such a conclusion is incorrect. Not only are there multiple possible biological pathways, but with respect to women, some of the strongest evidence for a biological pathway to same-sex sexuality (the CAH and DES data) suggests that this pathway produces a relatively unstable form of same-sex sexuality: periodic same-sex attractions and fantasies among otherwise heterosexual women! This finding indicates that we still have a lot to learn.

From Causation to Development

The biological data reviewed above support the notion that female same-sex sexuality has different etiological pathways than male same-sex sexuality. If this is the case, we would also expect female same-sex sexuality to unfold differently during childhood and adolescence, not only because the biological influences might differ for women versus men, but also because women and men face such dramatically different social contexts when it comes to sexual development. As the anthropologists Ellen Ross and Rayna Rapp argued, "Sexuality's biological base is always experienced culturally, through a translation. The bare biological facts of sexuality do not speak for themselves; they must be expressed socially. Sex feels individual, or at least private, but those feelings always incorporate the roles, definitions, symbols, and meanings of the worlds in which they are constructed."[94] In the domain of same-sex sexuality, this interbraiding of biological underpinnings and meaning-laden social contexts is vividly manifested in the process of coming out.

The phrase "coming out," as used by psychologists, typically refers to the process by which individuals come to realize, act on, and privately accept their same-sex orientation, even if they do not necessarily disclose it to others. There are multiple psychological models of this process, and though they do not predict the same exact sequence of events, they generally agree on the basic components of this process, at least within a contemporary Western cultural context. Almost all specify a period of early awareness of same-sex attractions followed by tentative exploration of a non-heterosexual identity. This exploration typically occurs through contact with lesbian, gay, or bisexual individuals, literature, films, or community resources. The most commonly assessed milestones include (a) childhood feelings of differentness that may or may not be associated with sexual issues; (b) gender-atypical behavior, appearance, or interests; (c) fascination with or sexual attraction to the same sex, perhaps manifested in friendship choices, fantasies, dreams, or sex play; (d) disappointment or lack of interest in the other sex; (e) gradual realization of sexual as well as romantic feelings toward the same sex; and (f) conscious questioning of one's sexual identity.

This "master narrative" of sexual-identity development is familiar to researchers and laypeople alike and is widely found not only in the academic literature but in popularized personal accounts from openly lesbian/gay/bisexual individuals.[95] The defining features of the master narrative are typically consistency across different areas (same-sex attractions and fantasies and romantic feelings) and continuity over time (that is, the same pattern of same-sex desire from early childhood to adulthood).

Before addressing the question of gender differences, it is important to note that this generalized model has been criticized over the years. The very notion of "prototypical" pathways of lesbian/gay/bisexual child and adolescent development has become increasingly suspect, as researchers have collected more data on diversity in developmental experiences. For example, though it was once thought that all sexual minorities experienced the emergence of their same-sex attractions before adolescence, we now know that this is not always the case. In fact, sexual minorities show a wide range of developmental histories, with different ages and contexts for the classic "milestones" of first same-sex attractions, first conscious sexual questioning, first same-sex contact, and first self-identification.[96]

A number of environmental factors can influence such differences. For example, consider the sharply different environments of a gay male teenager in a large urban center versus a young man living in an isolated rural town. The urban youth probably has many more opportunities than the rural youth to learn about same-sex sexuality and to seek same-sex contact. Culture and ethnicity are also particularly important. Studies of the United States have found that ethnic-minority communities tend to stigmatize same-sex sexuality more stringently than mainstream Anglo society, a finding consistent with the lack of positive or neutral terms for "lesbian," "gay," or "bisexual" in some languages.[97] As a result, ethnic-minority youths with same-sex attractions often grow up with a sense that nobody else shares their experiences; these factors can substantially influence the timing and context of sexual-identity development.[98]

The underlying reasons for the stigmatization of same-sex sexuality vary considerably across different ethnic groups, with different implications for young people's developmental experiences. For example, Latino, African-American, Asian-Pacific Islander, and South Asian communities typically place considerable emphasis on family ties, and same-sex sexuality is often construed as a violation and betrayal of familial cohesion and loyalty.[99]

In ethnic groups that have sharply demarcated gender roles, same-sex sexuality often carries the additional stigma of gender-role deviation.[100] For example, many Latino communities expect adolescent males to display the exaggerated masculine characteristics of "machismo" (courage, aggressiveness, power, and invulnerability) in order to gain status as mature, appropriately behaving Latino men. Adolescent females must display appropriate "etiqueta" (patience, nurturance, passivity, and subservience) to gain status as mature, appropriately behaving Latino women. Because these cultures typically construe same-sex sexuality as gender nonconformity, adolescents who pursue same-sex sexuality are viewed by their communities as having fundamentally failed as men or women.

Same-sex sexuality among African Americans is often associated with long-standing cultural stereotypes of African Americans as hypersexual and morally bankrupt. As a result, sexual minorities often feel pressured to hide their same-sex sexuality in order present an image of normalcy to larger Anglo society.[101] These pressures are particularly difficult for young people, who may view their same-sex desires as signs of sickness or moral failings.

For all these reasons, ethnic-minority youths may interpret and express their same-sex sexuality very differently from Anglo youths. For example, some might pursue exclusively sexual same-sex behavior with strangers to avoid thinking of themselves as gay, while maintaining their most important romantic ties to women. Others might identify as lesbian or gay and regularly pursue same-sex behavior but resist larger participation in gay culture, choosing to emphasize the cultural component of their identity in order to maintain their strong cultural ties.[102]

Despite all these sources of variability, the most important of all is gender. In fact, the past quarter-century of research on this topic suggests that very few features of sexual-minority development are *not* differentiated by gender. For example, whereas many gay men recall childhoods characterized by gender-atypicality, feelings of "differentness," and early same-sex attractions, fewer lesbian/bisexual women recall such experiences. Women also show greater variability than men in the age at which they first become aware of same-sex attractions, first experience same-sex fantasies, first consciously question their sexuality, first pursue same-sex sexual contact, and first identify as lesbian or bisexual.[103]

Women also grant a larger role to emotional versus sexual factors in the development of their same-sex attractions. Many women report feeling emotionally attracted to other women before being physically attracted to them.[104] This supports the finding that women generally place less emphasis on the sexual component of their lesbian or bisexual identification, both during and after the questioning process, and more on ideological factors, reference groups, and a rejection of or commitment to particular roles.[105]

Most important in terms of sexual fluidity, women show more discontinuous experiences of same-sex sexuality than do men. In other words, they report more changes in sexual attractions and behaviors over time and in different situations. Women are also more likely than men to report sexual behaviors or attractions that are inconsistent with their identity (for example, other-sex behavior in self-identified lesbians and same-sex behavior in self-identified heterosexuals) and to grant a role to choice and circumstance.[106]

There has been considerable debate over the years on what causes these differences between women and men. Traditional essentialist perspectives, which hold that sexual orientation is an early-developing and fixed trait, offer only two possible characterizations of sexual-minority women who report sharply discontinuous experiences of sexual attraction to men and women: either they were always lesbian/bisexual or they were never lesbian/bisexual.[107] According to the essentialists, experiences of discontinuity signal "false consciousness," a misperception of one's authentic attractions and orientation. Many commentators, for example, have offered this interpretation for Anne Heche's transition to lesbianism and back to heterosexuality; in other words, if she went back to men so easily after breaking up with Ellen DeGeneres, she obviously was not really a lesbian.

According to this perspective, women's variable and discontinuous experiences of same-sex sexuality might reflect the fact that they are more likely than men to show "false consciousness" about same-sex sexuality, perhaps because cultural suppression of female sexuality has hampered women's awareness of their own desires. This would seem to suggest that if researchers could "weed out" women with false consciousness and restrict their research samples to "real" lesbians, then perhaps we would not see such variability and discontinuity. But how exactly would this be done? Women's own self-reports might not provide reliable data: we could argue that even women who strongly perceive their sexuality as essential and fixed are simply reflecting the essentialism pervading both popular and scientific accounts of sexual orientation. Alternatively, those who experience their sexuality as more variable, emotionally based, or situationally influenced might arguably do so because they have not been socialized to view their sexuality as an essential, driving force the way men typically are.[108]

Another problem complicating our understanding of women's changing sexuality is that discontinuities in their sexual experiences and feelings over time are always assessed retrospectively. In other words, women are asked to think back to earlier feelings and relationships and explain how they arrived at their current sexual identity. This method introduces significant potential bias, since most individuals are highly motivated to tell autobiographical stories— especially about sexuality—that suggest a consistent, stable, "core" self.[109] Thus individuals subtlely and sometimes unconsciously revise descriptions of previous attractions and behaviors to conform to their current understanding of themselves. A woman who now identifies as lesbian might look back on previous, pleasurable relationships with men and conclude that she was in denial about her lesbianism. Similarly, a woman who currently sees herself as heterosexual might reflect on previous attractions to women and conclude that she was confused or simply going through a phase.

This differentiation between "authentic" and "inauthentic" experiences of sexuality has a long history in the scientific and popular literature on sexual orientation, and it continues to spark heated debate among sexual minorities themselves.[110] Given the greater discontinuity and variability in women's same-sex sexuality, these debates are particularly salient within the lesbian/bisexual community. They show how deeply scientists and laypeople alike have absorbed the assumption that "real" same-sex orientations always emerge early, produce consistent patterns of attraction and behavior, and stay the same over time and in different situations. This assumption is not entirely unreasonable given that it aptly characterizes the experiences of many gay/bisexual men.

Yet why should they be the norm? Perhaps the primary reason that women's developmental pathways appear so different and deviant, prompting us to develop convoluted explanations about misperceived, misremembered, and misunderstood experiences, is that we keep comparing them to the experiences of men. What if the very nature of female same-sex sexuality is fundamentally different?

The Next Step

This is exactly what I am suggesting. As the research has shown, women's sexuality is fundamentally more fluid than men's, permitting greater variability in its development and expression over the life course. We have just gone about studying it all wrong. We have been focusing on openly identified lesbian and bisexual women when we should be studying any woman with same-sex attractions or experiences. We have been ignoring "quirky" phenomena such as periodic other-sex attractions among lesbians when we should actually be paying close attention to such experiences. Perhaps most important, we have been relying on isolated snapshots of sexual feelings and behaviors at single moments in time when we should actually be tracking, over time, how women's feelings and experiences shift across different situations, relationships, environments, and developmental periods.

If we really want sex-specific models of female sexuality, we need detailed, longitudinal data on the multifaceted expression of same-sex and other-sex sexuality over long stretches of women's development. When I first entered the field of sexuality research in the early 1990s, no such information existed. So I decided to collect it myself.

CHAPTER 3

Sexual Fluidity in Action

When I began my longitudinal study on female sexuality, I was not looking for anything like sexual fluidity; I simply intended to study variability in women's sexual pathways. But my results showed that something more was going on than just variability. Over time, I came to see that most of what I thought I knew about female sexuality was wrong.

I undertook this project to answer several key questions sparked by the existing research: How much stability and continuity was there in female same-sex sexuality over time? Could we predict its long-term course from childhood and adolescent experiences? Was there any truth to the distinction between "born" lesbians (that is, "real" lesbians) and "political" lesbians (in other words, "fake" lesbians)? What could we say about the development of bisexual women, given that nearly all the previous research examined only lesbians?

In setting out to answer these questions, I first attended carefully to the handful of studies that had tried to examine same-sex sexuality over time.[1] Each had notable limitations that I hoped to correct in my own work. For example, none of them involved more than one follow-up assessment, and this follow-up took place after a relatively short period of time, typically around two years. I knew that if I really wanted to capture long-term patterns of sexual development, I needed to assess individuals repeatedly over much longer stretches of time.

Another shortcoming of the previous studies was that they focused only on adults who had self-identified as gay/lesbian/bisexual back in the 1970s and 1980s. That era was characterized by much less openness and visibility when it came to same-sex sexuality. As a result, we could never rule out the possibility that variability in sexuality was due to cultural repression and the fact that some women were not exposed to lesbianism or bisexuality until late adulthood. For this reason, I felt it was important to examine the sexual pathways of young women who were coming out now. These women had grown up with much greater exposure to ideas about same-sex sexuality than had previous generations. Thus they might be less likely to experience discontinuities in their sexual development owing to repression and lack of knowledge. I also wanted to include bisexual women and those who declined to identify themselves as sexual minorities, since such women had been drastically underrepresented in previous research.

Finally, I knew that previous studies had relied primarily on numerical measures of sexuality, such as Kinsey ratings of attractions and behaviors. Yet I wanted to understand the reasons behind sexual variability and to probe women's experiences and interpretations of their sexuality. The only way to gather such information was to conduct in-depth interviews, during which women could be prompted, with the assurance of confidentiality, to reflect on and reveal such deeply personal information.

I set out with the goal of conducting detailed one-on-one interviews with as large a group of young sexual-minority women as I could find, then reinterviewing them regularly over as many years as possible.

Although I felt strongly about giving voice to women who had been underrepresented in previous research samples, such as bisexuals and those who did not openly claim lesbian/bisexual labels, I was not sure how to find them. I had no research funding, so I was unable to place newspaper advertisements. The lack of funding also meant that I could not offer women financial compensation for their time (a standard practice for interview studies). I simply hoped that women would be motivated to participate in a study that took their unique experiences seriously.

I opted for a strategy of face-to-face recruitment across as wide a variety of settings as possible. I bought a used car and began taking road trips each weekend to a number of large urban cities and small rural towns in the large eastern state where I was attending graduate school. I visited lesbian/gay/bisexual community events (such as picnics and parades), lesbian/gay/bisexual youth groups, student groups at various colleges, and also college courses on gender and sexuality (such courses often attract individuals who are questioning their sexuality, but who might not identify as sexual minorities). In each setting, I approached individual women or made general announcements describing my research. I stressed that all women between the ages of sixteen and twenty-three who had same-sex attractions were eligible to participate, even if they did not identify as lesbian or bisexual. I have been careful to check for differences between women who were recruited from different settings (say, the youth groups versus the college courses), or between women who had different economic and political backgrounds. I have found no such differences.

The sampling strategy drew a wide range of women with different backgrounds and identities. Of the eighty-nine participants, 43 percent identified as lesbian, 30 percent identified as bisexual, and 27 percent did not claim a sexual-minority identity (though they considered themselves nonheterosexual). Their average age at the first interview was twenty, and they reported having first questioned their sexuality at an average age of sixteen. As with most sexual-minority research samples, the majority of participants (85 percent) were white. Five percent were African American, 9 percent were Latina, and 1 percent were Asian American. The sample was also largely middle class; three-fourths of the participants came from families in which at least one parent had completed college, and nearly two-thirds came from families in which at least one parent had a professional or technical occupation. By the ten-year point, more than 90 percent of respondents had completed college, and more than half had earned either a graduate or a professional degree. At that point, approximately 60 percent considered themselves middle or upper middle class. The majority came from intact families, with only about one-fourth growing up with divorced parents. About one-half described their family as politically liberal, one-third as conservative, and less than one-fifth as moderate. On average, respondents were open about their sexuality to more than 75 percent of their immediate family members, about half of their work colleagues, and more than 85 percent of their friends. Approximately 40 percent felt that their family disapproved of their sexuality. Nearly half reported having experienced stigmatization, harassment, and fear of victimization because of their sexuality, and 20 percent had actually experienced antigay violence.

Despite my best efforts, this sample cannot be considered fully representative of young sexual-minority women. Although I believe that the respondents have given voice to basic aspects of female sexuality that apply to women more generally, we need additional research to clarify just how typical their experiences are. In particular, we lack a full understanding of how sexual fluidity might manifest itself differently among women who have grown up with vastly different circumstances, in different geographic regions, from different social classes, and with different ethnic and cultural backgrounds. These are key directions for future study.

Another critical question is whether any of my findings apply to strictly heterosexual women as opposed to bisexually leaning heterosexual women who have had direct experience with same-sex relationships. If sexual fluidity is a property of female sexuality in general, how does it manifest itself in these women? What would the average heterosexual woman say—or think—if asked to reflect deeply on whether she could ever see herself with another woman? I began to consider this question more and more as I wrapped up the very first round of interviews in 1995. In the end, I decided to interview an additional eleven heterosexual women whom I recruited from a college course on sexuality. Because of the course they were taking (which addressed issues of same-sex sexuality), these women had already been prompted to think critically about notions of sexual identity, and I was curious to see how they viewed their own capacity for same-sex versus other-sex sexuality.

Of course, the very fact that these women were willing to sit down and talk to me about why they considered themselves heterosexual, and whether that might ever change, makes them unrepresentative of the average heterosexual woman! Most heterosexual women never even think about their sexual identity; the presumption of universal heterosexuality is so strong that they never have to question it. One heterosexual respondent likened sexuality to ethnicity: she noted that because she was white, she never thought of herself as having an ethnic identity—that was something that seemed relevant only to ethnic minorities. Similarly, she observed, if you are heterosexual then you grow up never thinking about your sexual identity; only nonheterosexuals are forced to consciously analyze their "differentness" from mainstream norms and to come up with a new sexual identity. This woman, like all of the heterosexual respondents, became aware of these issues when she took a college course that critiqued cultural assumptions about sex, gender, and sexuality. As a result, these women are more willing and able to reflect on the meaning of "heterosexuality," and to imagine alternatives to it, than the average heterosexual woman. So though I periodically discuss their thoughts and experiences in order to put my findings in a slightly broader context, I do not consider these thoughts and experiences representative of heterosexual women more generally. In truth, they raise more questions than they answer about how sexual fluidity operates in heterosexual women, and I hope to tackle that question in future research. For now, note that whenever I refer to "the participants" or "the respondents" of my study throughout this book, I am generally referring to the sexual-minority respondents. Whenever I shift to discussing the heterosexual comparison group, I explicitly say so.

I interviewed each woman five times over the past ten years (approximately once every two years). The first interview took place in person, and all subsequent interviews were conducted over the phone. As in all longitudinal research, I lost contact with some of the original participants, so that the final 2005 sample contains seventy-nine of the original eighty-nine sexual-minority women and ten of the original eleven heterosexual women. Only one respondent declined to participate in a follow-up interview after being recontacted.

At each assessment, the interview questions and study procedure were reviewed and approved by local institutional review boards charged with protecting the rights of research participants. All participants underwent a standard informed-consent procedure before each interview, during which they were told that their responses were confidential, that they had the right to refrain from answering any of the interview questions, and that they could stop participating in the study at any time. At the close of each interview, women were given the opportunity to revise their answers to any of the questions or to add additional remarks.

The initial interviews in 1995 lasted between 1 and 1.5 hours and covered a wide range of issues, including the process by which women first questioned their sexuality; early memories of sexual feelings and behaviors; current and prior patterns of attractions, friendships, and romantic relationships; the women's interpretation of their current identity; and expectations for the future. I asked the women directly whether they felt they were born with their sexuality, whether choice played any role, whether they felt their sexuality changed over time, and whether they felt they had been influenced by various environmental factors.[2] Owing to the sensitivity of the subject matter, I did not tape-record that first interview; instead I took detailed notes and recorded quotations by hand, which I typed up immediately afterward. During the second interview, I typed verbatim transcriptions while the interviews were taking place. All subsequent interviews have been tape-recorded and transcribed. Throughout this book, I present quotations from these transcriptions. To protect the women's privacy, I leave out all identifying information and use pseudonyms.

To provide a numerical representation of same-sex attractions, I asked women at each interview to estimate the percentage of their day-to-day attractions that were directed toward women versus men, so that 0 percent would represent exclusively other-sex attractions, 50 percent would represent equal attractions to men and women, and 100 percent would represent exclusively same-sex attractions. I asked them to provide separate estimates for physical-sexual attractions versus emotional-romantic attractions. Thus this "percentage" measure yields a rough estimate of the relative frequency of a woman's same-sex versus other-sex attractions, similar to the Kinsey Scale described in the last chapter. The advantage of the measure I used is that it permits finer-grained assessments, whereas the Kinsey Scale offers only 7 possible categories (represented by the numbers 0 through 6).[3]

To assess sexual behavior, I asked participants at each interview to report the total number of men and women with whom they had had sexual contact (defined as any sexually motivated intimate contact more substantive than kissing). With this information, I was able to calculate the exact percentages of same-sex and other-sex contact that women had pursued between successive interviews (in other words, between 1995 and 1997, 1997 and 2000, 2000 and 2003, and 2003 and 2005). As with women's attractions, 100 percent represents exclusive same-sex behavior and 0 percent represents exclusive other-sex behavior. I also asked about the number of romantic relationships they experienced with men and women, and about the gender of their current romantic partner, if they had one.

The Long-Term Course of Sexual-Identity Development

To address the primary question of the study—the degree of continuity and stability in female same-sex sexuality over time—I began by focusing on the long-term course of women's sexual-identity development. Recall that sexual-identity development refers to the sequence of stages by which sexual minorities are thought to come to acknowledge their same-sex sexuality. The process usually begins with gradual awareness of same-sex attractions and subsequent questioning of one's sexuality. It is supposed to end—sometimes months later, sometimes years later—with the adoption of a lesbian/gay/bisexual identity. Once this occurs, no further change is anticipated.

Some studies suggested, though, that women's identity development might not be so straightforward. For example, in the early 1990s, the sociologist Paula Rust found that among a sample of 400 sexual-minority women, 75 percent of the bisexual respondents reported that they used to consider themselves lesbian, and more than 40 percent of the lesbian respondents reported that they used to consider themselves bisexual.[4] This was exactly the sort of variability in female sexuality that I found intriguing, but it was hard to know how to interpret it.

Historically, researchers have viewed "switching" from a bisexual to a lesbian identity as just another part of the coming-out process. They have assumed that some individuals adopt "bisexual" as a transitional identity because they have not yet accepted their lesbianism. They have attributed switches in the opposite direction—from lesbian to bisexual—to the fact that bisexuality is still viewed with skepticism by both mainstream society and the lesbian-gay community.[5] For example, many lesbian/gay organizations and publications do not even include the word "bisexual" in their titles. Consequently, when first coming out, some individuals with attractions to both sexes might not realize that identifying as bisexual is even an option; others might fear the widespread prejudice against bisexuals that still persists in some segments of the gay and lesbian community.[6] Such individuals might initially adopt lesbian/gay identities until they discover the concept of bisexuality or find communities more supportive of bisexuality.

If these are the major reasons that women have historically switched between bisexual and lesbian identities, then we would expect fewer of these changes among young women today. After all, women now have access to far more information about same-sex sexuality, including bisexuality, than have women in previous generations. Straightforward discussions of bisexuality as a legitimate sexual identity can be found in mainstream publications like *Newsweek* and the *New York Times,* and numerous television dramas and reality shows feature bisexual characters.[7] But does this make it easier for young women to accurately match their sexual orientation to an appropriate identity label, eliminating the need for future changes and adjustments?

The answer, my study revealed, is not quite. Already at the first interview, about one-half of the lesbian women reported initially coming out as bisexual, and about one-third of the bisexual women reported initially coming out as lesbian. Thus the greater visibility of same-sex sexuality in general, and bisexuality in particular, had not necessarily made it easier for women to settle on the right identity from the very beginning. I was also struck, at that first interview, by the amount of self-reflection involved in women's selection of that initial identity. Respondents typically described having carefully thought about the frequency and intensity of their sexual and emotional feelings for women versus men, their satisfaction with different relationship partners, and their desires for the future.

Given how thoughtfully the respondents appeared to have selected their identities, I was surprised to find that two years later, an additional one-third of them had changed identities! Most of the women who switched went from the "unlabeled" category to a lesbian or bisexual label, a change that was consistent with traditional coming-out models. Yet other women had also switched from lesbian and bisexual identities, despite the fact that they were no longer in the beginning stages of the coming-out process. Surely this could no longer be transitional, could it?

The most unexpected finding was that five women actually *gave up* their lesbian or bisexual labels in favor of unlabeled identities, and an additional five women started calling themselves heterosexual! Yet every single one of them continued to acknowledge attractions to women. The women who started calling themselves heterosexual typically reported that their same-sex attractions simply were not strong or frequent enough to justify identifying as lesbian or bisexual. They were generally more interested in men and expected to end up with men down the line. As one woman noted:

> I don't like to label, but if I had to choose, it would be heterosexual. I just realized that the chances are that in my lifetime, I probably won't ever be with a woman. I don't think there was any incident that made me realize that, maybe it was just the people I hung out with before, and the fact that now everything feels more set. Things seem more definite in my life right now. My boyfriend knows I have "tendencies" toward women, but he sees that possibility for himself too, and so we both acknowledge that there are no boundaries. You can be with men, you can be with women, but we're together and so for the time being, I'm straight. I can acknowledge the attractions

and not feel I have to act on them. (twenty-year-old heterosexual, previously unlabeled)

The group of women who switched to unlabeled identities were more diverse. Some of these women were lesbians who had become unexpectedly involved with male partners and felt that neither "lesbian" nor "bisexual" accurately represented their own personal experiences; others were women with nonexclusive attractions who had begun to doubt the meaning and importance of any sexual-identity categories.

Switching to unlabeled or heterosexual identities completely contradicts standard identity models, in which everyone is supposed to move inexorably *toward* lesbian/gay/bisexual identification. Perhaps, I speculated, the process of identity development was simply a lot slower than researchers have assumed. After all, the respondents in my study were still fairly young (between eighteen and twenty-four), so maybe their identifications would stabilize from this point on.

I was wrong. Between the second and third interviews, another 25 percent of women switched identities. As before, there were changes in all directions. Three lesbians switched to bisexual; one bisexual and one unlabeled woman switched to lesbian; three lesbian and three bisexual women switched to unlabeled; six bisexuals now identified as heterosexual; and three of the women who had adopted heterosexual labels at the previous interview changed their minds and now considered themselves nonheterosexual but unlabeled.

The next two assessments brought more of the same: about one-third of women changed identities between the third and fourth interviews, and another one-third changed identities between the fourth and fifth interviews. Clearly, there was more going on here than just slow development—after all, the respondents were now ten years out from the first interview. Moreover, it was not the same subset of women changing each time: though some women changed their identity more than once over the ten-year period, most of the changes were one-time-only transitions. By 2005, more than two-thirds of the women in my sample had changed their identity labels at least once after the first interview. The women who kept the same identity for the whole ten years proved to be the smallest and most atypical group!

Reasons for Identity Change

What motivates these changes? Were some women more likely to change than others? I had my own ideas about the answers to these questions, but they turned out to be wrong. The real answers were far more interesting.

My first hunch was that women's attractions were changing as well, in which case study participants might be switching identities to correspond with their "new" orientation. Chapter 5 addresses the thorny question of change in sexual attractions in much greater detail, so here I provide only a rough picture of the results. Basically, though women's self-reported same-sex attractions did fluctuate from assessment to assessment, sometimes by as much as 20 percentage points, the women almost always stayed within the same general category of lesbian, bisexual, or heterosexual. So though women's specific degrees of same-sex attraction were changing, their overall orientations were not. This finding sent me back to the drawing board in terms of explaining why women changed identities.

I then considered whether younger women might be more likely to change identities than older women, given that late adolescence and young adulthood are often periods of great transition. But I found no association between a woman's age and her likelihood of identity change. I then speculated that women who had been out for shorter periods of time might be more likely to change their identities, because they might still be working through the coming-out process. I calculated the exact number of years that each woman had considered herself nonheterosexual, and tested whether this number was smaller among women who had changed their identities. It was not. Furthermore, the age at which women reported first experiencing same-sex attractions and the age at which they first questioned their sexuality were also unrelated to identity change: women who had their first same-sex attractions at the age of nine were just as likely to change their identities as women who had their first same-sex attractions at age twenty.

What about women's actual relationship histories? Perhaps identity change was motivated by specific experiences with female and male partners. I examined the ratio of same-sex to other-sex relationships that women pursued between successive interviews (both short-term sexual liaisons and longer-term romantic relationships) and whether women had a romantic partner at the time of their identity change. Here the findings were more promising. At any given interview, women who were currently involved with a man were more likely than those currently involved with women and those unattached to report changing their identity since the preceding interview. Similarly, at each interview, women who changed identities reported a larger percentage of sexual and romantic relationships with men since the last interview (around 60 percent) than did women who kept the same identity (around 35 percent). Did this mean that women were changing their identities specifically to accommodate attractions and relationships with men?

If so, I reasoned, then certain patterns of change should be more common than others. Specifically, women should be switching to identities that accommodated other-sex attractions, for example, going from lesbian to bisexual instead of vice versa. Sure enough, this was the case. Of all the identity changes undertaken over the course of the study, more than 80 percent accommodated attractions to and relationships with men (that is, switching to a bisexual or an unlabeled identity, which took place more than two-thirds of the time, or switching to a heterosexual label, which took place 16 percent of the time). Thus when women undertook identity changes, they typically did so in a way that broadened rather than narrowed their potential range of attractions and relationships. I was struck by the fact that this pattern corresponded directly to observations made back in the 1960s, in which women's sexual experiences were viewed as "broadening" as they got older, whereas men's tended to become narrow and more specialized.[8]

Moreover, I found that this same broadening characterized women's sexual and romantic relationships. This was especially true for the women who identified as lesbian in 1995. At the beginning of the study, these women reported that 90 percent of their sexual contact was pursued with women, but this figure dropped to 74 percent at the ten-year point. Those with the largest changes in behavior were the ones who changed their identities: on average, women who stopped identifying as lesbian reported that their same-sex behavior dropped by about 40 percent over the course of the study, whereas women who stayed lesbian-identified the entire time showed no drop in same-sex behavior at all (averaging 92 percent same-sex sexual contact throughout the study).

I found significant shifts toward more nonexclusive sexual behavior in all the other groups as well. Women who identified as unlabeled or bisexual in 1995 showed an average drop of 16 percent in their same-sex sexual contact. The largest changes took place among the women who reidentified as heterosexual by 2005: more than one-third of their sexual partners were women at the beginning of the study, but by 2005 they were sexually active only with men. In contrast, women who were unlabeled or bisexual in 2005 had begun the study pursuing around 55 percent of their sexual contacts with women, but this figure dropped to 35 percent in 2005.

It became clear that the sample could be divided into two groups:

(1) lesbians who had been exclusively attracted to and involved with women throughout the study, and who were least likely to change their identities; and (2) everyone else. The other participants reported consistently nonexclusive attractions, increasing other-sex behavior, and were most likely to change their identities. Clearly, the women who were changing identities were not undergoing changes in their orientations. They had been attracted to both women and men all along.

The Importance of Nonexclusivity

The association between nonexclusivity (attractions to both sexes) and identity change underscores how much researchers have been missing by failing to include bisexual women in previous studies of identity development. I address the issue of nonexclusivity and bisexuality in greater detail in the next chapter, but several points bear mentioning here, in the context of identity change. Specifically, women who are drawn to both sexes face a more complex set of issues when adopting an identity label than women with exclusive same-sex attractions and relationships. In order to settle on the "right" identity, women with nonexclusive attractions have to go beyond just *acknowledging* their same-sex attractions—they must consider exactly how strongly they lean toward women versus men; whether sexual and emotional feelings are equally important; whether behavior trumps fantasy or vice versa; and whether social networks and ideological beliefs should play a role in their self-identification.[9]

Consider the example of Ellen. Now thirty-three years old and heterosexually identified, she reflects back on the single same-sex relationship that she had, at the age of twenty: "When I reached this more intimate level with this one particular woman, I knew I was still attracted to men, so I was sort of forced to really question, Is this sort of the pattern that I want to follow through my life, or is this just going to be a bisexual type of thing, or am I more comfortable with men or women, or . . . what?" Other women who experienced nonexclusive attractions made different choices. Amy, for example, is a bisexual woman who initially identified as lesbian; in recalling her initial coming out, she noted that though she always experienced periodic sexual attractions to men, her substantive emotional bonds were formed with women. Because she felt that these emotional bonds were more important than sporadic sexual desires, she was initially most comfortable with the label of lesbian. Yet as the years went by, she met a number of men to whom she bonded strongly on an emotional level. She realized that she could not completely rule out the possibility of falling in love with a man. She therefore switched to a bisexual label in her late twenties despite feeling that she might never actually act on her feelings for men.

Carol, age twenty-seven, reported similar feelings but reached a different conclusion. Instead of switching to a bisexual identification, she simply adopted a broader, more flexible understanding of lesbianism:

> I would say that the way that I define lesbian is probably the same, but I have become more flexible. I think I have become more comfortable in looking at it as a continuum instead of discrete categories. Partly from meeting more people and talking with them about their preferences, identities, how they define things and just being more exposed. Also realizing that all of my life I have been attracted to both men and women and coming to a comfortable place calling myself a lesbian in spite of that.

Some women maintained a lesbian label despite attractions to both sexes because they were dismayed by the negative stereotypes that both heterosexuals and lesbians harbor about bisexuals. As one twenty-five-year-old unlabeled woman remarked about her transition from identifying as bisexual to unlabeled, "I feel sort of uncomfortable calling myself bisexual because if I'm talking to a guy, it's the usual thing: 'Oh, so do you do this and that and the other thing?' And if I'm talking to a gay woman, then she's like, 'Oh, Really. I can't trust you.'" Another respondent noted, "A lot of people I talk to say, 'Well, you know, bisexuality is just one step up from one or the other, so you're not actually bisexual, you're actually on your way to becoming either straight or gay.'"

Other women with nonexclusive attractions would routinely change their identity labels in accordance with their current romantic partner or social network. If they were seriously involved with a woman, they identified as lesbian. If they were seriously involved with a man, they identified as bisexual or heterosexual, all the while acknowledging that they remained attracted to both sexes. "At this point in my life," a twenty-five-year-old bisexual woman explained, "I'm starting to think about a long-term, permanent partner, so I think if I met somebody and made that kind of lifetime commitment, then I would also be committing to that particular sexuality. But it could go either way, it could be a man or woman."

My findings suggest that for women with nonexclusive attractions, fixed identities may never completely succeed in representing the complicated, situation-specific, and sometimes relationship-specific nature of their sexual self-concepts. Perhaps for these women, adopting a *flexible, changeable* identity is the most mature, adaptive way of understanding their sexuality, as Paula Rust has suggested in her own research on women's diverse identity pathways.[10] In such cases, even a bisexual identity may not capture the complexity of their desires.

Do Different Types Have Different Histories?

The findings presented above raise a broader question about whether there are fundamentally different "types" of same-sex sexuality, with different origins and outcomes. This notion has a long history in the research literature on sexual orientation, and it has generated many studies aimed at testing whether the kind of sexual-minority individual you are is related to how you got that way. Most of the research on this question has focused on sexual-identity "precursors" and "milestones," such as the existence of childhood gender atypicality, the timing and sequencing of same-sex and other-sex attractions and sexual contact, the timing of first sexual questioning, and the factors that first prompted that questioning.[11]

The basic idea behind these studies is that early-developing sexual minorities, whose same-sex sexuality began to emerge at a young age in the form of same-sex attractions or gender atypicality, might be more "essentially," "biologically," or "authentically" gay than individuals who had unremarkable childhoods and whose same-sex sexuality emerged much later in response to situational factors such as meeting lesbian/gay/bisexual people or becoming familiar with lesbian/gay/bisexual issues (through college courses, media exposure, or political involvement).

This distinction between more and less authentic or essential forms of same-sex sexuality has emerged repeatedly in the research literature under different guises: real versus spurious homosexuality, constitutional versus opportunistic homosexuality, and born versus elective lesbians.[12] Individuals with essential same-sex orientations are presumed to become aware of their same-sex sexuality earlier because of the biological basis of these orientations. This view rests on two false assumptions: that biologically based traits reveal themselves earlier rather than later (as a counterexample, consider schizophrenia, which typically does not become expressed until late adolescence), and that situational factors have more influence on later-developing feelings and behaviors than on earlier-developing feelings and behaviors (many developmentalists would argue that, to the contrary, children are much more malleable than adults).

Researchers have traditionally assigned bisexuality to the "less essential" category. For example, in an early and influential psychological investigation of same-sex sexuality, the authors claimed outright that bisexual orientations were "much less strongly tied to pre-adult sexual feelings. . . . Exclusive homosexuality tends to emerge from a deep-seated predisposition, while bisexuality is more subject to influence by social and sexual learning."[13] Some members of the lesbian community have always been skeptical about the authenticity of bisexuality and critical of bisexuals for "choosing" to experiment with women despite eventually returning to heterosexuality.[14]

None of these presumptions about different types of same-sex sexuality is supported empirically. For example, though some early studies seemed to suggest that bisexually identified women were less likely than lesbians to report experiences like early "tomboyism," or that they experienced their first same-sex attractions at later ages, later studies failed to confirm these findings.[15] No published research has tested whether the *context* of a person's first sexual questioning (for example, having same-sex fantasies versus reading about lesbians in a women's studies class) is related to identification as lesbian as opposed to bisexual. Given that no studies have followed sexual-minority individuals over long stretches of time, there has been no systematic test of whether certain patterns of early versus late milestones predict certain long-term patterns of same-sex sexuality.

So do they? In my study I examined the following potential developmental predictors: recollections of early gender-atypical behavior or feelings of being different from the other girls; age of first same-sex attractions; age of first same-sex sexual contact; age of first sexual questioning; and the context of first questioning (through distinctly sexual routes, such as same-sex fantasies or attractions, or through situational routes such as taking classes on sexuality, meeting sexual-minority individuals, and so on).

In brief, none of these developmental variables was shown to predict anything about women's later experiences. They failed to predict whether women identified as lesbian, bisexual, or unlabeled at any of the five assessments; they failed to predict the degree of a woman's same-sex attractions across the five assessments; they failed to predict whether women changed or kept their identity labels over time; and they failed to predict whether women considered their sexuality something they were born with, something that was influenced by their environment, something that they chose, or something that might change in the future.

Although we might learn something by dividing sexual-minority women into subtypes on the basis of how they *currently* experience and think about their sexuality (exclusive versus nonexclusive, stable versus fluid, more or less environmentally influenced), none of these distinctions appears to be related to how women's same-sex sexuality first developed. Some of the women who were most exclusively and consistently attracted to women over the ten years of the study had been "late bloomers" with no awareness of same-sex attraction until they took a class on sexuality or joined a political organization at age twenty; some of the women with nonexclusive attractions who changed identities multiple times had been tomboys who recalled experiencing their first same-sex sexual fantasies before they even reached puberty.

Thus the widespread notion that a woman's sexual milestones provide clues about the long-term expression of her sexuality appears misguided. In the end, we simply do not know why one woman's same-sex sexuality develops early and another's much later, or why it is sometimes triggered by private experiences of sexual attraction and other times by environmental or situational factors. But it certainly seems inappropriate to pronounce certain women's experiences of same-sex sexuality less "authentic" simply because they run counter to societal stereotypes.

Notably, other researchers are beginning to reach the same conclusions. Some have argued that instead of distinguishing between essential and situational forms of same-sex sexuality, we need to acknowledge that all complex behaviors are generated by a range of essential, biologically determined propensities interacting with a range of situational and environmental factors.[16] Given these interactions, we may never accurately predict the future course of a woman's sexuality on the basis of her current or prior experiences.

Women themselves reported an increasing awareness of this fact. Some respondents noted that though they had begun the study convinced that they understood their sexuality, they gradually realized that they did not know as much as they thought, and that they could not necessarily predict how they might feel in the future about certain people or relationships. As one woman said, "I've been wrong about so many things about it in the past, I've no idea what to say about the future." Some women dealt with this uncertainty by changing their identity labels to conform with their experiences; others adopted flexible definitions of their current identity that could accommodate unexpected changes. Yet one of the most fascinating findings of the study was the fact that many women dealt with the perceived fluidity and unpredictability of their sexuality by casting off all identity labels.

Becoming Unlabeled

We might expect women who wanted to acknowledge the potential for unexpected patterns of attraction and behavior with both women and men to simply adopt bisexual identities. This was not the case. Although approximately one-third of identity changes involved the adoption of a bisexual label, a slightly larger number involved the eschewal of lesbian or bisexual labels altogether in favor of an "unlabeled" identity. Moreover, if we include the women who considered themselves unlabeled at the very beginning of the study, then about two-thirds of women in the sample have considered themselves unlabeled for some period of time in the past ten years. The unlabeled category is thus the single most popular identity in the study! Such a finding is particularly striking given that, as noted, unlabeled women have been systematically excluded from all previous research on sexual orientation. As with the exclusion of bisexuals, it now appears that this omission may have seriously distorted our current understanding of women's experiences.

But what exactly does it mean to be unlabeled? Traditional coming-out models would characterize the adoption of such an identity as a sign of internalized homophobia or repression, for these models assume that healthy sexual-identity development always concludes with the adoption of a lesbian, gay, or bisexual label.[17] Yet when I asked women to explain their reasons for "unlabeling," I found something quite different. None of them denied or discounted their same-sex attractions, and most remained completely open about their same-sex sexuality to friends, family members, and coworkers. For them, switching to an unlabeled identity did not constitute a return to the closet.

Instead, women explained that they gave up identity labels because they realized that their sexuality did not fit an existing label, and they were increasingly skeptical about the rigid and arbitrary nature of any sexual categorization.

Why did so many women feel that neither lesbian nor bisexual labels fit their experiences? As with identity change in general, non-exclusive attractions played an important role in respondents' decision to forgo labels. Women who gave up their identity labels described their sexual attractions (averaged over the ten years) as about 60 percent directed to women, compared with 78 percent among women who had never been unlabeled. So why not simply identify as bisexual? Some unlabeled women felt that the bisexual label implied a greater degree of interest in men than they actually felt. Most of these women had switched to unlabeled identities from lesbian identities, often after realizing that though they were predominantly interested in women, they could not rule out periodic attractions to—or even involvement with—men:

> I've been in a committed relationship for almost seven years, and I've never thought about anyone else. But I think I'm more comfortable now with the idea that I could be attracted to a man, and that's OK. . . . It's OK for it to be a little bit fluid. (age twenty-eight, lesbian)

> I think these days I'm much more comfortable just allowing myself to feel whatever I feel. Growing up, there was society around me telling me to date boys, or whatever, and then I came out as a lesbian and there was an equal pressure to date women. Now I am mainly going through life and seeing who I meet, and I'm much less panicked about the whole thing. Whatever I feel is all right, you know? (age twenty, unlabeled)

> Every time I feel comfortable with a label, something happens that makes me think that that's not an appropriate label. . . . I guess I went through a period where I thought I should probably label myself as lesbian and live according to that. Then I fell radically in love with a man. . . . I think labeling my sexuality is dangerous and I should just experience it. (age twenty-seven, bisexual)

In these cases, the adoption of an unlabeled identity was a compromise between the poor fit of both the lesbian label (which presumes exclusive same-sex attractions and behavior) and the bisexual label (which presumes a significant degree of sexual interest in both men and women).

Another commonly cited reason for the poor fit of existing labels was discrepancy between physical and emotional attractions. At first glance, the notion of such discrepancies might seem strange—aren't emotional and physical attractions two sides of the same coin? This view is certainly the most popular, but it is inaccurate. Although most of the women I interviewed felt that their sexual attractions paralleled their emotional attachments, this was not always the case. In fact, women reported that on average, the percentage of physical same-sex attractions they experienced differed from their emotional same-sex attractions by about 15 percentage points in either direction (in other words, some women were more emotionally than physically drawn to women, whereas others were more physically than emotionally drawn). A small number of women reported discrepancies of up to 40 percentage points.

Like women with nonexclusive attractions, women with significant gaps between their emotional and physical feelings often faced challenges in selecting a comfortable identity label. They had to decide whether their sexual identity was better categorized by patterns of "love" or patterns of "lust," and they had to forecast what sort of relationships they might desire in the future. Many of these women found it difficult to make these determinations. Sue, for example, felt that her attractions were riddled with contradictions: "I prefer to make out with men, but the idea of having sex with a man utterly repulses me. I would, however, like to marry a woman, and that's who I want to make a long-term commitment to."

Other women worried that no single resolution would ever emerge. As Jen noted, "Sometimes I worry that I will never settle down with anyone, because the way I feel about guys is mainly sexual, and the way I feel about women is mainly emotional. So I'm always going between the two, and I don't know *what* to call that, you know?" Her confusion is understandable. After all, conventional models of sexual identity typically presume that sexual and emotional attractions always match, and so decisions about lesbian versus bisexual identities are simply about degrees of attraction. Yet many women had a hard time weighing the different types of attractions they felt for women and men and deciding which best captured their sexual identity:

> I feel that I am mostly drawn to women, but it is certainly possible that I could be drawn to a man again. But I wouldn't identify as bisexual mainly because I haven't felt the *kind* of attractions to a man that would make me really want to be in a relationship with him, the way I have felt with women for the past six years. So I guess technically I would consider myself bisexual, but that gives more weight to the male end than I really want. (age twenty-four, unlabeled)

Because traditional models of sexuality make no provision for discrepancies between physical and emotional feelings, women experiencing these gaps often conclude that no existing identity labels adequately represent their unique experiences.

Notably, many of the women in the heterosexual comparison group also experienced disparities between their physical and emotional attractions. Every single one of these women reported having a current or past pattern of emotionally intense bonds to female friends. In some cases they described these friendships as bordering on romantic or physical intimacy. For many of these women, their capacities for same-sex emotional affection and their predominant other-sex physical desires motivated them to volunteer for my study. Many reported a long-standing curiosity about just what their same-sex friendships meant, given that they were certain of their heterosexuality:

> I have always had really strong emotional bonds to women, but I never really felt funny about it because our society sort of expects strong emotional bonds between women, so I never thought that I shouldn't pursue that. I'm rarely physically attracted to a woman, but sometimes I have this strong urge to get to know a woman better. . . . I'm so much more emotionally drawn to women than men that for a while I worried that I would never get close to a man,

and I was actually surprised that I ended up connecting with a man as strongly as I did with my current boyfriend. (age twenty, heterosexual)

This lesbian relative said to me, "Come on, you have all these really close women friends, haven't you ever thought about it? I said no, but I did spend some time thinking about it. But I finally decided that I wasn't lesbian or bisexual, because although I love my friends so much, I really just don't have sexual feelings for them. I know people that define themselves as lesbian based only on their emotional feelings, but I think you really need that sexual element to be a lesbian. (age nineteen, heterosexual)

At the end of my sophomore year I started to think things like, "Am I heterosexual or not? Why do I do certain things? Whom am I physically attracted to, whom have I been attracted to in the past? . . . Especially, I thought of the feelings of jealousy and possessiveness I sometimes have for my female friends. But in the end, I decided that because I'm physically attracted to men, I'm not gay. (age twenty-five, heterosexual)

Thus fluidity appears to manifest itself similarly in both heterosexual and sexual-minority respondents, the primary difference being that heterosexual women take the gap between their physical and emotional attractions more seriously than do sexual-minority women: in their estimation, if their attractions to women are exclusively emotional, then they are probably not gay.

For some of the sexual-minority women who gave up their identity labels, unlabeling was part of a larger process of questioning or rejecting the very notion of sexual categorization, often directly in response to a greater awareness of sexual fluidity. These women typically reported that over the years, they had increasingly come to realize that they had no idea what sort of attractions and relationships they might desire in the future. Accordingly, the only way to make sufficient space for the full range of future possibilities was to set labels aside and leave themselves open to different experiences:

> The reason why I haven't labeled myself is because I feel like I'm putting myself in a box. I don't want to close off any possibilities. I'm with a woman now, but I'm not sure about what will happen in the future, and that's okay. (age twenty-six, unlabeled)

> I guess because I feel that you just never know how someone will affect you, and I just never know who my soul mate is going to be. (age twenty-four, unlabeled)

> I think [labeling as a lesbian before] was right for me at that time, but I feel like it hasn't answered all my questions . . . I haven't found my true life partner so far, so I guess . . . I just don't want to be so specific. I just kind of want to be open to life now. (age twenty-seven, unlabeled)

Others described a more radical questioning of sexual categories and indicated that dividing up sexuality according to "gender pairings" (that is, same-sex, other-sex) had little to do with the way they experienced different types of relationships:

> I don't really think that labels adequately or accurately describe anybody. I think you can be with a man your whole life and still be a lesbian, and I think you can be with a man and a woman, back and forth, and still not be bisexual. (age twenty-five, unlabeled)

> I hate boxes. Hate them, hate them. And I hate this whole dichotomy paradigm that our society tends to revolve around. It's black, it's white, it's male, it's female, it's straight, it's gay, whatever. None of those fits. (age twenty-four, unlabeled)

> When I'm with a woman, I'm not really a lesbian, and when I'm with a man, I'm not really straight. Maybe if I spent ten years with a woman it would change the way I thought, and I would call myself a

lesbian. I think your definition changes based on your experiences.
(age twenty-two, bisexual)

Six years later, this same woman noted:

I date both men and women, but I don't like the word "bisexual,"
because I think it implies polarity. I guess I started thinking about
this around 4 1/2 years ago, when I was involved in a long-term
committed relationship with a man, but a *queer* man. And it made
me redefine things, because I didn't believe that a queer man and a
queer woman together in a relationship like ours was conventionally
heterosexual. (age twenty-eight, bisexual)

Other women rejected the implication that once they adopted a sexual-identity label, it was a statement about their "essential nature."
As one unlabeled woman protested, "I just feel like I have no idea
what my sexuality would 'naturally' be. I have no idea how much is
constructed by me at this point, and been constructed by how I've
lived. . . . It makes me uncomfortable calling myself anything . . . I
would rather just not have to name it at all. I shouldn't have to
think about it" (age twenty-seven, unlabeled).

Many women indicated that it took them a number of years and
considerable self-reflection to reach these conclusions. These respondents began the study with more stringent notions about sexual categorization. As one woman mentioned at her ten-year interview, "I think I'm comfortable with the idea that I could be
attracted to a man, and that's OK. I think that's something that I
never would have thought when I was, say, eighteen or twenty"
(age twenty-eight, lesbian).

Interestingly, sexual-minority teenagers today appear to be reaching the same conclusions at earlier ages. Recent studies have found
that many such youths describe themselves as "questioning" rather
than as lesbian, gay, or bisexual.[18] Some of these young people are,
in fact, actively engaged in the process of figuring out the sexual-

identity label that best suits them. Others embrace the "questioning" label in order to explicitly reject society's classification of sexuality into fixed heterosexual, bisexual, and homosexual categories, and to signal their openness to discovering ever-changing possibilities in their sexual attractions and behaviors. This attitude toward questioning is exemplified by Ann, who thought she might never be completely certain about her sexuality; nor did she necessarily want to: "For those of us who question, your whole life becomes a question. Do you then reach some level of understanding, and then it's static? I don't think so" (age twenty-two, unlabeled).

Many respondents came to view sexual-identity labels not as expressions of essential sexuality but as social, cultural, and cognitive "creations" that served different functions in different environments. Women who adopt unlabeled identities are not repressed or self-loathing; to the contrary, many of them have a more nuanced perspective on sexuality than those who unquestioningly treat "lesbian," "bisexual," and "heterosexual" as fixed and essential sexual types.

Putting It All Together

So what does all this mean? If we step back to look at the big picture, four findings stand out as particularly important. Each of these findings contradicts existing models of sexuality, and yet they emerged so strongly and consistently across the ten years of this study that they demand explanation.

Change in sexual identity. Traditionally, sexual-identity development has been considered a straightforward process with a clear outcome: identification as lesbian/gay/bisexual. The results of my study directly contradict this view. Over the ten years of the study, the majority of women repeatedly changed their sexual identity.

The rate of these transitions did not decline over time, so it seems likely that they will continue in the future.

Lack of closure. According to traditional models of sexual-identity formation, the years after coming out bring increased certainty and stability in sexual identity. Yet the women in my study became increasingly willing to acknowledge the potential for future change in their attractions and relationships. Many of them gave up identity labels altogether because they felt that no single label could encompass the complexity of their feelings and experiences, and because they did not want to close off future possibilities.

The prevalence of nonexclusivity. Lesbians, with their presumably exclusive same-sex attractions, have always been considered prototypical sexual minorities. Bisexuals, in contrast, have fit no neat categories and thus have been viewed with skepticism. Yet the results of this study suggest that nonexclusive attractions are the norm rather than the exception, and they are consistent with findings from large-scale representative surveys. Over time, the majority of women in the study—including lesbians—acknowledged the possibility that they might experience attractions to or relationships with both sexes. Moreover, they underwent identity changes (such as adopting bisexual or unlabeled identities) specifically to accommodate such possibilities.

Early experiences do not predict later ones. Researchers studying the development of sexual orientation have typically assessed early indicators and milestones of same-sex sexuality—such as gender-atypical behavior and early-appearing same-sex attractions—on the assumption that these factors predict the subsequent expression of sexual orientation. Specifically, women whose same-sex sexuality emerges early have been considered more "essentially gay" than those whose same-sex sexuality emerges later in life or is triggered by situational factors. My findings do not support this distinction. In my study indicators and milestones predicted nothing about women's eventual development, nor did the types of factors that initially caused women to question their sexuality.

The task now is to develop a new model of female sexuality that successfully explains the fascinating twists and turns the respondents experienced. If the traditional model of sexual orientation is inaccurate, then what is the alternative? A revised model has to balance the fact that women do appear to possess relatively stable overall patterns of sexual attraction with the fact that they nonetheless show variability in feelings and experiences over time and across situations. A model positing *female sexual fluidity* is the best solution.

Sexual Fluidity

My understanding of female sexual fluidity includes four elements:

1. Women do, in fact, have a general sexual orientation: most are predominantly attracted to men; some are attracted to both sexes; and some are mainly attracted to women. As noted, there are many possible causes of these orientations, and they might unfold at various points in development.
2. In addition to their sexual orientation, women also possess a capacity for fluidity. Think of this as a sensitivity to situations and relationships that might facilitate erotic feelings. An example might be an intense emotional relationship (with either a man or a woman) or exposure to environments that provide positive experiences with same-sex relationships. Fluidity can trigger either same-sex or other-sex attractions.
3. The sexual attractions triggered by fluidity may be temporary or long-lasting, depending on how consistently a woman en-

counters the facilitating factors. For example, a heterosexual woman who becomes unexpectedly involved with a close same-sex friend might experience her newfound same-sex attractions as long-lasting if the relationship develops into a stable, long-term bond. Alternatively, the attractions might disappear altogether if the relationship dissolves. The key point is that the attractions triggered by fluidity do not alter a woman's basic orientation, though they might function like an orientation in terms of consistency.

4. Not all women are equally fluid. Just as women have different orientations, they have different degrees of sensitivity to the situational and interpersonal factors that trigger fluidity. As a result, though two women may be exposed to the same set of potential "triggers," one will experience the development of unexpected same-sex attractions whereas the other may not.

In Chapter 7 I provide much more detail about this model and how it operates. For now, I want to focus on the *phenomenology* of fluidity. Specifically, how does this model provide a coherent explanation for the main findings of my study? Let's take the findings one by one.

Change in sexual identity. Traditional models of sexual-identity development suggest that the process involves acknowledging and accepting your same-sex sexuality (heterosexuals, of course, never really have to go through this process, since heterosexuality is universally assumed). Once you discover, accept, and openly claim your true sexual orientation, the process is finished. But if women's fluidity makes it possible for them to experience unexpected attractions under certain circumstances, imagine how this fact might complicate the identity-development process. You might generally feel that you are oriented toward women, but if sexual fluidity facilitates periodic attractions to your male best friend, you might find it uncomfortable—either personally or socially—to maintain a lesbian label. This dilemma is exactly what many of the lesbians in my study described.

Alternatively, consider the women who eventually re-identified as heterosexual. Many of them reported gradually realizing that they were, in fact, generally oriented toward men, even though their same-sex attractions and relationships had been powerful and genuine. I would argue that their same-sex experiences were made possible by sexual fluidity—they were neither "phases" nor "choices" but authentic desires facilitated by the availability of the right person in the right situation. This would explain why such women feel fairly certain of their overall heterosexuality despite acknowledging the power and pleasure of their prior same-sex experiences and remaining open to the possibility of such experiences in the future. As one woman explained, "Your core sexuality probably stays the same, but if the moment that you're living in is strong enough for you, then that's your sexuality at that moment" (age twenty-six, bisexual).

Lack of closure.   Sexual fluidity also provides an apt explanation for the fact that many women became increasingly reluctant to make definitive predictions about their sexuality as the years went by and increasingly ambivalent about fixed identity labels. We might expect that with the passage of time women would come to understand their own capacity for fluidity, casting doubt on the relevance of fixed identity labels and the very notion of fixed sexual selves. This is consistent with the fact that many women *independently* mentioned the notion of fluid sexuality when asked to explain their ambivalence about labeling:

I feel like for a great majority of people, sexuality is very fluid. I think that there are definitely people who are just one way, like either lesbian or straight. It's like a curve, there are some people who flow on the ends, but most people flow in the middle. (age twenty-two, lesbian)

I hate labels; I think they're stupid. Well, they're not stupid, they're limiting, and I think that especially around sexuality things are really much too fluid to try to place a concrete label on it. (age twenty-five, bisexual)

Historically, ambivalence about labeling one's sexuality has been treated as a sign of maladjustment, confusion, or inauthenticity. Researchers have traditionally eliminated "unlabeled" respondents from research samples, unsure whether they were repressed lesbians or "dabbling," misguided heterosexuals. We now know that it is our rigid categories that are misguided, not these women. Women who wrestle with sexual-identity labels give voice to an important consequence of sexual fluidity that deserves more systematic study.

Along the same lines, sexual fluidity requires us to rethink the very notion of identity. Instead of assuming that sexual identities represent enduring sexual "truths," it may be more productive to think of identity as "the choice of a particular perspective from which to make sense of one's sexual feelings and behaviors."[19] This definition allows for multiple, culture-bound, context-specific solutions to the ever-present "problem" posed by same-sex attractions and behaviors. It also allows for the fact that the same solution might not be equally appropriate for all individuals. Whereas one person might avoid labeling his or her sexual identity solely to avoid social rejection, another might do so as an affirmation of sexual fluidity; yet another might do so because Western sexual-identity labels have little meaning in that person's cultural tradition. These strategies might be beneficial for some women and less so for others, but we need to examine them on a case-by-case basis.

The prevalence of nonexclusivity. As noted, most women in the study acknowledged nonexclusive attractions, but the way they experienced those attractions was not the same. Some respondents reported desires that were consistent with a bisexual orientation producing regular attractions to both sexes in varying degrees. But other women described nonexclusive attractions more in terms of potential or capacity. In other words, they reported being generally oriented toward one sex on a day-to-day basis, but they acknowledged that once in a while they encountered individuals who sparked unexpected desires. This is perfectly consistent with the notion that women possess generalized orientations in concert with a capacity for fluidity, and it suggests that the nonexclusivity brought about by sexual fluidity is not quite the same as a bisexual orientation.

Early experiences do not predict later ones. Researchers have assumed that women whose same-sex sexuality develops late in life or proves sensitive to situational factors are not quite as "authentically" or "essentially" gay as women who describe their same-sex sexuality as early-developing and impervious to situational influences. They assume that women whose same-sex sexuality is first triggered by situational factors will eventually abandon it for the safety of heterosexuality. This expectation has spawned colloquial terms such as "LUG"—lesbian until graduation—in reference to women who identify as lesbian *only* in the accepting, progressive environment of college.[20]

Yet the existence of sexual fluidity would mean that all women are sensitive to interpersonal and situational influences on their sexuality, albeit to differing degrees. Accordingly, we should not expect women who first questioned their sexuality because of situational or interpersonal factors to be significantly different from women who questioned their sexuality without such triggers. Furthermore, because situational influences *interact* with dispositional factors, potentially "speeding up" or "slowing down" the expression of various traits, we should not expect the timing of a woman's early attractions or sexual questioning necessarily to predict the eventual course of her attractions, behavior, and identification over time. Rather, the distinction between women whose sexual questioning is triggered late as opposed to early, or by sexual fantasies as opposed to feminist theory courses, might simply depend on a woman's specific degree of fluidity combined with the availability of the right triggers at the right time.

The need for appropriate triggers provides a potential explanation for the fact that over time, the majority of women in the study pursued increasing rates of other-sex sexual contact. Even lesbians who were nearly exclusively attracted to women pursued periodic other-sex sexual contact as the years went by. Such patterns might be attributable to corresponding changes in women's environments. As they left college and joined the working world, nearly all the women reported that they were moving into environments that were less populated with fellow sexual-minority women and more populated with male friends and colleagues. As one thirty-year-old lesbian said, "I just meet far more men on a day-to-day basis than I ever did in college." Another lesbian, who had attended an all-women's college, remarked at age twenty-seven, "I moved back into the co-ed world." It makes sense that as these women became exposed to more men, dramatically increasing the situational triggers and opportunities for other-sex attractions and relationships, fluidity would shift their feelings and behaviors in the same direction.

One of the most important reasons for integrating the notion of sexual fluidity into our understanding of female sexuality is that we might then provide young women themselves with more accurate information about these issues. Many of the women in this study expressed embarrassment when explaining changes in their sexual feelings, relationships, or identities because they had internalized the prevailing cultural message that such experiences were highly atypical. As one twenty-year-old told me before recounting her complex sexual history, "I'm not sure I'm a very good example of a lesbian, and I don't want to mess up your study or anything, so it's okay if you don't want to interview me after all."

Little did she know how common her experiences were! Psychologists, clinicians, and policy makers are increasingly designing educational programming for schools and social service agencies aimed at dispelling myths about sexual orientation and providing support to sexual minorities as they embark on the identity-development process. For women to benefit from these efforts, the science behind these messages should speak to the full range of women's actual experiences and not just presume—as has long been the case—that women simply undergo "female versions" of the types of experiences that have been documented among males.

My aim is to place sexual fluidity in its proper place at the center rather than on the margins of our understanding of female sexuality and its development over the life course. Toward this end, the next three chapters provide detailed investigations of the three primary manifestations of sexual fluidity: nonexclusivity in attractions, changes in attractions, and the capacity to become attracted to "the person and not the gender." For each phenomenon, I use case studies from my longitudinal research to convey how fluidity is experienced and interpreted by women themselves.

CHAPTER 4

Nonexclusive Attractions and Behaviors

Which, if any, of these women from my study would you consider bisexual?

Abigail has been attracted to both sexes ever since she was a child. Her old high school friends like to remind her that she used to come back from movies talking about *both* the cutest guy and the cutest girl. She covered her bedroom wall with pictures of beautiful female models and also male bodybuilders. She now pursues casual sex with men and sometimes watches gay male pornography, but she has only fallen in love and formed meaningful relationships with women.

Monica admits that she sometimes thinks the only reason she is *ever* attracted to men is that she has been socialized to find them attractive. But other times, she feels that those attractions are authentic. Her emotional bonds with women are more intense and satisfying, but she has never been involved with a woman. Her friends convinced her that because she gets involved only with men, she cannot legitimately consider herself bisexual. They urged her to "come out as heterosexual." She is now happily married to a man who considers her to be "100 percent straight—end of story." Her husband is not aware that she is still attracted to women and fantasizes about them several times a week.

Suzanne has been preoccupied with women's bodies since high school, when she was heavily involved with classical dance and used to admire her fellow dancers' bodies. She has always formed "borderline" intense attachments to her female friends, and after becoming familiar with lesbian/gay/bisexual issues and individuals in college, she became intrigued by the possibility of having a sexual relationship with a woman. It never happened. She says that for reasons she still does not fully understand, her aesthetic appreciation of women and her intense bonds with them never quite cross over into sexual desire.

Gwen, who is now married to a man, never considered herself a very sexual person. When she was nineteen, she became unexpectedly romantically and sexually involved with a close female friend, and they carried on an intense affair for more than a year. She thinks that most women probably have some degree of attraction for women, whether or not they acknowledge or act on it. But Gwen thinks it is unlikely that she will ever again be involved with a woman. Most of her attractions are focused on her husband these days. When she does find herself drawn to a woman, the desire is not nearly as intense as her feelings for her husband. Nonetheless, she still has more sexual fantasies about women than about men.

Ann's job requires her to maintain multiple residences in different cities: she currently divides her time between one European city and two large American cities. She has different lovers in each location, some male and some female. Each of her partners is aware of the others, and they are all comfortable with the situation. Ann used to have a primary male partner to whom she was more intensely bonded and with whom she expected to maintain a long-term committed relationship, but they broke up. She feels that she will probably always need both men and women in her life, and she hopes to find another long-term primary relationship, with either a man or a woman.

Ellen came out as a lesbian in high school and can remember being strongly attracted to women from an early age. Nonetheless, she can still imagine falling in love with a man. In her view, you fall in love with whomever you happen to fall in love with. She cannot see herself ever having sex with a man, but she is open to the possibility.

Nicole had her first full-fledged romantic and sexual relationship with her female best friend when she was fifteen. The affair distressed her parents, who sent her off to therapy. The therapist reassured Nicole that there was nothing unhealthy about her relationship. She told her that it was impossible to determine what the relationship meant for her sexual identity: maybe she would conclude that she was lesbian or bisexual, maybe not. Nicole found the therapist's open-minded attitude reassuring. She continued the love affair for another year. Toward the end of high school she became involved with a man with whom she stayed through her college years. But she also remained active in her college's lesbian/gay/bisexual community. She eventually married her college boyfriend and is very happy with him. She does not have any specific label for her sexuality, though she is still attracted to women.

Diedre has never understood sexual categorization. She explains that she becomes attracted to a person's soul, and does not consider their biological sex. She has had satisfying relationships with both men and women and has no idea who she might settle down with in the future. She has trouble relating to the concept of bisexuality because it emphasizes the existence of two genders, which she finds irrelevant to her own sexuality.

Pinpointing Bisexuality

The diversity of these examples is perplexing. Are all these women bisexual? Are some of them? Sex researchers have not devised any guidelines for making such determinations. The simple truth is that academics have found it just as difficult as everyone else to define the hotly debated, frequently stereotyped, much-maligned notion of bisexuality. No single definition seems to capture adequately all the experiences listed above, and yet every single one of these women experiences the hallmark of bisexuality: *attractions to both men and women.*

But what exactly do we mean by "attractions"? Do they have to be sexual attractions, or do romantic feelings count? How many different men and women do you need to find attractive to qualify as bisexual? Is one single crush enough? Does it have to be current, or does a single attraction in high school (or elementary school, or college, or the military, or that yoga retreat you attended two years ago) count too? Do the feelings have to be long-lasting? What about a single erotic dream, a tipsy kiss, or several nights of deep conversation and intense fireside flirting during a camping trip? What is the role of sexual behavior? Is a person's bisexuality more authentic if she actually acts on her attractions? What about fantasies? Are they more or less defining than attractions? Does considering the prospect of same-sex relationships make a person bisexual or just open-minded?

No wonder there is so much confusion about bisexuality—even researchers who have been studying the topic for decades disagree on the answers to these questions.[1] Some see bisexuality as a straightforward sexual responsiveness to both sexes; others view it as the potential for such responsiveness. Some view bisexuality as a form of "gender-free" sexuality in which the femininity or masculinity of a partner is irrelevant. Others see it as a heightened appreciation for *both* masculinity and femininity. Still others view bisexuality as humans' basic sexual nature, before socialization molds us toward one gender or the other. Others believe that there is no such thing as bisexuality, and that all individuals are basically oriented toward men versus women, regardless of what they might like to believe or how they might have experimented over time. Then there are the long-standing stereotypes that have proliferated in both the lesbian-gay community and mainstream society, portraying bisexuals as promiscuous, incapable of commitment, closeted, cowardly, repressed, flighty, indecisive, oversexed, and mentally unstable.[2]

Despite the persistent confusion about bisexuality, it has gained visibility and research attention over the past ten to fifteen years.[3] Especially among the youngest generation of sexual minorities, bisexuality is increasingly popular as both a sexual identity label and an overarching philosophy promoting open, flexible understandings of sexuality instead of rigid homosexual and heterosexual categories.[4] It was once difficult to find the word "bisexual" in the titles of academic articles or lesbian-gay organizations and publications, but now it is generally considered politically incorrect *not* to include the word. Mainstream magazines and newspapers have featured cover stories on bisexuality, and there is even a social science journal devoted exclusively to the topic.

In the academic realm these changes are partly a result of the increased attention that has been paid to female same-sex sexuality over the past decade. As the research has increasingly documented, women are more likely than men to have bisexual identities, attractions, and behaviors. Thus it has become clear that we cannot hope to fully understand female sexuality without a more thoroughgoing understanding of bisexuality. In fact, we might argue that the gaps in our scientific understanding of bisexuality stem not only from society's preoccupation with rigid sexual categories but also from the fact that the prevailing models of sexual orientation have been based on the experiences of men.

We have a long way to go in filling these gaps. Despite the increased awareness of bisexuality, it remains poorly understood, largely because it has so many different manifestations. There is no typical form of bisexuality—all the dueling conceptualizations are "true" to some extent, for some individuals. For this reason, I prefer the term "nonexclusivity" to "bisexuality" because it is general enough to capture a wide range of experiences, and because it does not come with the same historical and cultural baggage attached to the word "bisexual." I still use "bisexual" to denote bisexually identified individuals and "bisexuality" to denote a *consistent pattern* (or "orientation") of nonexclusive attractions, but I generally prefer "nonexclusivity" because it makes no presumptions about the relative balance of one's same-sex and other-sex attractions.

By speaking of nonexclusivity, I intentionally sidestep questions about what bisexuality "really" is, who "has" it, and whether some types are more authentic or intrinsic than others. My goal, instead, is to describe and understand the phenomenon of nonexclusivity in all its forms, and to explore their implications for female sexual fluidity. The downside to using the term "nonexclusivity" is that some people might associate it with infidelity, since the term "exclusive" is often used to refer to monogamous relationships. Let me reiterate that this is *not* the usage I intend. Even in the context of sexual behavior, I use "nonexclusive" simply to describe a woman who has pursued sexual behavior with both women and men *over the course of her own sexual history,* not at the same moment in time. I have been troubled enough by potential misinterpretations of the term "nonexclusivity" to have spent a good deal of time searching for alternatives, but to no avail. So I continue to use this term.

In this chapter I briefly review what scientists know and do not know about bisexuality and nonexclusivity. I then turn to findings from my longitudinal study to explore how women's diverse experiences of nonexclusivity have played out over a ten-year period. Recall that many of the stereotypes and unanswered questions about nonexclusivity concern its long-term stability. Is bisexuality a transitional phase or a permanent sexual orientation? Do most bisexual women eventually revert to their "true" lesbian or heterosexual natures? Until now, researchers have never followed sexual-minority individuals for long enough periods of time to find out. Now, however, we can begin to address this question.

Definitions and Populations

In the past, scientists and laypeople alike assumed that individuals with exclusive same-sex attractions were the most common types of sexual minorities. In contrast, individuals with nonexclusive patterns of desire were routinely overlooked. Men and women who openly claimed bisexual identities have also been excluded from lesbian-gay social and political organizations because their "real" identities were matters of suspicion. This was particularly true within the burgeoning lesbian-feminist communities of the 1970s, in which bisexually identified (or bisexually behaving) women were often distrusted because of their supposed access to heterosexual privilege.[5]

Even now, scientific studies of sexual minorities routinely exclude bisexual individuals, often for practical reasons. In many research samples, there are too few openly identified bisexuals to group together and analyze as a separate category. At the same time, grouping them with either lesbians or heterosexuals obscures the findings.[6] What if some of the bisexuals are really closeted lesbians and others are confused heterosexuals? The only way to avoid these problems is to restrict research samples to clear-cut lesbians and gay men, setting the bisexuals aside. After all, they are just flukes, right?

Wrong. A groundbreaking, nationally representative study of sexuality among American adults conducted by the sociologist Edward Laumann and his colleagues found that among both women and men (but especially women), more individuals reported experiencing attractions for both sexes than attractions exclusively for the same sex.[7] Moreover, this finding has been replicated in a number of other nationally representative studies of American adolescents and adults.[8]

The gender differences are even more interesting: in the survey by Laumann's group, slightly more than 6 percent of American men and 4 percent of American women reported some degree of attraction to the same sex. Yet these groups of men and women proved to be notably different from each other. Among men, about the same percentage reported being attracted mainly to women as reported being attracted only to men. Combined, these two groups account for about 40 percent of men with same-sex attractions. In contrast, only 10 percent of men with same-sex attractions were attracted to both sexes and 11 percent were attracted mostly to the same-sex. If we plot out these percentages, we get a big letter "U," with "spikes" at the two extremes representing the large numbers of men with exclusive same-sex *or* other-sex attractions, and a big drop in the middle representing nonexclusivity.

Women could not look more different. The largest group of women with same-sex attractions turned out to be the group with predominantly—but not exclusively—other-sex attractions. More than 60 percent of women with same-sex attractions fell into this category, meaning that the most common type of sexual-minority woman is someone whose attractions "look" heterosexual (some researchers have referred to these women as "Kinsey 1s," since a Kinsey score of 0 would represent exclusive heterosexuality). As we examine groups of women with progressively more exclusive same-sex attractions, the numbers get smaller and smaller. Altogether, 20 percent of women with same-sex attractions reported being attracted to both sexes, 14 percent reported being mostly attracted to the same sex, and only 7 percent reported being exclusively attracted to the same sex. So whereas four times as many men were attracted only to the same sex as were attracted to *both* sexes, among women this pattern was basically reversed.

Could this stark gender difference stem from the study's self-report methodology? After all, maybe women are less comfortable admitting to exclusive same-sex attractions than to nonexclusive attractions, even on an unconscious level. As many feminist scholars have pointed out, women's sexual involvement with men—or lack thereof—has always had stark social and political implications. Back in 1980, Adrienne Rich coined the term "compulsory heterosexuality" to identify the invisible, pervasive system of social control that has historically granted privileges to women (such as social status and economic security) on the basis of their sexual availability to men.[9] Hence, though both sexes are stigmatized for same-sex sexuality, total withdrawal from the institution of heterosexuality is socially "dangerous" for women in particular. As a result, we might argue that women with exclusive same-sex attractions are unconsciously motivated to claim that they are still attracted to men as well. The only way to rule out this possibility is to somehow "get inside" men's and women's heads so that we can assess their desires without requiring them to report their feelings openly.

One way to do this is to examine individuals' physiological experiences of sexual arousal along with their psychological experiences. This is a valuable strategy not because the body provides a "truer" measure of desire but because physiological responses are more difficult for the average person to control consciously. A team of researchers headed by J. Michael Bailey at Northwestern University has conducted a series of studies on gender differences in men's and women's genital responses to same-sex and other-sex erotic stimuli. In men, this involves placing a sensitive elastic strip around the penis which measures the degree of penile erection. In women, it involves inserting a small, tampon-sized device inside the vagina to measure the degree of increased blood flow to the vaginal walls (this measurement is a classic indicator of female sexual arousal and is directly analogous to the male measure because erections are caused and sustained by increased blood flow). In one study led by the psychologist Meredith Chivers, the Northwestern team measured the physiological and self-reported arousal of four different groups: gay men, straight men, lesbian women, and heterosexual women.[10] Each individual was placed alone in a private room and hooked up to the measurement equipment. They then viewed videos of women having sex with women, men having sex with men, men having sex with women, and some neutral videos of landscapes, as a control condition.

The results were startling. Both gay and heterosexual men responded mostly as we might expect: gay men were most physiologically and subjectively aroused by the male-male videos, whereas heterosexual men were most physiologically and subjectively aroused by the female-female videos. Women, however, showed a completely different pattern. There was much lower correspondence between women's genital responses and their self-reported ratings of arousal, a finding that has emerged in other, similar studies.[11] But more important, on average women had roughly equivalent genital responses to the different sexual videos. So whereas gay men did not tend to develop erections in response to the female-female video, and heterosexual men did not tend to develop erections in response to the male-male video, most lesbian and heterosexual women became physiologically aroused in response to all the videos. Importantly, this was not equally true for every woman. Some lesbians showed substantially more arousal to the female-female videos and some heterosexual women showed substantially more arousal to the male-male videos. But on average, women's responses were "nonspecific," in the authors' words. Women's *self-reported* arousal, however, was more in line with their self-described identities: lesbians reported the greatest arousal to the female-female video, and heterosexual women reported the greatest arousal to the female-male video. Notably, similar findings were found in a separate study of female sexual response by a different researcher, supporting the validity of the effect.[12]

The Northwestern team then conducted an additional study that contrasted the sexual-arousal patterns of self-identified heterosexual and gay men with self-identified bisexual men.[13] They found that though self-identified bisexual men reported sexual attractions to both women and men, they tended to become physiologically aroused by either one sex or the other. So though the men felt that their attractions were bisexual in nature, their bodies responded as if they were either gay or heterosexual. The researchers have concluded from this provocative series of studies that there appears to be a fundamental sex difference in the nature of sexual arousal, with men's arousal more "category-specific" than women's. In other words, men tend to respond physiologically to categories of individuals—males versus females. Women, however, do not appear to be sensitive to these categories. Although they may subjectively prefer one sex over the other, their bodies respond to both. In interpreting these findings, it is important to remember that physiological arousal is not necessarily more accurate than subjective arousal. We do not fully understand the link between these two types of sexual arousal, so discrepancies between them are difficult to interpret. I revisit this issue in more detail below.

The psychologist Richard Lippa has provided further confirmation of this basic gender difference by examining the role of sex drive.[14] Lippa studied how "classic drive theory" applied to human sexuality. According to this theory, high levels of sex drive should increase individuals' desires for the types of sexual partners they usually desire, instead of increasing their desires for sex with just anyone. In terms of sexual orientation, this would mean that gay men with high sex drives should be particularly interested in sex with men, but their high sex drives should have no effect on their interest in sex with women. Correspondingly, heterosexual men with high sex drives should be particularly interested in sex with women, but their high sex drives should have no effect on their interest in sex with men.

Lippa examined this theory in a series of studies investigating associations between the sex drives of gay, lesbian, and heterosexual individuals and their interest in female and male partners. His findings paralleled those of the Northwestern team. Specifically, high levels of sex drive in men were associated with higher levels of sexual interest in one's "preferred" gender (men for gay men, and women for heterosexual men). But for most women (with the exception of the lesbian subsample in one of his studies), high sex drive was associated with increased sexual attraction to *both* men and women. Like the Northwestern team, Lippa believes that his results suggest a fundamental difference between the way sexuality and sexual orientation are organized for women versus men.

But what do all these findings imply at the level of day-to-day experience? Especially perplexing, of course, is the fact that women's fairly broad physical responses to same-sex and other-sex stimuli differed from their subjective responses. Are women intentionally misrepresenting their desires? This is possible, but it seems unlikely in the context of these studies given that the women knew their genital responses were being monitored. A heterosexual woman might want to hide the fact that she was becoming aroused by the same-sex video, but she would know that the researchers would be able to tell by examining her genital responses.

It seems more plausible that the discrepancies between women's genital responses and their subjective feelings of desire are real: sometimes women are physically aroused without knowing it, and sometimes their subjective feelings of desire are not matched by genital arousal. Notably, similar discrepancies have occurred in other psychophysiological research. For example, many studies of stress reactivity have found that though individuals report feeling stressed in response to laboratory stressors, they show no physiological arousal; others show physiological arousal in the absence of self-reported stress.[15] In this case, however, women's responses were generally more discrepant than men's. Why? One possibility is that society's ever-present double standard for female and male sexuality (boys who have strong sexual desires are normal, while girls with this profile are sluts) leads adolescent girls to ignore their own experiences of arousal, so that they have few opportunities to "match up" their psychological and physiological experiences of desire.[16] This might be exacerbated by the fact that young boys are more likely than young girls to explore their own bodies and engage in sex play.[17] By the time they reach adulthood, these factors may coalesce to produce notable gaps between women's psychological and physiological experiences of arousal.

We are implicitly assuming, of course, that these experiences are supposed to match up, but perhaps we are wrong about that as well. Just as you might be attracted to different people for different reasons (one person is physically beautiful, another is warm and funny, another is complex and mysterious), maybe diverse types of desire become activated in different circumstances. Sometimes they might correspond, sometimes not. We do know that the overall degree of correspondence is far greater among men. Perhaps, then, discrepancies between psychological and physiological arousal represent yet another manifestation of women's distinctive capacity for fluidity. In other words, perhaps fluidity allows women to experience situation-specific sexual arousal that diverges not only from their overall orientation but also from their concurrent psychological experience as well. This might help to account for cases in which women go for years without any awareness of same-sex attractions at all, and then abruptly develop such attractions in the context of a specific same-sex relationship.[18] Maybe such women always possessed a fluid capacity for such arousal (in other words, if they enrolled in Chivers's study they would have had a robust genital response to the same-sex stimuli), but they required direct involvement in an intimate same-sex relationship to transform that physiological capacity into a conscious experience of attraction.

If this is the case, then many women might be far more fluid than they realize. Most likely the participants in Chivers's study would never have expected their genital responses to be as broad as they turned out to be. But do such responses matter if they are outside a person's conscious experience? This question, of course, harks back to the debates about who "counts" as bisexual. If your *physiologi-*

cal pattern of arousal is nonexclusive (in other words, you would respond genitally to both men and women in Chivers's study), but your *subjective* desires are clearly categorical, then are you lesbian or bisexual? Is the physiological measure a better index of your underlying orientation, or does it simply assess a capacity that remains meaningless unless it is integrated with conscious experience? After all, consider your own feelings of desire. When you meet someone and think, "Wow, that person is attractive," where exactly is that response coming from? Are you aware of your own physical arousal at that moment, or are you responding psychologically? What if you found out that though you think Chris is more desirable than Pat, your body responded more strongly to Pat than to Chris. Would that change your decision about whom to approach? If Chris and Pat were of different genders, would you then change your sexual-identity label?

In truth, we know so little about the phenomenology of desire and the specific connection between its physical and psychological components that it makes no sense to pronounce some forms of arousal more authentic than others or better indicators of a person's "true" orientation. The complex nature of the existing data should serve as a potent reminder of just how complex attractions are. When we toss around simplistic definitions of homosexuality and bisexuality—"attracted to the same sex, attracted to both sexes"—we imply that "attraction" and "desire" are straightforward phenomena and that all we need to do is figure out who is attracted to whom.

The situation is much more complicated than that. One way to break down this complexity is to look closely at the real-life, day-to-day, year-by-year experiences of the women in my study. Virtually all of them—even the lesbians—have been attracted to both men and women to some degree, at some point in time. Yet they differ dramatically with regard to how they experienced same-sex and other-sex attractions (physical versus emotional, immediate versus gradual, intense versus weak, and so on) and in how they interpreted them. Exploring the diversity of their experiences helps to reveal the multifaceted nature of nonexclusivity. Furthermore, tracking different women over time allows us to explore questions that researchers have never before been able to address: How stable are nonexclusive attractions over the long term? Is bisexuality a phase or an orientation? Do most women eventually gravitate toward one gender, or are women with nonexclusive attractions consistently compelled to seek relationships with both sexes? My respondents' experiences speak directly to these controversial issues.

Nonexclusivity over Time

The best place to begin is with women's identity labels. What distinguishes women who identify as bisexual or unlabeled from women who identify as lesbian? Is the difference between these groups a matter of degree or a matter of kind?

As noted, when I began my study nearly 60 percent of the participants considered themselves either bisexual or unlabeled. At the time I was unsure how to categorize or interpret the unlabeled women, so I compared them with the lesbian and bisexual women on a number of measures to see whether they resembled either group. I found that their reported percentages of same-sex attractions closely mirrored those of the bisexually identified women. In other words, "unlabeled" seemed to function as an alternative way to represent an individual's capacity for nonexclusive attractions.

Recall, as well, that among the two-thirds of women who changed their identities over the ten years of the study, most undertook changes that accommodated a broadening of their attractions rather than increased exclusivity. Specifically, women were more likely to switch to unlabeled and bisexual identities than to heterosexual or lesbian identities over the ten years of the study. In fact, by 2005 fully 80 percent of the sample had identified as bisexual or unlabeled for at least some period of time. But were they doing so for the same reasons? Did they interpret the label "bisexual" in the same way? Exactly what range of attractions did the respondents consider to be consistent with a bisexual versus a lesbian label? They obviously thought that a woman did not need to be exclusively attracted to women to identify as lesbian. Across the ten years of the study, only three women reported that they were 100 percent attracted to women at each assessment, and only seventeen women reported 100 percent same-sex attractions at any assessment. This means that only one-third of the women who *ever* adopted a lesbian label reported consistently exclusive same-sex attractions, showing that most women thought it was acceptable for lesbians to experience periodic attractions to men.

But this was the case only if most of their attractions were directed toward women. The majority of women who consistently identified as lesbian reported experiencing between 90 and 95 percent of their attractions for women. In contrast, the majority of women who identified as bisexual at each assessment reported that between 40 and 60 percent of their attractions were for women. Unlabeled women showed a wider range of same-sex attractions, between 30 and 80 percent, but most unlabeled women fell in the same range as the bisexuals.

Remember that these percentages represent relative ratios of attraction, that is, how often a woman is attracted to women versus men on a day-to-day basis. Because there are other ways to compare attractions to women versus men, at the ten-year point I asked women a broader range of questions about their attractions, such as the intensity of their attractions and how many different women and men they generally found themselves drawn to. After all, someone might report being 100 percent attracted to women simply because her attractions were directed to her current partner. That situation seems quite different from a case in which a woman is attracted to a wide range of different women from day to day.

Using labels from 2005, when I asked the question, the majority of self-identified lesbians rated the intensity of their attractions to women as approximately 7.5 on a scale of 1 to 8. The average rating for bisexually identified women, in contrast, was around 6, and for unlabeled women it was less than 5 (which puts them slightly below the midpoint of the scale). As for attractions to men, self-identified lesbians rated the intensity of those attractions at around 2 (the second lowest scale point), bisexuals as slightly over 6, and unlabeled women as a little over 5.

On average, bisexual and unlabeled women reported that attractions for men and women were about equal in intensity. But these figures are group averages—what about individual women? If some bisexual women feel that their same-sex attractions are more intense and others feel that their other-sex attractions are more intense, those differences would cancel each other out once we took the group average. So I took each woman's ratings and subtracted her intensity rating for men from her intensity rating for women. If the ratings were identical (meaning her same-sex and other-sex attractions were equally intense), this would yield a score of 0. If her attractions to women were more intense than her attractions to men, this would yield a positive number; if her attractions to men were more intense, this would yield a negative number.

The average among the bisexually identified women was −.6, meaning that on average, bisexual women tended to give very similar ratings of intensity to men and women, differing by less than one point on the 1 to 8 scale, with men receiving slightly higher ratings. Yet there was quite a bit of variability, and in fact one-third of bisexual women rated their attractions to women as more intense than their attractions to men. Interestingly, if we compare bisexual women's ratings of *intensity* with their reports of the *frequency* of same-sex versus other-sex attractions (the now-familiar 0 percent to 100 percent figure), an unexpected picture emerges. The subset of bisexual women who had more intense attractions to women also had more frequent attractions to women, which seems to make sense. A similar pattern was found among the bisexual women who had more intense attractions to men. Most of these women were also more frequently attracted to men. Yet about one-third of these women were more frequently attracted to women. In other words, on a day-to-day basis, they were more often drawn to women than to men, but when they did become attracted to a man, the feelings were more intense. Perhaps this explains another interesting fact about this group: despite reporting that they were more frequently attracted to women, they tended to have more sexual contact with men!

What about the number of different women and men the respondents found attractive? Over the preceding six months, lesbians reported having been strongly attracted to about three different women and only one man. Bisexuals reported becoming attracted to an average of four different women and two men. These numbers are not very different from those reported by the lesbians, and they again underscore the fact that bisexuals tended to be more frequently attracted to women than to men, even if the attractions themselves were not always maximally intense.

When asked why they were more frequently attracted to women, bisexually identified women often indicated that women were more likely than men to have the characteristics they found desirable, such as political consciousness, sensitivity, empathy, or sheer aesthetic beauty:

> I find that it's a lot easier to bond with women, and there's also something really deeply satisfying, there's an understanding that exists with women that doesn't automatically exist with men. . . . I was recently getting out of this last relationship with a man, and I remember thinking, "Why do men lack that understanding and intuition that women seem to have naturally?" (age twenty-five)

> I can't generalize to all guys, but it's very hard to find guys that have the political feminist background that I need to deal with someone.

They have this cluelessness about women's issues, and cluelessness about the way society is structured around misogyny. (age twenty-two)

Other participants noted that women were generally better lovers than men, and that being with women had raised their standards for sexual satisfaction:

I don't put up with as much anymore, you know. I guess in terms of actually being sexual with men I expect them to take the time to really please me, and to do what I need because I know what that is now, and I can communicate that, and if they don't listen it's their problem. (age twenty-six)

Yet despite some of these female advantages, several bisexually identified women found that men continued to draw their erotic attention:

I think before, I underestimated the power of male sexuality, you know, traditional sexuality within this culture, that idea of male sexual power. I underestimated its pull for me. It's really hard being someone who's a feminist and acknowledging that. (age twenty)

Of course, whether such feelings eventually motivated women to participate in same-sex versus other-sex sexual behavior is a different issue. It is no surprise that bisexually identified women sought sexual contact with men as well as women over the ten years of the study. However, the number of lesbian-identified women who also sought sexual contact with men was unexpected.

Most people assume that women who come out as lesbian never again have sexual contact with men. Yet this was not the norm. Rather, about 60 percent of the women who identified as lesbian at the initial 1995 interview had some sort of sexual contact with men (from "fooling around" to sexual intercourse) during the next ten years, and more than 40 percent did so within two years of that first interview. Some of these women eventually changed their identity to bisexual or unlabeled, often in direct response to these experiences. But even among lesbians who remained lesbian-identified for the entire ten years of the study, more than 50 percent had some form of sexual contact with a man by 2005.

This finding is not unprecedented, but these figures are larger than those reported in previous research. This might be due to the fact that previous studies never followed lesbians over such long stretches of time. For example, Paula Rust's survey of more than 300 adult lesbians found that over 40 percent of them had participated in other-sex relationships since identifying as lesbian.[19] A large survey of African-American lesbians conducted in the 1980s found that 12 percent of lesbian respondents had had heterosexual intercourse in the previous year, and a public health survey conducted in San Francisco in the early 1990s found that one-fourth of self-identified lesbians had had sexual contact with a man in the previous three years.[20]

Historically, lesbian participation in other-sex sexual behavior has been attributed to the pressure that women have faced to engage in traditional marriage and family arrangements at the expense of their own sexual gratification.[21] Another potential explanation is that the pervasive stigmatization of same-sex sexuality might lead some lesbians to consider returning to the safety of heterosexual relationships and identities. This might explain Paula Rust's finding that women who had come out as lesbian in the relatively repressive 1970s were more likely to engage in subsequent other-sex behavior than were women who came out in the more tolerant 1980s or 1990s. It is also possible, though, that some of the women who came out as lesbian in the 1970s had always been aware that they were attracted to both men and women but did not know that the category "bisexual" even existed as an option.[22] Back then, if you were attracted to women at all, you were a lesbian.

Yet cultural pressure does not appear to be a sufficient explanation for the other-sex behavior of the lesbians in my sample. For one thing, they were all immersed in environments that offered substantially greater tolerance for same-sex sexuality, and less pressure to marry, than did previous generations. This should lead to lower rates of other-sex sexual behavior among self-identified lesbians, not greater rates. Furthermore, if lesbians were pursuing other-sex behavior as a result of social pressure or fears of stigmatization, then we would expect the highest rates of other-sex behavior among the lesbians who reported the most disapproval from family and friends and the greatest stigmatization and harassment. But this was not the case at all. Lesbians with accepting families and tolerant communities had the same rates of sexual contact with men as did lesbians with disapproving families and intolerant communities.

The only thing that did predict a lesbian's other-sex sexual behavior over the ten years of the study was—sensibly enough—her self-reported attractions to men back in 1995. All but one of the lesbians who reported in the beginning of the study that at least 10 percent of their attractions were directed to men acted on those attractions at some point in the future. Hence, periodic other-sex behavior among self-identified lesbians appears to be a straightforward outgrowth of periodic other-sex attractions. And given that most lesbians report at least some other-sex attractions, Rust concludes, "the question is . . . not whether self-identified lesbians will ever again find themselves heterosexually involved, but *how they will react to heterosexual involvement.*"[23]

So how did they react? Did sexual contact with men prompt lesbians to migrate to bisexual and unlabeled identities? Not always—lesbians' responses to other-sex sexual contact depended on whether they pursued such contact casually, for sexual release, or whether it took place within a significant love affair. Of course, the notion of lesbians' seeking sexual release with men might seem surprising. If they are more attracted to women, then wouldn't *same-*

sex contact be more gratifying? The trouble, according to many lesbians, is that it is hard to find women who are interested in casual sex. Because men are generally more comfortable pursuing uncommitted sex, and because well-defined social scripts make it easy to progress quickly from male-female friendship to sexual activity, many lesbians found that it was just easier to have casual sex with men than with women. As one lesbian remarked, "I can't say that I have any strong attractions for men at all, but men are just a lot easier to obtain than women are" (age twenty-three). Other lesbians said that they could not engage in casual, purely sexual relationships with women because they would not be able to separate out their emotions:

> It's not that I'm completely uninterested in sex with men, but I generally don't feel any sort of emotional bond with them. So if it happens, it's purely sex and that's it. Which I'm absolutely incapable of doing with a woman. (age twenty-three)

> I could never dissociate emotion and sex with a woman, but I could very easily dissociate that with a man. . . . With women I'm looking for a relationship and something meaningful and, you know, potentially being this person's girlfriend, or whatever. Whereas, honestly, in guys, I'm just kind of looking to have a little fun sometimes. (same woman six years later, age twenty-nine)

> Maybe every couple of years I find myself attracted to a guy enough to kiss someone, but I don't feel that I would ever be in *relationship* with a guy. I don't emotionally feel like I can be with a guy. (age twenty-six)

> I've had physical relations with men, but no other types of relationships. Just random, stupid things, no emotional ties. But I feel that when I meet a woman, it's going to be forever, but with a man, I know that it's not going to be long-term. (age twenty-three)

In general, lesbians did not think that such encounters were inconsistent with their lesbian identification. As one woman remarked when describing her sporadic sexual involvement with a good male friend, "I don't feel like anybody is going to take my 'lesbian license' away or anything." This woman, like many other lesbian-identified respondents, felt that the most important component of their lesbian identity was their emotional connection with women:

I guess I don't entirely think sexuality, even though it has the word "sex" in it, is all about sexuality. I don't entirely conceptualize it as "who I want to have sex with." It's who I love, and who I'm attracted to. I think the physical and the sexual stuff yes, definitely plays a role, but I think that the emotional and mental attraction for me personally is so much more important, and that's what I primarily have with women. (age twenty-three)

I would say a large portion of choosing a lesbian identity relates more to the emotional connection. . . . I've had sexual interactions with both men and women, but I don't really feel that "bisexual" is accurate—well, it's an accurate behavioral label, but I don't feel like it's an accurate reflection of how I actually feel. I feel much more fulfilled and connected and intimate with women. So I feel that "lesbian" is probably a better term for it. (age twenty-nine)

Given the emphasis that so many lesbians placed on the emotional component of their sexual identity, those who fell in love with a man found it far more difficult to continue identifying as lesbian. In fact, all of the women who identified as lesbian in 1995 and went on to develop full-blown romantic relationships with men (which amounted to a surprisingly high 30 percent of the lesbian group) eventually switched to bisexual or unlabeled identities. Most notably, they changed their labels even if they felt that their true orientation was still lesbian. But how could they possibly think that? If they were emotionally and physically satisfied by a man, didn't this prove that they weren't lesbian?

The answer is no if the man was an exception. And this was exactly how many lesbians understood their unexpected other-sex love affairs—as flukes. In the words of one woman, "I don't really feel like I'm bisexual, because all of my other attractions are for women, and I feel like he is sort of an exception" (age twenty-five). Many of these women were rejected and stigmatized by their own lesbian communities when they embarked on these unexpected relationships, a phenomenon that has been described at length in memoirs by other high-profile lesbians who fell in love with men, such as the activist and author Jan Clausen and the singer Holly Near.[24]

Interestingly, not one of the lesbians who experienced an abrupt, unexpected transition disavowed any of her previous feelings, relationships, or identities, or characterized them as false or misguided. Rather, they all acknowledged the inconvenient reality that sometimes it was impossible to tell what would unfold in the future. Even if you were attracted to men only 5 percent of the time, if that 5 percent happened to include *the one,* that relationship might become 100 percent of your future. In Chapters 6 and 7 I revisit such cases in more detail to explore how and why they occur.

Given that so many of our preconceived notions about bisexuality are inaccurate, it is useful to re-examine some of the most common stereotypes. The three most prevalent misconceptions are that (1) bisexual people are inherently promiscuous, and hence incapable of monogamous commitment to one partner; (1) they are really just repressed lesbians; or (2) they are really just confused or "curious" heterosexuals. Having tracked the sexual and romantic relationships of bisexual and unlabeled women for ten years, does my study support any of these characteristics?

The stereotype about promiscuity and nonmonogamy appears soundly refuted by my data. By 2005, the majority of all women in my study were involved in committed monogamous relationships, and women with nonexclusive attractions were no different in this regard. Among women who had ever identified as bisexual or unlabeled during the ten years of the study, more than 80 percent were involved in a committed monogamous relationship by 2005, and of these, 60 percent had lasted for at least four years. So much for the notion that bisexual attractions are incompatible with commitment! Two out of three of these committed monogamous relationships were with men, and of these, half resulted in marriage. Interestingly, the negative stereotypes about bisexuality and promiscuity had seeped into women's own homes: a number of bisexual women reported having to reassure their husbands that just because they were attracted to women did not mean that they needed to act on those feelings. As one bisexual woman put it, "I can choose between a red car and a black car, but I've only got a one-car garage!"

What about the notion that bisexuals are repressed lesbians or curious/experimenting heterosexuals? Notably, over the ten years of the study not a *single* woman reinterpreted her previous identity in this fashion. Even the bisexual and unlabeled women who eventually switched to lesbian labels still described themselves as "technically" bisexual and simply indicated that the predominance of their same-sex attractions was more consistent with a lesbian than a bisexual label.

Thus the "repressed lesbian" and "confused heterosexual" stereotypes also appear to be false. At the same time, we can see how such stereotypes arose, given that women's relationship patterns became more "lesbian-like" or "heterosexual-like" as the years went by and they began to settle down into stable, long-term relationships. A bisexual woman who marries a man certainly resembles a garden-variety heterosexual, and a bisexual woman who settles down with a woman seems like the average lesbian.

The gradual trend toward "specialization" among bisexual and unlabeled women is most evident in the women's ratios of same-sex to other-sex sexual behavior. Here, the most surprising finding was that bisexual and unlabeled women pursued progressively more sexual contact with men than with women over the ten years of the study. About 57 percent of bisexual-unlabeled women reported increases in their other-sex sexual contact as time went by, whereas only about one-third reported decreases (the rest showed no consistent pattern of change). The same trends emerged in women's romantic attachments: those who gravitated toward more sexual contact with women also pursued more romantic ties with women, whereas those who gravitated toward more sexual contact with men also pursued more romantic ties with men. About one-fourth of the bisexual-unlabeled women switched to either lesbian or heterosexual identities in line with their behavioral changes, but most felt that their bisexual or unlabeled identities still did a good job of describing their overall sexual profile.

But could we have predicted which bisexual and unlabeled women would eventually gravitate toward women as opposed to men? At first I thought that their 1995 self-reported percentages of same-sex versus other-sex attractions might have foreshadowed their futures, since this had been true of the lesbians. But this did not turn out to be the case for bisexual and unlabeled women. Two bisexual women with the exact same degree of same-sex attractions in 1995 often made very different choices ten years later: whereas one would have settled with a woman, the other would have ended up with a man.

Interestingly, this "prediction failure" was true only for women's 1995 reports. The percentage of same-sex attractions that bisexual and unlabeled women claimed in 1997, 2000, 2003, and 2005 did correlate with their eventual degree of same-sex behavior, such that women who reported more frequent same-sex attractions pursued progressively more sexual contact with women, and those with more frequent other-sex attractions pursued progressively more sexual contact with men. Most likely, later reports did a better job of predicting women's eventual behavior than did earlier reports because attractions and behavior are known to influence and reinforce each other.[25] Women's sexual fluidity is likely to enhance this process: a woman who is attracted to both women and men but becomes involved in a satisfying same-sex relationship is likely to find that this experience enhances the frequency and intensity of her same-sex attractions, while it probably also draws her attention away from other-sex attractions and opportunities. This might motivate her to seek progressively more same-sex relationships in the future, and over time this tendency might solidify into a stable pattern.

As for the fact that more bisexual and unlabeled women gravitated toward men than toward women, social factors also proved important. Specifically, women repeatedly mentioned two factors that influenced them to seek male partners: (1) the composition of their social networks, in terms of both the number of women versus men and the number of lesbian/gay/bisexual versus heterosexual friends, and (2) the relative ease and social acceptability of pursuing other-sex versus same-sex relationships.

Many women found, for example, that as they moved from college into the working world or changed cities for career purposes, they sometimes ended up with fewer lesbian/gay/bisexual friends than they had before. At the same time, many women found that their jobs put them in much greater day-to-day contact with men than had been the case before. As one bisexual woman noted, "These days, probably 90 percent of the people that I see every day are men, so in terms of meeting somebody and having them also be interested in you, that's just more likely now to be a guy. I've just encountered way less bisexual and gay women. That's probably why my last few relationships have been with guys."

This was true even for women who had started out strongly attracted to women. Willa provides a salient example. She had identified as bisexual since high school, when she had been extremely active in raising awareness about lesbian/gay/bisexual issues. Willa's coming-out story was among the most dramatic in the entire sample: she had been vaguely aware of same-sex attractions since around age fourteen, and by the time she was sixteen they were fairly consistent. Yet she was still trying to push them out of her mind. One day while standing in line in the high school cafeteria, she noticed an extremely attractive girl. She was so immediately and strongly drawn to the girl that her legs started to tremble and become weak. Her knees abruptly locked and she fell down on the floor, lunch tray flying. She recalls thinking to herself at that point, "Okay, I don't think I can deny this any longer."

During her college years, she was very involved in the lesbian/gay/bisexual community. But after she graduated, she found herself "hanging around more men than women, more than I'm used to," and she became involved in a serious relationship with a man. Their relationship went on and off for the next couple of years, and over time she simply found that though she was still open to becoming involved with an attractive woman, that possibility became less and less likely. She found herself fantasizing less often about women and seeking out fewer opportunities to date female partners. By the fourth interview, she had gotten back together with her longtime boyfriend, and by the fifth interview they were happily married.

Another factor that influenced some women's decision making was the prospect of having children. As they grew older, some participants began thinking about having a family, and they were forced to ask themselves whether they wanted to take such a step with a man or a woman. Rita provides an example of the type of decision making that some bisexually identified women went through:

> I really like the idea of being able to have a kid that's both part of me and part of the person that I love, and to see that come to fruition and turn into a whole new person. . . . If I broke up with Bob and I

met a woman and fell madly in love, then yeah, I would live with her, adopt a kid, but I just see it more easily, you know what I mean, when I look to the future I see myself more easily falling into a relationship with a guy. But it's funny because I do still think of myself as bisexual, so I guess I'm leaning more toward men these days due to more practical reasons, societal reasons. (age thirty)

Many bisexual and unlabeled women felt that as long as they had some degree of choice over whether to have children with a man or a woman, it made sense to take the "easier" path for the sake of the children. Nonetheless, women with this view were often ambivalent about it. This was especially true for those who found their relationships with women to be more emotionally gratifying than their relationships with men. For such women, the flexibility made possible by their nonexclusive attractions could sometimes be a heavy responsibility, because it prompted them to actively and repeatedly question not only their attractions but also their own susceptibility to traditional expectations about marriage and family life. Many bisexual women found that as they moved through different life stages and made different decisions about career and family, the conventional ideal of a husband and kids continued to hold sway for them, no matter how much they were aware of its restrictiveness.

Judith provides a compelling example of how some bisexual and unlabeled women struggled with conflicting desires for a conventional life and the satisfaction of same-sex attractions and relationships.

Judith

When I knocked on Judith's dorm-room door to interview her, the person who peeked around the door to greet me was not Judith but—to my surprise—her wide-eyed, curly-haired three-year-old son.

Judith had given birth to him when she was seventeen. The father had never been in the picture, and Judith was somehow managing a full college course load as a single mother.

If she found the challenge stressful, she certainly did not show it. Judith possessed an unusual combination of warmth and exuberance, such that being around her was both comforting and uplifting. Her deep affection for her son and his adoration for her were compelling. As we spoke, he alternately clambered around her legs, wandered over to see what I was writing, and busied himself with his toys. Judith's gentle, freckled face was almost always smiling, even when she discussed difficult experiences and decisions.

Judith had first started questioning her sexuality in an abstract way when she was twelve years old and her parents enrolled her in a progressive school that offered an extensive program on racism and prejudice. She remembers realizing at some point that if everyone was supposed to love everyone else regardless of ethnicity, social class, and so on, then why should gender matter? She excitedly told her close friends about this realization, and their response was, "Duh, that's called bisexuality."

By the time she was fourteen she was aware of clear-cut attractions for women, and some of her older lesbian/gay/bisexual friends gave her pamphlets about coming out. She did not even look at them until she was eighteen, at which point her on-and-off sexual questioning had started up again in full force. By that point she had given birth to her son and was no longer involved with the father. It was the summer before she was supposed to leave for college, and she finally pulled out the dusty "coming-out" pamphlets that her friends had given her four years earlier. She quickly ruled out the possibility that she was a lesbian, since she was undoubtedly attracted to men. The notion of bisexuality immediately made sense, and she started attending meetings at the local lesbian/gay/bisexual center "to see if they were human!" By the time she entered college in the fall, she had started identifying as bisexual and immediately joined the campus lesbian/gay/bisexual group. Six months later, she was thrilled to have her first relationship with a woman.

Although Judith never went through the self-hatred that characterizes so many lesbian/gay/bisexual youth, by the time of our first interview she was deeply uncertain about what sorts of relationships she wanted and expected to have in the future. She tended to form strong and satisfying emotional bonds with women, but she had "a gut feeling" that she would end up with a man: "I know I'll still be attracted to women, even if I married a guy, but I don't really want to start a relationship with a woman right now because that's not where I see myself going. I just wish I felt more of an emotional attraction for men."

Over the next eight years, Judith vacillated between her persistent attractions to women and her motivation to find "the right guy" to settle down with, someone with whom she could have the same sort of strong emotional connection that she tended to form with women. At times she tried to focus on finding a potential male partner, and at other times she relaxed and allowed herself to enjoy her attractions and relationships with women. At one point, when she was in a male-focused stage, she recalls having sex with her boyfriend and actually becoming jealous of his enjoyment of her body. She thought to herself, "Damn! I remember how great it is to be with a woman! I want to have that, too!"

Throughout this time, Judith remained self-conscious about the degree to which her motivation to settle down with a man was exactly what conventional heterosexual society would expect her to do. Even though she felt that her own motives had more to do with her personal situation than with social acceptability, she noted that she did not generally discuss these issues with other people. She did not want to be judged; nor did she want people to draw the wrong conclusions about bisexuality based on her experience. As she said, "It's my own individual process I'm going through. I don't talk about it much, because I don't want straight people to think that all bisexuals will 'grow out of it' or that they will eventually want to marry a man."

The big question with which she continued to struggle, however, was whether her motivation to get married would lead her to "settle" for a heterosexual relationship that was not as emotionally satisfying as she wanted. Moreover, as she began to contemplate the possibility of having additional children, she became aware that there might be something special and satisfying about raising a child with another woman. Although Judith struggled with these conflicts, she retained a sense of humor about them:

> I joke with my friends that, you know, men don't live as long as women, and so maybe I can have a good, long, wonderful, committed, deep, enriching, long-lasting marriage, and then it would be nice if he could just pass away early, and then I can spend the rest of my days with a woman! My friends are like, "What did you just say?" And I say, no, no, it's not that I want him to die, this hypothetical guy, it would just be convenient, you know, so I could experience a long-term relationship with a man and I can also experience a long-term relationship with a woman. . . . I have great curiosity, what it would be like to raise a child with another woman. But I also know that life would be so much easier to just go ahead and have kids with a guy. . . . So given the option to go one way, I would probably do that.

At the ten-year point, Judith felt that she was still leaving her options open for the future; she still wanted to find "the right guy" and settle down, but she was also extremely satisfied with her career and with how much she had grown as a parent. Although she was wistful about eventually having to choose one gender over the other, she felt that the ongoing "push and pull" of her attractions to—and distinct appreciation of—men versus women was a satisfying and important part of her. She likened it to the enjoyment that she got from ballroom dancing, and specifically from alternating between being the leader and being the follower: "I feel like my sexuality is sort of a subset of my mental perspective, which is, you know, like my dancing, and feeling satisfied and enriched by both leading and following, and so then my sexuality is a subset of that, being attracted to both men and women. It's a perspective that's kind of over my whole life. . . . I just always enjoy knowing that my brain and my body work that way."

How Does Gender Matter?

Judith's appreciation of her capacity for attractions to both women and men raises interesting questions about the specific role that gender plays in nonexclusive attractions. Judith's remarks consistently demonstrated a keen awareness of the distinct characteristics of women versus men, physically, emotionally, and psychologically, and her own distinct way of responding to these gender-linked characteristics.

Similarly, numerous bisexual women in my study noted that when it came to men and women, their attractions were sparked by different physical and psychological characteristics. Eleanor, for example, liked "athletic, stocky" women but "tall, gentle" men. Suzanne said that she noticed the way women dressed but the way men acted.

Other women found the same basic traits attractive in both men and women but felt that these traits were substantially more common in one gender than in the other. Chris, for example, remarked that she had always had trouble with the idea that "gender didn't matter": "I mean come on, everyone is attracted to some traits more than others, and those traits just aren't equally distributed in women and men. If you like really emotionally sensitive people, well then you're just going to find that more often in women than men, so gender *does* matter" (age twenty-two, bisexual).

Because of such differences, some women found that their overall patterns of desire tended to alternate between men and women. As one unlabeled woman remarked, "Some days I wake up and I really want a man's touch. . . . Other days I wake up and I really want a woman's touch" (age twenty). Another respondent noted, "I need women *and* I need men, both physically and emotionally. But I need them in different degrees and in different levels depending on where I am in my life" (age twenty-eight, bisexual). Some respondents noted that this need was manifested in relationship patterns: "I don't plan it that way, but it seems that whenever I get out of a relationship with a woman, I want to be with a man, and when I get out of a relationship with a man, then I want to be with a woman" (age twenty-six, bisexual). For some women, being with one gender tended to heighten their appreciation of the distinct characteristics of the other. The hardness of a man's muscles made them appreciate the softness of a woman's breasts and belly; women's smaller size made them appreciate a man's height.

Other bisexuals emphasized that the erotic and emotional dynamics they experienced with women were altogether different from those they experienced with men:

I think I've become more of an essentialist as I've gotten older. My bisexuality before was "love knows no barriers, love is genderless," but I think now I'm aware of fundamental differences between men and women, a lot of it being reinforced by socialization, but a lot of it being fundamental, and I'm not sure I felt that way before. (age twenty-two)

Another woman noted:

I don't like to view people first as their gender, but that's definitely a big factor, and I don't want a gender-free world. I believe in differences between men and women much more than I used to. I used to believe they were pretty much the same, you know, blah blah blah, but now I totally see the differences and believe that they are based on energetics, your basic spirit, as well as society, or how your energy interacts with your body, I don't know. . . . And though I'm pretty much fifty-fifty attracted to both, I have to say that my physical attraction for women, for women's bodies, is much stronger than for men's. (age twenty-six)

This experience, of course, diverges sharply from that of women who claimed that the defining attribute of their sexuality was that they were completely inattentive to a partner's gender, and that their attractions to a particular man or woman were based on everything *except* gender: personality, chemistry, intellectual rapport, and so on. (I discuss this phenomenon in detail in Chapter 6.) Interestingly, this stark difference—between women whose nonexclusive attractions involve a heightened appreciation of each gender and women whose nonexclusive attractions disregard gender altogether—is reflected in many of the long-standing academic debates about whether bisexuality threatens or reinforces categorical models of sexuality.[26]

For example, many theorists have argued that an understanding of bisexuality as an independent orientation between heterosexuality and homosexuality, involving attractions to both sexes instead of just one, does not deviate much from conventional models of sexuality—it is just a matter of having an extra category. But an understanding of bisexuality as a form of "gender-free" eroticism is noticeably different because it challenges the traditional privileging of gender that is inherent in conventional models of sexual orientation. After all, if bisexuals do not attend to the gender of their partner, then the very distinction between "same-sex" and "other-sex" attractions no longer makes sense. We might just as well distinguish between attractions to older versus younger partners, or to extroverts versus introverts, or to artists versus intellectuals. Conventional models of sexuality have taken for granted that gender is the only category that matters; gender-free forms of bisexuality force us to question whether this is so.[27]

It makes no sense to argue that one of these conceptualizations of bisexuality is more accurate than the other; both exist at the level of women's subjective experiences, and we simply do not know whether these patterns have different causes or long-term implications. The important point is to put the question of gender on the table, to treat its influence on desire as a scientific question rather than as a given. Until now, sex researchers have not devoted much attention to figuring out exactly how gender structures individuals' experiences of desire and what exactly we respond to when we become aroused by a man versus a woman. I address these questions in more detail in Chapter 6, when I describe the experiences of women who claim that they become attracted to "the person, not the gender."

But we need to address a more basic question first, one that underlies all the complexity, ambiguity, variability, and nonexclusivity in women's attractions that we have seen so far. What exactly do we mean by "sexual attraction"?

So Just What Is an Attraction, Anyway?

The problem with trying to define sexual attraction is that researchers know very little about how individuals experience sexual feelings. Although we take pains to assess how often people experience same-sex versus other-sex attractions, the relative balance between them, the age at which they first emerged, and so on, we rarely stop to ask what a particular respondent means by the word "attraction" and what sorts of subjective thoughts and feelings are bundled together in this experience.[28] Instead, we presume that everyone defines and experiences sexual attraction in the same way. This seems as naive as Potter Stewart's famous 1964 assertion that though he could not specifically define pornography, "I know it when I see it."[29] Sexuality researchers seem to have assumed that, analogously, we all "know" same-sex and other-sex attractions when we feel them, so one person's report of same-sex attractions is equivalent to another's. This thinking reflects an implicit biological bias: if we assume that experiences of sexual attraction are wholly biologically determined, then they should be roughly equivalent from person to person, governed by the same species-wide neurobiological and hormonal events.

But human sexuality is substantially more complicated than that. Although experiences of desire and attraction have biological underpinnings, they are nonetheless powerfully shaped by social, cultural, and interpersonal contexts. As Edward Laumann and Jenna Mahay pointed out, "We must all *learn* what to regard or understand as being sexual or nonsexual."[30] I would argue that this learning process also takes place at the level of subjective experience. In other words, culture and society teach us not only what "sexual" means but also what it feels like, and these determinations vary widely as a function of social and cultural norms, expectations, and socialization practices.

Sure enough, once I began prompting the respondents in my study to describe their experiences of "attraction," I was met with a diverse range of responses that seemed utterly incomparable to one another. Women's descriptions ranged from specifically genital sensations *(tightness in my groin; wetness)* to full-body physical sensations *(warm feeling all over; high energy, fluttery feeling in my belly; a sort of chemical connection)* to psychological states *(liking to look at the person's face or body; longing for nearness; not caring about the person's personality; wanting to have sex)*. Are these really the same thing? No wonder the Northwestern team found consistent discrepancies between individuals' subjective reports of arousal and their physiological responses—"desire," "arousal," and "attraction" have a wide range of possible cognitive, emotional, and physical manifestations, and different women likely focus on different aspects.

Which are the most important? Nobody seems to know. In my study respondents often expressed doubt about what "counted" as an attraction, especially when they experienced differences between their same-sex and other-sex attractions. Attractions to one gender were often described as more or less "automatic," "clear," "all-encompassing," "cognitive," "fleeting," "intimidating," "motivating," "intimate," "lasting," "powerful," "emotional," "pleasurable," "heartfelt," and "electrifying." Many women drew distinctions between same-sex and other-sex attractions that specifically centered on emotional as opposed to physical aspects of attraction. Amy, for example, indicated that her attractions to men were "gut-level, immediate, physical responses," whereas her attractions to women were slower to develop, more emotional in nature, and more dependent on the specific quality of her relationship with the woman in question. Other women drew exactly the same sort of distinction in reverse, so that attractions to women were more "gut-level" and immediate. Overall, however, the majority of respondents attributed "gut level" reactions to men and "emotional" reactions to women.

Some women noticed differences between what they wanted to do in response to same-sex and other-sex attractions. Beth, for example, noticed that when she was strongly attracted to a woman, she felt sexually charged and wanted to pursue the woman in question. But when she was drawn to a man, the feeling was less urgent and dissipated on its own fairly quickly. As with the physical-emotional distinction noted above, some women described a very similar pattern but in reverse, such that attractions to men were experienced as more sexually motivating than attractions to women.

Numerous women confessed that they sometimes questioned the authenticity of their attractions to women or men, suspecting that they might be distorted by cultural conditioning, social pressure, aesthetics, or emotional attachment. Cara, for example, remarked:

I have always *noticed* women more than men, but my attractions to women confuse me because I don't know whether they are physical or emotional. I can easily look at a guy and think, "He's good-looking . . . I'm attracted to him . . ." but I can't do the same with women. What really makes me question, with women, is that I always have these intense relationships with my female friends, and emotionally it *feels* like we're dating. But I don't know if that's the same as an attraction—I don't know, sometimes I feel like I don't have any attractions at all! (age twenty, unlabeled)

Other women expressed similar doubts about the authenticity of their attractions to men: "Most of my relationships with men have evolved out of really good friendships, so I already had an emotional bond with them, and that made it hard for me to tell if I was really physically attracted to them, or whether I simply had strong emotional feelings for them." Some women were unsure of the true nature of their feelings for men because they were aware of the fact that they had been socialized to eroticize men: "It's like there's this track for men, and it's just easier to get on that track. But because of society, there *is* no track for my feelings for women" (age nineteen, bisexual). Another woman asked, "Am I attracted to a particular man because he's great, or because society has just conditioned me to be turned on by men?" (age twenty, unlabeled).

Many women also brought up social conditioning when they analyzed their appreciation for female beauty. Numerous participants reported that when they first became aware of their attractions for women, they initially had difficulty distinguishing between simply finding a woman attractive and being attracted *to* her. As one woman remarked, "My best friend happens to be really beautiful, although I don't know if I'd say that I'm sexually attracted to her . . . I'm not sure how to classify my feelings for her. I know that I think she's beautiful, and so I feel like I definitely have *physical* feelings for her, but they're not as strong as the sexual feelings I've had for some guys." Others mentioned that they had become so accustomed to analyzing and envying women's faces and bodies in magazines, television shows, and films that they could no longer be sure why they enjoyed looking at images of attractive women. Some articulated an awareness that such images had been designed to appeal to men and to show women how to attract male attention (usually by buying a certain product). After years of chronic exposure, some women found it difficult to disentangle their own attractions from their conditioned desire to be attractive. As one eighteen-year-old bisexual woman recounted, "I don't know if I want her, or if I want to *be* her." Similarly, a thirty-year-old heterosexual woman remarked, "It's hard to separate when I'm looking at someone and thinking, gosh, I wish I had that butt, and kind of also *looking*, you know, like that's a nice butt. So, I'm sort of . . . I think I have a little of both going on."

These snapshots just hint at the complexity surrounding the issue of sexual attraction. Despite all the attention that sex researchers have devoted to understanding sexual orientation, we do not yet have good theories about how and why different attractions feel the way they do, and why some are more motivating than others. Although there have been some attempts to explain how individuals develop their own idiosyncratic patterns of desire, including the psychologist John Money's notion of "lovemaps," such models tend to be fairly deterministic and may not appropriately account for the sorts of evolving changes that female sexual fluidity makes possible.[31] We also need more specific attention to the role of gender in individuals' subjective experiences of attraction (a question I revisit in Chapter 6). This is a particularly important issue when it comes to understanding the diverse forms of nonexclusivity that I have described above, and a key direction for future research. After all, if some bisexual women experience attractions to men as automatic genital responses and attractions to women as emotional attachments, whereas others show exactly the opposite pattern, isn't this potentially as important as knowing the relative frequency of their same-sex versus other-sex attractions?

Subtypes of Nonexclusivity?

This brings me to my final point: Are the diverse experiences documented above simply random, reflecting the fact that nonexclusive attractions can be pushed and pulled in virtually any direction by circumstantial, personal, or situational factors? Or are there systematic patterns at work? This question has a long history in the sexuality literature. Numerous sociologists and psychologists have differentiated between bisexual "types" with different degrees of same-sex and other-sex attraction and behavior, different degrees of personal masculinity and femininity, different preferences for social contact with men versus women, different triggers for their sexual feelings, different contexts in which nonexclusive behavior might be expressed, and so on.[32] Notably, no single overarching typology has ever won out, but certain distinctions do seem consistently relevant.

For example, studies have consistently found that, as with the women in my sample, some bisexually identified individuals describe their attractions as gender-neutral, whereas others are highly responsive to gendered traits in both men and women.[33] Moreover, there appears to be a distinction between women with *consistent* attractions to both sexes and women with a "bisexual potential" that might never be expressed unless triggered by the right person or opportunity.[34] "Bisexual" is an appropriate label for women with consistent nonexclusive attractions, but perhaps not for women who simply feel that they have a capacity for bisexuality.

Consider, for example, that the random, representative survey of American adults conducted by Laumann and his colleagues found that a greater percentage of American women (5.6 percent) reported "finding the idea of same-sex contact appealing" than reported currently experiencing same-sex attractions (4.4 percent). Among men this was not the case: more men reported being attracted to the same sex (6.2 percent) than found the idea of same-sex contact appealing (4.5 percent). We might characterize women who lack current same-sex attractions but do find the idea of same-sex sexuality appealing as those who possess a potential for nonexclusive attractions. Outside the context of an actual opportunity, they might not consciously experience same-sex desire, but they have a sort of "readiness" for it.

Interestingly, this was true of some of the women in my heterosexual comparison group. None of the women had any childhood or adolescence experiences of same-sex desire, but the strength of their current emotional attachments to women made them open to the idea of same-sex relationships:

> I have talked with friends about the fact that two women can often know each other and understand each other so much better than a man and woman can, because there is that empathy. So in that sense, it's not out of the realm of all possibility that I could want to be involved with a woman. I don't anticipate that I would ever *identify* as a lesbian, but I guess I'm open to the possibility of being with a woman. (age twenty-two)

> The only thing that ever makes me really think about it is the fact that I form such close friendships with women. It's like they're more than friends, but they're not sexually charged. It's like there's this nebulous level between friendship and intimacy. But I'm only sexually attracted to men, and I don't really see myself straying from that. . . . With one of my friends, we have had talks about how we could, if we wanted to, take our relationship further. But it was enough to just be aware of that potential, to acknowledge that we were that important to each other. We didn't need to go further. On some level, I think everybody has the potential to love both women and men. (age thirty)

> Generally I'm totally certain about being heterosexual, but there are women that I have met that I find so incredible that I'm not sure if I

find them attractive because I find them incredible or if I find them attractive *and* incredible. I think I have always found women attractive, but not necessarily in a sexual way. (age twenty-three)

Although these women do not appear to be bisexual, their "version" of heterosexuality is flexible and fluid. Even though none of them anticipated seeking same-sex relationships in the future, they were nonetheless honest with themselves about their own capacity to enjoy such relationships, especially in the context of an existing emotional attachment.

Two of the women acted on this potential, but with casual acquaintances rather than close friends. One of them ended up "making out" with a female coworker during a business trip; another actually went so far as to have sex with several women. Both of them found the experience enjoyable, but neither found it compelling enough to make her consider identifying as bisexual. In fact, the second woman specifically chose not to identify as bisexual because she knew that she was fundamentally drawn to men, and she did not want to inadvertently contribute to negative stereotypes portraying bisexuals as "curious" heterosexuals. Her sensitivity regarding these issues—and her openness to same-sex contact—was heightened by the fact that her sister was bisexual:

I've spent a lot of time with gay friends, largely through my sister, and at a party one night, I just ended up sleeping with this woman. It wasn't all that great, but I didn't know if that was because I didn't like women, or if I wasn't really into this particular woman. So I ended up trying it again. Of course, my gay friends keep wanting me to come out as bisexual, but actually I think my experiences with women clarified for me that I'm actually heterosexual. And I didn't want to make a mockery of the bisexual label by claiming it just because I've been with a woman. I didn't want to be one of those women who just calls herself bisexual in college. (age twenty-five)

Are these women more fluid than other heterosexual women, or are they simply more willing to openly acknowledge their fluidity? This question has long preoccupied research on bisexuality: Does *everybody* possess some potential for nonexclusive attractions, regardless of whether they acknowledge that fact, or do only a subset of people? Freud certainly believed in a universal human "ambisexuality" that is molded by culture and experience into homosexuality or heterosexuality, and other theorists have adopted and expanded these views over the years.[35] The studies I reviewed at the beginning of this chapter, of course, suggest that women are particularly likely to possess a flexible erotic potential, a view supported by the results of my study.[36]

This erotic potential, heightened among women, is what I have been describing as female sexual fluidity. By now, it should be clear that though the concept of fluidity overlaps with the phenomenon of bisexuality (since fluidity, by definition, makes nonexclusive attractions possible), they are not the same things. Whereas bisexuality can be conceived as a consistent pattern of erotic responses to both sexes, manifested in clear-cut sexual attractions to men and women (albeit not necessarily to the same degrees), possessing a potential for nonexclusive attractions (or, as we have seen, finding the "idea" of same-sex contact appealing even if you currently have no same-sex desires) is clearly different.

The women in my study intuitively grasped this distinction. Although the vast majority showed growing understanding and appreciation for sexual fluidity as the years went by, and increasingly used terms such as "fluid," "flexible," and "plastic" to describe their sexual feelings and explain their multiple sexual transitions, they did not interpret this fluidity as universal bisexuality. I asked them outright to indicate whether they agreed or disagreed with the statements, "Deep down, most heterosexual women are probably bisexual," and "Deep down, most lesbians are probably bisexual." Nearly 60 percent disagreed with the characterization of heterosexuals as bisexual, and nearly 70 percent disagreed that most lesbians were actually bisexual. Overall, women endorsed a notion of fluid potential but did not endorse a notion of universal bisexuality. Perhaps this is why so many women responded to changes in their sexual trajectories by identifying as "unlabeled" instead of "bisexual." Deviations from their usual sexual patterns were not interpreted as evidence for a "true," underlying bisexual orientation. Rather, they were interpreted as evidence that one's orientation did not provide the last word on one's lifetime experiences of love and desire. Because of sexual fluidity, unexpected transformations remained ever-present possibilities. In the following chapters I explore two such transformations in depth: changes in patterns of attraction over time and attractions that develop specifically for single individuals.

One of the reasons bisexuality continues to be a topic of such heated debate is that there is no uniform experience of non-exclusivity. Doubtless ten and twenty years from now, scientists and laypeople alike will continue to argue about the fact that some bisexuals seem to be "really" gay, whereas others seem to be "really" straight; that some are strongly attracted to both genders, and others are inattentive to gender altogether; that some experience their bisexuality as a distinct orientation, and others as the lack of an orientation; that some experience it only in the realm of emotional feelings, and others only in the realm of sexual feelings; that some experience nonexclusive attractions all the time, and others only under certain circumstances. There is no point in trying to figure out which one of these characterizations represents true bisexuality—*they are all true.* Each type represents a legitimate manifestation of nonexclusive attractions that requires our attention. No single definition of bisexuality could ever cover them all.

Furthermore, these different types of nonexclusivity probably have notably different causes, different rates of prevalence, different developmental trajectories, different cultural meanings, and different long-term implications for an individual's desires, relationships, behavior, and self-understanding. Take another look at the excerpts with which I began this chapter, drawn directly from the women in my study. Many of these women would have a difficult time relating to the experiences of the others, and yet each represents a real and important "slice" of the total phenomenon of nonexclusivity. Our goal should be to develop models of female sexuality capable of understanding all these diverse experiences. A greater scientific and social understanding of female sexual fluidity is critical to this goal. Now that so many studies, using different methods and subject populations, have definitively documented the centrality of nonexclusive attractions for women, it would be irresponsible for scientists not to place this phenomenon at the top of our research priorities.

CHAPTER 5

Change in Sexual Attractions

Perhaps no topic in sexuality research is as controversial as the question of change in sexual orientation. Regardless of how individuals come to think of themselves as lesbian/gay/bisexual, can they "switch back"? Can a heterosexual person "turn" gay, even well into adulthood?

These questions are often raised in the context of debates about whether sexual orientation is a fixed trait (in which case, presumably, it should not be changeable) or a lifestyle choice (in which case, presumably, it should). Unfortunately, these debates are more frequently taken up in a political context than in a scientific one. Antigay activists have historically maintained that same-sex sexuality is a lifestyle choice that should be discouraged, deemed illegitimate, and even punished by the culture at large. In other words, if lesbian/gay/bisexual people do not *have* to be gay but are simply choosing a path of decadence and deviance, then the government should have no obligation to protect their civil rights or honor their relationships; to the contrary, the state should actively condemn same-sex sexuality and deny it legal and social recognition in order to discourage others from following that path.[1]

Not surprisingly, advocates for gay/lesbian/bisexual rights see things differently. They counter that sexual orientation is not a matter of choice but an inborn trait that is as much beyond an individual's control as skin or eye color.[2] Accordingly, since gay/lesbian/ bisexual individuals cannot choose to be heterosexual, it is unethical to discriminate against them and to deny legal recognition to same-sex relationships.

Many activists and researchers, myself included, have expressed ambivalence about linking debates over social and legal recognition with debates over "choice" and "change." After all, plenty of inborn traits are viewed as highly undesirable, so why should the notion of sexual orientation as a biological trait make it more socially acceptable? After all, the common view of race and ethnicity as inborn traits certainly has not eroded racism or necessarily promoted racial harmony.[3] Perhaps instead of arguing that gay/lesbian/bisexual individuals deserve civil rights because they are powerless to change their behavior, we should affirm the fundamental rights of all people to determine their own emotional and sexual lives.[4]

Debates about choice and change also have implications for advocates of "reparative therapy," who claim that people with same-sex attractions can eliminate deviant desires through a series of therapy sessions.[5] Both the American Psychological Association (APA) and the American Psychiatric Association maintain that same-sex sexuality is normal and natural, and on this basis they view reparative therapy as unethical and inappropriate.[6] Moreover, it just does not seem to work. Researchers have consistently found that individuals who have undergone reparative therapy—even those who are happy with the overall outcomes—continue to experience same-sex attractions, though they might develop useful strategies for distracting themselves from unwanted desires or enhancing the emotional quality of their heterosexual marriages despite such attractions.[7]

Yet despite the fact that these therapies do not appear to alter individuals' underlying same-sex sexuality, practitioners still market them to potential clients as if they do. This practice violates APA guidelines, which mandate truth in advertising: clinicians are not supposed to promise therapeutic outcomes they cannot deliver.[8]

Reparative therapists also routinely misrepresent the risks associated with such therapy (such as increased distress and shame) and
its controversial techniques (which sometimes include "aversion"
therapies that incorporate electric shocks or the administration of
medications to induce nausea). The most fundamental breach of
APA ethics, of course, concerns the fact that same-sex sexuality is
neither a mental disorder nor an indicator of one, and consequently
it is unethical to attempt to eliminate it.[9]

Against this backdrop, scientific data on longitudinal change
in same-sex attractions are potentially explosive and ripe for misin-
terpretation. To avoid this possibility, I want to clarify some key
terms from the start. First, consider the controversial question of
"choice." Many people inappropriately equate change with choice
when thinking about sexual orientation. In other words, they assume that if sexual orientation is an inborn trait, it must be rigidly
fixed and impervious to conscious control. Conversely, if sexual attractions show any variability at all, then orientation must be not
an inborn trait but a consciously chosen lifestyle.

These assumptions are illogical, unscientific, and just plain
wrong. Change, choice, and control are three totally separate phenomena. Individuals undergo plenty of drastic psychological
changes that they did not choose and over which they have little
control. Consider puberty: Who would choose the perplexing, confusing, sometimes overwhelming changes in sexual feelings that
come with that stage of development? Can they be stopped? What
about the notable decline in sexual attraction that often happens in
a failing marriage? Most individuals feel powerless to rekindle their
former passions (or to extinguish attractions for a new and more
desirable partner). And what about the well-documented declines
in sex drive that often accompany late life; are those chosen?

Researchers have documented considerable variability in aspects
of sexuality other than sexual orientation, yet no one ever claims
that these changes are chosen.[10] We speak in commonsense terms

about moments of sexual *reawakening, discovery,* or *decline,* during which individuals begin desiring different amounts or forms of sexual release from day to day, month to month, or year to year. Yet in the context of same-sex sexuality, we presume that perfect stability and consistency should be the norm. This is simply a cultural bias with no scientific support.

The confusion is understandable, given how little scientists know about when and why sexual desires change. In recent years, researchers have begun to show more interest in this topic, mainly because of the growing attention paid to sexual dysfunction. Ed Laumann's large-scale, random survey of American adults generated controversy because it found that nearly 30 percent of American women reported low or nonexistent sexual desires.[11] With such a large potential market, pharmaceutical companies have been feverishly searching for effective treatments to change—in this case simply increase—women's desires. Yet the more we learn about women's desires, the more obvious it becomes that they involve complex interplays among biological, environmental, psychological, and interpersonal factors.[12] Relationship context appears to be particularly important to women, so much so that some clinicians have suggested reframing the term "low sexual desire" as a "desire discrepancy" between partners. After all, maybe a woman's sex drive seems low only when her partner wants sex more often than she does. If that is the case, who has the problem? Clearly, there is no simple reason that one woman might have stronger and more frequent desires than another, or why one woman might experience a decline in the intensity of her desires over time while another might experience a resurgence.

We do have substantial evidence, however, for three important points about desire. First, variability in sexual desire is both hormonally and situationally driven, such that variation in androgens and estrogens as well as in cultural norms and social environments must be taken into account.[13] Second, individuals are often completely unaware of the full range of their sexual desires. As indicated in the previous chapter, people's physiological responses to same-sex and other-sex erotica do not always agree with their subjective responses.[14] Such findings make it tricky to assess change in sexual predispositions. Which dimension should we assess? Mind or body? And how would researchers ever know whether an individual's desires actually changed or whether our relatively crude methods tapped into a different *type* of desire, one that might have had a different pattern all along?

Finally, as I have repeatedly emphasized, *women's sexual desires show more variability than do men's,* both over time and across situations. Roy Baumeister published an exhaustive review of all the published data on this topic.[15] Notably, most of these data focused on aspects of desire other than the gender of one's preferred partner. Collectively, the results conclusively demonstrated that women show greater variability than men in a wide range of sexual phenomena, including desired frequency of sex, desired sexual acts, preferred contexts for sexual behavior, types and frequency of fantasy, and judgments of desirable partner characteristics. Thus, though everyone is capable of some sexual variability, given the intrinsic flexibility of our sexual-response system, some individuals are clearly more variable than others, and women are disproportionately represented in that group.[16]

Extensive evidence also points to greater variability in female same-sex sexuality than in male same-sex sexuality. How much of this evidence specifically speaks to the possibility of actual change? Some of the relevant data come from research on how women first became aware of their same-sex attractions. As noted in Chapter 2, traditional sexual-identity models suggest that sexual-minority individuals usually begin experiencing same-sex attractions at an early age, even if they subsequently try to repress or deny them. But over the years, numerous researchers have documented cases in which women report no awareness of same-sex attractions until mid- to late adulthood.[17] The easy explanation, of course, is that these women always had same-sex attractions, but they remained dormant because of cultural stigmatization.[18]

Over the years, however, studies of such late-life transitions have suggested that this "dormancy" or "latency" model might be overly simplistic. The psychologist Sophie Freud Loewenstein, Sigmund Freud's granddaughter, studied the other-sex and same-sex "passions" of more than seven hundred adult women. Some of these women described novel and unprecedented same-sex passions that developed late in life, and which they interpreted as true shifts in their erotic desires. Loewenstein knew that these women might make such claims in order to maintain a façade of heterosexuality, but after carefully examining their cases, she concluded that they might be right, and that they might in fact be undergoing "a genuine shift in love object orientation. . . . Some respondents were bona fide heterosexual women who switched in midlife to a lesbian orientation."[19] Similarly, the British psychologists Celia Kitzinger and Sue Wilkinson interviewed eighty adult lesbians whose first sexual questioning took place in adulthood rather than in adolescence. More than two-thirds of these women had been previously married. The average age of their first same-sex experience was eighteen, and the average age of their first lesbian identification was thirty-four. Although some women said that they suppressed their lesbianism for many years, others experienced the transition to same-sex sexuality as a sudden transformation which they described in terms of "rebirth," a "quantum leap," a "conversion experience," or "emerging from a chrysalis."[20]

The psychologist Carla Golden has written persuasively about women's potential for erotic change. She became interested in this phenomenon when she was on the faculty at an all-women's college. She noted that many of the women who enrolled in her courses on feminism and sexuality seemed to be undergoing profound changes, not only in how they thought about sexuality, but in their actual sexual feelings. She began interviewing a wide range of women—lesbian, bisexual, and heterosexual. After more than one hundred interviews, she concluded that actual change sometimes does occur.[21] Although a subset of the "late-blooming" lesbian-bisexual women whom Golden interviewed described their heterosexual pasts in terms of repression and falsehood, another subset maintained that though they had, in fact, been "truly" heterosexual in the past, they were just as "truly" bisexual or lesbian now. Yet importantly, these women did not feel that they *chose* these transitions; rather, they typically described the onset of their same-sex desires as strong, spontaneous, and surprising. This finding underscores the point I made earlier: although mainstream society tends to confuse change with choice, they are completely different experiences.

Of course, all the studies mentioned here were retrospective. Women reflected backward on how they identified and felt in the past. This approach has plenty of problems, especially when investigating something like change in attractions, in which individuals might be strongly motivated to reinterpret their pasts. That makes the longitudinal design of my study particularly informative. Regardless of what women thought about themselves and their attractions back in 1995, and how they might like to think of themselves now, ten years later, how much change actually took place during this time?

Conceptualizing Change

Women in my study did report changes in their attractions, but rarely to a degree that pushed them into a different category of sexual orientation. Let's examine this finding in detail to see how those changes were experienced, what triggered them, and whether they had long-term effects on women's identities.

To begin, we need to consider the different ways that change can be measured. One straightforward approach is simply to compare women's self-reported percentages of same-sex attractions in 2005 to their self-reported percentages in 1995. We can do this by subtracting 1995 percentages from 2005 percentages. A difference of zero indicates no change; positive-difference scores indicate that same-sex attractions have increased; negative-difference scores indicate that same-sex attractions have decreased. If we compute each woman's difference score and then take the average across all women, we get −5, meaning that women's same-sex attractions declined by an average of 5 percentage points. But this is not a very meaningful result: since we averaged all the individual difference scores together, positive scores and negative scores tend to cancel each other out. If same-sex attractions increased by 40 percentage points in half of the sample but *declined* by 40 points in the other half, the average difference score would be zero, and we would (wrongly!) conclude that no change occurred.

The solution is to look at the absolute size of changes; that is, the magnitude of each change regardless of whether it was "toward" men or "toward" women. That would give us an estimate of just how much change took place overall. But here we face another hurdle in interpreting the magnitude of change: What counts as a big change versus a trivial one? If a woman goes from 60 percent same-sex attractions to 65 percent, is that change really meaningful, or does it simply reflect "wiggle room" in her own self-perceptions (what statisticians call *measurement error*)? After all, when women are reporting these percentages, they are not actually counting up each and every attraction they have experienced in the past year and calculating exact percentages. They are providing rough estimates, and so a bit of error is to be expected.

One way to get a sense of what constitutes big versus small change is to look at prior studies that have used analogous measures of same-sex attraction. Several earlier studies have examined short-term changes in individuals' ratings on the Kinsey Scale (the 0–6 scale that represents, like my 0–100 percent scale, the ratio of a person's same-sex attractions to his or her other-sex attractions). Many of these studies have considered *any* change in rating (that is, moving up or down by at least 1 point on the Kinsey Scale) large enough to merit attention. It turns out that changes of this sort are fairly common. One group of researchers collected Kinsey ratings five years apart from about fifty bisexual men and women living in San Francisco in the 1980s.[22] They found that two-thirds of participants gave different ratings at the two assessments. In another study of bisexual men recruited through community activities and print advertising, approximately 50 percent of respondents changed their rating of sexual attractions over a one-year period.[23] A study that averaged women's Kinsey ratings of sexual attraction, fantasy, behavior, and self-identification found that over an eighteen-month period, about 20 percent of women changed Kinsey categories.[24]

We can easily compare my ten-year findings to these prior studies by dividing my 0 to 100 percent measure into sections representing the 7 Kinsey categories (0, 1, 2, 3, 4, 5, and 6), such that a change of 1 Kinsey point is equivalent to about 15 percentage points. So how many women experienced a shift of that magnitude, in either direction, over the course of the study?

Prevalence of Change over a Ten-Year Period

Altogether, a little less than half the women reported changes in their attractions equal to 1 Kinsey Scale point from 1995 to 2005. This puts my findings in the same general range as prior studies, even though I observed women for much longer periods of time. As for larger shifts—those equivalent to 2 Kinsey Scale ratings—about one-fourth of the women reported such changes. Yet it is more interesting to look at the direction of change: of the women who underwent changes of at least 1 Kinsey point in magnitude, twice as many had become more attracted *to men* as had become more attracted *to women.* This finding parallels what we saw with sexual-identity transitions, in which more women undertook identity changes that accommodated attractions and relationships with men (that is, switching to bisexual, unlabeled, or heterosexual labels) than switched to lesbian labels.

So how should we interpret these shifts? Are any of them substantial enough to represent change in a woman's overall sexual orientation? Does the trend toward nonexclusivity indicate that a sizeable proportion of lesbian women will become bisexual over time, or that all women are really bisexual? As with interpreting changes in sexual identity, it is helpful to examine which women are changing the most. If we examine correlations between women's initial percentages of same-sex attraction (in 1995) and the size of their subsequent changes, we find a strikingly consistent pattern: the more same-sex attractions a woman reported in 1995 (and, in fact, throughout the rest of the study as well), the less her attractions changed over time, in either direction. Thus women who reported predominant or near-exclusive attractions to women in 1995 tended to remain pretty much the same. The women with more nonexclusive attractions—those who identified as bisexual or unlabeled—underwent the most sizeable shifts.

The consistent differences that emerged between the lesbians and the nonlesbians are particularly interesting. They suggest that though most lesbians experience some degree of attractions to men—only three women reported 100 percent same-sex attractions at every interview—these data are not consistent with the notion that all women are bisexual. The degree of lesbians' same-sex attractions and their stability over time render them meaningfully distinct from the bisexual and unlabeled women, even if this distinction is one of degree rather than of kind.

If we use these changes in attractions to make inferences about changes in sexual orientation, we must conclude that there is not much evidence for change in orientation. The small shifts experienced by lesbians nonetheless kept them in the lesbian range, and even the sizeable shifts experienced by unlabeled and bisexual women kept them in the bisexual range: they almost never jumped to near-exclusive same-sex attractions or plummeted down to near-exclusive other-sex attractions. Note, in particular, that the women who had reidentified as heterosexual by 2005 did not undergo much change either: they had always reported less frequent same-sex attractions than the rest of the sample; they simply came to label and interpret these feelings differently over time.

Thus the most accurate conclusion is that though women's sexual orientations are fairly stable, they nonetheless accommodate an increasingly broad range of attractions as time goes by. This raises the larger question of whether changes in identity and attraction tended to correspond: Were women who reported greater changes in their attractions more likely to switch their identity labels? The answer is no. Women who reported changes in their attractions of 1 or more Kinsey points were not disproportionately likely to change their identity labels. Yet this does not mean that changes in attractions and identity were totally unrelated; rather, it appears that the *direction* of change in attractions proved significant. Women who reported large changes toward men were more likely to switch identities than those with large changes toward women. This is consistent with the fact that most of the post–coming-out identity changes I observed accommodated greater nonexclusivity (for example, switching from lesbian to bisexual or unlabeled identities, rather than vice versa).

Another interesting factor to consider is the specific ratio of women's same-sex to other-sex attractions. Some previous studies have suggested that sexual-minority women follow an implicit 75 percent boundary when identifying as lesbian versus bisexual. In other words, those who experience at least 75 percent of their attractions for women tend to identify as lesbian, whereas those who experience less than 75 percent of their attractions for women tend to identify as bisexual. There is no stated "rule" about such matters; people just seem to follow this norm without being consciously aware of it. Accordingly, we might expect women whose attractions cross this implicit 75 percent boundary to be disproportionately likely to change their identity label. In fact, this is the case. When we examine women's successive reports of same-sex attractions (for example, from 1995 to 1997, from 1997 to 2000, and so on), we see that women's attractions crossed over (or under) this 75 percent boundary about one-fifth of the time. In the majority of these cases, women also changed their identity label.

Karen provides a vivid example of such an experience.

Karen

Karen contradicted all the popular stereotypes about lesbians: although she wore very little makeup, she had slight, feminine features framed by soft blond hair that curled in naturally at her shoulders. Her bangs made her look even younger than her nineteen years. At our first interview she wore a pastel sweater and neatly fitting jeans. As we spoke, her hands were gently folded on the table in front of her, the very model of feminine propriety.

Yet this conventional appearance masked a forthright, assertive woman who was bursting with excitement about recently coming out as a lesbian and beginning her first same-sex love affair. Karen had first begun to think about sexuality issues during her junior year of high school, when she became involved in AIDS activism and educational programs designed to combat homophobia. She met an older lesbian activist who inspired her and who spoke candidly about what it was like to live openly as a lesbian. Karen had never met a lesbian before, and she described the experience as enlightening. At that time, however, she still considered herself completely heterosexual.

Once she got to college she found herself becoming attracted to women, and she met many more openly identified lesbians. Fairly quickly, she became close friends with her current girlfriend, and their relationship blossomed into a love affair. At the time of our interview, they had been together for nine months. Some of Karen's friends thought that her transition to lesbianism was unusually abrupt. They asked her, "How can you possibly know for sure so soon?" Even her current girlfriend, who had been an openly identified lesbian when she met Karen, wondered whether Karen could really be certain of her lesbian orientation.

Karen acknowledged that she sometimes felt "odd" because of her rapid transition. Whereas many of her lesbian friends recalled years of private questioning and self-doubt, Karen had none of that. Nonetheless, she felt 100 percent certain of her lesbianism. The relationships she had with men in high school were both physically and emotionally unsatisfying, whereas she was completely enthralled with her current girlfriend. Although she still felt that she could develop emotional bonds with some men and appreciate "the beauty of some male bodies," she had no desire to act on those feelings. As far as she was concerned, women were *it*. When she talked about her current girlfriend, she beamed.

This is not to say that her transition was effortless; some of her high school friends flatly rejected her when she came out to them, and others made no effort to hide their disapproval. But she responded to these experiences by developing a stronger network of college friends who either accepted or shared her sexuality. Over the next few years, as she became involved with a number of different women and became more politically and socially aware, she grew even more certain of her sexuality.

By the time of the third interview, however, things had changed. Karen was now twenty-five years old and out of college. She had recently ended a two-year relationship with a woman. As the relationship wound down, she found herself reflecting on her attractions more generally, and she realized that she was more open to the possibility of men than she had previously thought. As she explained: "It wasn't so much that I found myself attracted to men, but it really just started to open me to thinking of people as individuals and not so much according to their gender." Soon this openness went from theory to reality: "I became close friends with a man I played soccer with. . . . I think I was really strongly attracted to his personality. Physically, I was attracted, but it wasn't sexual. I just knew that he was good and fun and I guess we became really close friends, and the attraction developed later on. Now he's my partner. It was startling in some sense. I hadn't been in a relationship, or even sexually attracted to a man in five years. But it felt right."

Some of her lesbian friends did not see it that way. Karen encountered the same kind of rejection from them as she had encountered from her heterosexual friends back when she first came out as lesbian:

> Overall, people have been supportive, but I've definitely seen some nastiness because of it. One lesbian I know, she said that it was just a phase, that I was misguided, that she didn't want him in her house. It made me angry, it made me cry, it made me question—I mean, these were the same types of things I heard from straight people when I first came out about having relationships with *women.*

Although Karen now strongly felt that she was attracted to both men and women, she did not feel comfortable identifying as bisexual; she was still most comfortable thinking of herself as a lesbian: "I don't want to say, well, because I'm with a man, I'm bisexual now. I think in the very basic definition, it comes down to, okay, I've been with this amount of women, this amount of men, and I'm with a man now, and I'm still attracted to women, it's still completely open. So what it comes down to for me is that lesbianism is still where I am most closely aligned." When asked what type of relationship she would seek if the current one ended, she was uncertain: "Overall, my attractions to women haven't changed, and it's more like my attractions to *him* have, but it's still not like this has just opened up a whole other world, or that I'm now *just* as attracted to men as to women, because I'm not."

At our eight-year follow-up interview, Karen reported that after three and a half years together, she and her boyfriend had gotten engaged. Interestingly, not only does her fiancé know everything about her lesbian past, but he, too, is attracted to both women and men. They have talked openly about the fact that though they are making a monogamous commitment to each other, they will probably always experience bisexual attractions.

But Karen still felt that the kinds of attractions she had for women were different, and generally more intense, than the attractions she had for men. In particular, she felt that she had "emotional, spiritual connections" with women, characterized by feelings of trust and comfort, which she had never quite experienced with men other than her fiancé. But she no longer identified as lesbian, and in fact no longer identified as anything. Over the years, she had become very skeptical of identity labels:

> Yeah, I'm just so sick of the homo, hetero, bi thing. I'm really sick of those sort of three categories that we have. I just think there's so many points along the continuum and I don't really think we have enough words for it all, even for gender. . . . And you know in my experience I have known a lot of women who have dated both genders and have even ended up marrying men. So in my experience there have been a lot of other women that have done the same thing that I did, or had similar experiences to mine.

At the ten-year interview, Karen was happily married but ambivalent about the fact that it was so easy for friends, family members, and colleagues to "erase" her lesbian past. To compensate, she had started openly identifying as bisexual—a label that she had previously resisted—in order to communicate that she was still attracted to women and expected that she always would be. She reported finding subtle ways to mention her previous same-sex relationships in order to keep people from assuming that she was just "totally heterosexual."

In making sense of Karen's experiences, it is interesting to look closely at how she described her overall pattern of sexual and emotional attractions while she was going through these unexpected transitions. At the first interview, when she had just come out, she reported that 90 percent of her physical attractions and 95 percent of her emotional attractions were directed toward women. At the second interview, her emotional attractions had increased to 99 percent and her physical attractions to 95 percent. At the third interview, when she had become involved with her husband, her emotional attractions were still high—now 97 percent—but her physical attractions had dropped to 75 percent. She was clearly still more attracted to women than to men, but not as predominantly as before. This trend continued over the next two interviews, and by 2005 she reported that 75 percent of her emotional attractions and 50 percent of her physical attractions were directed toward women. And not all her other-sex attractions were directed toward her husband. When I asked her how many different men and women she was typically attracted to in the average month, she said about three men and three women. Yet the intensity of her attraction to her husband was stronger than her attractions to other women.

Thus Karen provides one of the few examples in my study of women whose changes took them across the conventional lesbian/bisexual divide. Yet notably, even as she became increasingly committed to her husband, she continued to profess uncertainty about what might have happened if she had not met him. She continued to describe him as "unusual" compared with other men. In addition to being bisexual, he had a "feminine energy" and a way of connecting with other people that she generally found more typical of women than of men.

So would Karen have stayed firmly lesbian-identified if she had never met this particular man, and if she had settled down with a woman? Possibly. Her experiences demonstrate the importance of individual relationships in triggering women's fluidity. Perhaps she would always have had some "openness" to men, but it might have remained inconsequential—to her identity and her overall experience of her sexuality—if she never met anyone to activate it. This fact was further reflected in her own understanding of her sexuality as being both something that she was born with and something that was strongly influenced by the environment. She thought that environmental circumstances had changed the types of people she encountered, thus triggering different feelings, but she was certain that she had little control over the feelings themselves: "I just don't think attraction is something that we can control. I mean, maybe people can control whether or not they want to be in a relationship, and maybe some people know an attraction is happening but they choose not to pursue it, because they know it's not acceptable, but I don't think we choose who we're attracted to."

Was It a Phase? Reidentifying as Heterosexual

Just as Karen shifted from considering herself lesbian to considering herself unlabeled, some bisexual women experience such significant shifts toward men that they reidentify as heterosexual. Altogether, 17 percent of women in my sample readopted heterosexual labels at some point during the study. Some of them subsequently went back to bisexual or unlabeled identities, so that in 2005 only 9 percent of the women called themselves heterosexual. Such cases bring up a fascinating but controversial set of questions: Do these examples prove that lesbianism or bisexuality is sometimes just a phase, and that some individuals are actually wrong when they proudly come out? Or do they suggest that the cultural stigmatization of same-sex sexuality is strong enough to lure women back into the closet at any time, even after years of open lesbian or bisexual identification?

A closer look at the women who readopted heterosexual labels shows that both of these characterizations are inaccurate. All of these women had been very comfortable discussing their same-sex attractions and did not report any ongoing concerns with social stigma—thus the notion that they were going back into the closet seems misplaced. So does the notion of a phase: all the women continued to report some degree of erotic interest in women, and only one participant characterized her previous bisexuality as a "curious phase."

So what, then, explains their transitions? Two patterns seemed to emerge, and both reflect the ambiguity that sexual fluidity introduces to our understanding of sexual orientation. The first pattern concerned women who were certain of their attractions to other women but decided to identify as heterosexual because they had settled down with men and expected men to remain the focus of their future attractions and experiences. Paula provides an example of this pattern. From the very first interview, she was certain of her bisexual attractions, but she stopped seeing this pattern as highly relevant to her sexual identity when she became engaged to a man, about midway through the study. Her attractions had always leaned more toward men than toward women, and so at that point she felt it made sense to consider herself heterosexual rather than bisexual. As she said, "My attractions are always focused on the person that I'm currently involved with anyway, and right now that's just him." By the eight-year follow-up interview, she had come to see the entire labeling process as having more relevance for individuals' relationships than for their independent identities: "I do still have an attraction to women. But it's hard to label myself other than in a relationship. So I guess I see my sexuality as centered around my relationship itself and not about outside factors as much as I used to. I still find my strongest *emotional* attractions to women—well, maybe that's not true anymore, it's really split down the middle . . . with my husband, it was just the right place, right time. I'm in a relationship with a man because of who he is and not because he's a man."

The second group of reidentified heterosexuals had always been predominantly interested in men, and had actually expressed consistent doubts over the years about whether the quality or degree of their same-sex attractions was "enough" to suggest that they were bisexual. For this reason, many of them had initially been unlabeled. Eleanor provides a fascinating example of this pattern.

Eleanor

At the very first interview, Eleanor described herself as "questioning," but unlike some of the other questioning women I had interviewed, who came across as relatively quiet and internally focused, Eleanor had an outgoing, vivacious demeanor. She had a broad, engaging smile and a self-deprecating sense of humor.

I could tell that Eleanor would be a little different from the other respondents when she flatly refused to characterize her same-sex attractions on my 0–100 percent scale. She threw up her hands and exclaimed, "I can't make any sense of that at all! There are too many variables involved when I'm attracted to someone, so there's no way for me to divide it up that way." Eleanor was twenty years old and had first begun to question her sexuality about a year earlier, when her boyfriend told her that he was bisexual. She had been aware of sporadic same-sex attractions since the age of thirteen, and, in her words, "they scared the hell out of me." Yet the quality of her attractions had always confused her. As she described it, most of her "gut level," immediate sexual urges were in response to men, but she found women much more aesthetically and emotionally desirable:

> I prefer to make out with men, but the idea of having sex with a man utterly repulses me. I would, however, like to marry a woman, and that's who I want to make a long-term commitment to. . . . When people ask me if I'm straight and I say yes, I know I'm being dishonest, and I can't tolerate that dishonesty. But if somebody asked me if I

was a lesbian, I'd also feel dishonest saying yes. I guess I might be bisexual. I'm annoyed by the uncertainty. I know I'm not straight, it's just a matter of defining my not-straightness. . . . You could probably extrapolate straightness, lesbianism, and bisexuality, all from me.

Eleanor felt that she "failed the lesbian authenticity test" because her feelings for women were more emotional and aesthetic than sexual. But she wondered if that was just a result of cultural conditioning. As she stated, "Maybe the pathway from liking someone as a friend to being sexually attracted to them just isn't as well worn for women as it is for men. . . . I don't know. My idea is for my emotional and physical attractions to match. Right now they don't."

By the second interview Eleanor had settled on the compromise of a bisexual identification, despite the fact that her feelings for women remained relatively ambiguous. She was eager for more certainty about her sexuality, but she resisted the common approach of looking to her childhood for clues:

I still go through this whole explanation when I tell people I'm bisexual, because the truth is that my attraction to women isn't really all that sexual. It's more aesthetic. Women are just so much better looking than men. I guess I find women magnetic. That's not quite the same as a sexual attraction. . . . Last time I thought things would resolve themselves. I expected that over time I'd either feel clear sexual attractions and I'd identify as bisexual or I wouldn't feel them at all and I'd identify as heterosexual. But now I realize that won't happen—I still feel the same, and I've accepted that. . . . I *was* an insane little tomboy, looking back. I climbed trees and stuff. But I don't think that has anything to do with it. I think mostly I didn't care what others thought. I know a lot of women who come out and then they go back and reconstruct their whole childhood, but I really don't think that being a tomboy had much to do with it.

At the third interview, at age twenty-five, Eleanor finally reconciled with the fact that her emotional and aesthetic appreciation for women did not really qualify as sexual attraction. Yet contrary to the notion that this might just be a rationalization for not identifying as lesbian or bisexual, Eleanor actually expressed great disappointment that she was not gay:

> I've kind of straightened out! I still call myself bisexual but I'm on the edge of heterosexual, which I'm not pleased about. I mean, straight culture—yuck, bad! I never really wanted to be heterosexual but I don't have much choice in the matter. . . . It was this gradual realization that, in fact, as a rule, I wasn't all that sexually interested in other women anymore. I would date other women, but it would never be serious because I wasn't all that sexually attracted. And I'm thinking, well, if it's a sexual-orientation thing, isn't actual sexual attraction sort of one of the things that theoretically goes along with that? . . . I feel self-conscious because I still identify as bisexual, but I'm aware that my identity and my actual orientation don't really match anymore, so that's highly disconcerting. I think sexuality definitely changes, because it's not that I'm just more aware of the straight parts of me, I've actually *become* more straight, but I don't have any idea what causes those changes.

Eleanor reported the same basic perspective at the eight-year and ten-year follow-up interviews, when she characterized herself as "reluctantly heterosexual." At the ten-year point, now thirty years old, she noted, "I'm living proof that sexual identity is not something that you pick, because I never actually wanted to be straight!" Her experience shows that sexual fluidity can make it possible for a heterosexual woman to develop an erotic *appreciation* for other women that might periodically spill over into desire, but her basic pattern of attraction is unlikely to change completely, no matter how much she might wish that it would.

Eleanor did, by the way, eventually relent to characterizing her same-sex attractions along my 0–100 percent scale. At the second interview, when she considered herself bisexual, she described herself as 65 percent physically and emotionally attracted to women.

At the third interview, by which point she had reconciled herself to the fact that her attractions to women were not really sexual, she reported experiencing 15 percent of her emotional attractions for women, but only 5 percent of her physical attractions for women. Her rating of physical attractions stayed around that level for the next two assessments, but her percentage of *emotional* attractions to women actually shot up to 70 percent at the ten-year assessment, exemplifying the long-standing discrepancy between her physical and emotional attractions.

In retrospect, Eleanor felt that the intensity of her emotional attractions, and the sometimes confusing boundary between physical and emotional feelings, had led her to question her sexuality from the very beginning. As we will see in Chapter 7, overlap between emotional and physical feelings is a key component of sexual fluidity that can lead many women to experience sporadic, ambiguous attractions that run counter to their overall sexual orientation.

Sheila

Sheila provides a compelling example of a woman who initially shifted toward the other sex and reidentified as heterosexual, but then shifted back toward a same-sex orientation. Sheila was a confident, sixteen-year-old African-American girl with an unusual coming-out story. She first began to question her sexuality at the age of fifteen, when she gradually became attracted to a friend of hers. Her feelings neither alarmed nor worried her. She was already familiar with lesbian/gay/bisexual individuals because her parents were actively involved in progressive politics and had numerous lesbian/gay/bisexual friends. Sheila does not recall any big revelation about her sexuality, just a slow realization that "this was a piece of me." She soon announced to her parents that she was bisexual, and their (unbelievable!) response was to jump up, hug her, and congratulate her. Sheila's mother even drove her to our first interview and patiently waited outside in the car during our ninety-minute conversation. Perhaps as a result of this unwavering support, Sheila seemed wise beyond her years, able to analyze and articulate her feelings with surprising forthrightness and insight.

At the first interview, Sheila felt fairly equally drawn to both men and women and described her emotional and physical attractions as split down the middle, 50–50. Yet by the second interview, she had become more interested in women and described her physical attractions as 75 percent same-sex (her emotional attractions remained 50–50). When I asked her to explain what exactly had changed, she said that she had become involved in a substantial same-sex relationship. In her opinion, "when you're involved with someone, that has a big effect on what types of attractions you feel."

Yet for Sheila, the effect of becoming involved with someone could clearly operate in both directions. By the third interview, at age twenty-one, she had become seriously involved with a man, and he had just asked her to marry him. She had said yes, and she currently considered herself heterosexual. At that point, she reported that her same-sex physical attractions had dropped to around 20 percent, and her emotional attractions had pretty much flatlined, since all her emotional feelings were now focused on her fiancé. When I remarked on the abruptness of her transition, she noted that it probably had something to do with the way her relationship with her last girlfriend had ended. Sheila had been deeply in love, but they broke up when the woman moved to a different city. Sheila was heartbroken and said that the experience "took the fight out of me." At that point, she simply stopped seeking out other girlfriends, since no one could compare to her former lover. Eventually she started to wonder, "Maybe I'm not as gay as I think I am," and she started focusing more on men. But even though she was now engaged to be married, she was still open to the possibility of becoming involved with women in the future; she added that even her boyfriend found the idea appealing! As she put it, "If it comes to me, it comes to me. I stopped trying to reinvent or reidentify myself."

Two years later, things had changed yet again, and she was back to considering herself bisexual. The relationship with her fiancé had not worked out, and she had called off the engagement. Since that time, she had been dating both men and women but had not had any other long-term relationships. She still remained open to both men and women, and her physical and emotional attractions to women were back around where they used to be—about 40 percent of her physical attractions and 60 percent of her emotional attractions. In general, though, Sheila felt that she was more drawn to an individual's personality than to his or her gender.

This might explain why in 2005, at age twenty-six, Sheila's attractions had shifted even more toward women. As she got older, she found herself less and less tolerant of what she perceived as immaturity on the part of many of the men she met (as she noted, "They have to be smart enough to hold a conversation with me!"), and she had generally found it easier to meet attractive women. But she still considered herself open to both sexes. She felt that the most satisfying thing about her sexuality was that she could "walk into a room anywhere and find someone that I could possibly in some way have a relationship with."

Sheila provides an example of the degree to which the simple availability of different partners can shape the way a woman sees the direction of her sexual and emotional interests. Another compelling aspect of Sheila's story is the fact that her parents' unwavering support of her bisexuality did not appear to push her in any particular direction. Rather, it allowed her to explore and analyze her *own* desires, and to conclude confidently that she could ultimately have whatever type of relationship she wanted.

The Nature of Change

In considering these diverse examples, what kinds of conclusions can we draw about changes in sexual attraction and, more broadly, in orientation itself? One important conclusion is that though women do, in fact, experience transformations in their sexual feelings, often brought about by specific relationships, these changes do not appear to involve large-scale "switches" in their overall sexual orientation. Rather, their sexual and emotional attractions typically fluctuate only within a general range. This may mean that the overall range of a person's potential attractions is set by her orientation, but her degree of fluidity determines exactly where she will end up within that range.

In other words, it is altogether false to assume that if a woman's sexual orientation is an essential trait, then her sexual attractions must be fundamentally rigid. Sexual orientation can have an inborn basis and yet still permit variation in desire over time. The amount of variation a woman experiences is determined by two factors: (1) her specific degree of fluidity, which varies from woman to woman, and (2) her exposure to the types of environmental, situational, and interpersonal factors that might trigger her fluidity. This provides an apt explanation for the variability observed in my study. Although all the respondents underwent significant changes in their social and geographic environments, living situations, intimate relationships, and jobs over the ten years of the study, some women's attractions remained relatively stable throughout these transitions (for example, those of the committed lesbians), whereas other women's attractions fluctuated, to some degree, with each and every assessment.

For such women, the simple number of men and women they encountered on a day-to-day basis was often an important factor in driving such fluctuations. As one bisexually identified woman said, "My attractions are very dependent upon who I'm coming into contact with. Two years ago I had more men in my life, and now it's more women. I'm involved with a woman now, and that influences me. Last time I was with a guy, and that influenced me." One lesbian who had come out in her women's-only college noted that her attractions to men increased immediately after she graduated:

After I graduated I was surprised to find myself attracted to guys. And I thought, "You know, I can't ignore this," and it wasn't primarily one guy, but guys in general. And initially I still identified as lesbian and I thought this was just an exception to the rule. After that, I think I saw the futility in labeling because it can really restrict your boundaries and make people assume things that may or may not be true about you. . . . I mean, it wasn't a phase at all, being a lesbian, and I still feel mainly toward women, but in some ways I'm less rigid with regard to my claims to lesbianism. Society is heading more toward seeing sexuality as fluid, and I go along with that. I mean, my attractions *have* changed—I used to feel *nothing* for men. (age twenty-two, unlabeled)

Lena provides another salient example. When I first interviewed her, she had just begun to question her sexuality. She had close friendships with both women and men, and she had difficulty determining whether she was more strongly drawn to one than the other. Over the next two assessments, her peer group had become more female-dominated, and she felt that her attractions to women had become more numerous, whereas her attractions to men had diminished. She also became involved in a substantive relationship with a woman, which further intensified her same-sex attractions. But then she entered business school and broke up with her longtime girlfriend. Suddenly, her attractions shifted, and she started dating men again:

I feel like I'm much more aware of men around me than I have been before, and I think a lot of that has to do with, you know, being in business school, I'm surrounded by many more men than I have been in the past, and so I think some of that contributes, so I guess I'm still . . . I would say I'm still just as aware of the women around me as I was before; that hasn't diminished, but I'm much more aware of the men around me than I have been before. (age twenty-four, bisexual)

Yet several years after Lena graduated from business school, her attractions changed yet again. Her social network now included a substantial number of women. She had also become involved with the woman of her dreams, and they were currently planning a commitment ceremony. Did Lena's orientation change? No, but her opportunities and environment certainly did. Her physical attractions to women hovered fairly consistently around 70 percent, except for her time in business school, during which they dropped to 55 percent. Thus Lena provides a good example of how sexual fluidity can permit temporary changes in a person's attractions without necessarily affecting her overall orientation.

Jennifer, an openly identified bisexual, eloquently summarized her own view of how immediate environment can change a person's experience of his or her essential sexuality:

> Here's the thing about the nature versus nurture thing. I definitely believe that there's some inherent thing that I was born with that makes me bisexual. But the thing is that my whole sexuality is way bigger than just being bisexual. Everything that's influenced it, and how I've come to understand it, and the fact that I *ever* came to understand it, all of that is an environmental thing. I don't think that any environment would have changed the fact that I'm bisexual, but I do think that various different environments could change the way I came to *realize* it, and that I ever came to realize it at all, and how I ever chose to experience and express it. (age twenty-nine)

Awareness and the Question of Choice

What about cases in which women experience change, not in their environments, but in their awareness of different erotic possibilities? In my study such changes in awareness proved to be recurrent themes in women's sexual development. Across the entire sample, nearly half the women said that their initial sexual questioning was triggered not by straightforward, free-floating experiences of same-sex attraction but by exposure to or contact with lesbian/gay/bisexual ideas or individuals (for example, meeting lesbian/gay/bisexual friends, taking a class that covered sexual-minority issues, or seeing these issues discussed on television or in books), which triggered subsequent self-reflection and, eventually, awareness and experience of same-sex attractions.

Because such experiences involved so much thought and reflection, some people might interpret them as examples of women choosing their sexual orientation. But this is not consistent with women's own reports. Rather, they describe a complicated dynamic in which a cognitive "openness" leads to a larger psychological and physical "openness" to unexpected feelings and experiences. Thinking about same-sex sexuality did not change people's attractions, but cognitive openness did appear to create a space for fluidity to operate:

> I wouldn't say [my attractions] changed so much as they flowered, that I feel more comfortable with my attraction to women, so that I have had more real relationships with women, so I can let myself go more freely sexually and notice my attractions more readily. . . . I'm more free letting them happen. (age twenty-six, bisexual)

> I don't know if my attractions ever really changed. In some sense, it's like I'm constantly changing, constantly evolving, constantly bending and flexing. But is that me finding more dimensions myself, or is that me actually changing? I think I see it as becoming more aware, and recognizing more. . . . I feel like it is somewhat biological and somewhat environmental, but I don't think the environment has *that* much strength. (age twenty-seven, bisexual)

Other women, however, questioned the distinction between having an attraction and being aware of it. After all, what does it mean to have an attraction that you are not aware of? Does it even count as an attraction? If an experience of sexual attraction is partially constituted by a person's awareness of it, then changes in awareness *are* changes in sexuality:

> For me the awareness is part of the experience of feeling the attraction. . . . The moment I say that I'm aware of being attracted to women, the more I start to notice myself being more attracted to women. (age twenty-five, unlabeled)

> I think they go hand-in-hand. If your sexuality changes over time, then you become aware of it, but also as you become more aware of yourself as a sexual being, then maybe your perception of your sexuality changes. (age twenty-three, bisexual)

In many ways, the notion of awareness exemplifies why fluidity is such an apt metaphor for women's sexuality. Fluidity successfully conveys the capacity of women's sexuality to fill an available space the way a body of water takes the form of its immediate boundaries. Sometimes the available space is created by a particular environment, opportunity, or relationship, but sometimes it is created by the process of self-reflection. Either way, when the attractions develop, they may be experienced as an expansion and a blossoming rather than as a discovery of something that was always there but just repressed.

The phenomenon of sexual fluidity also provides a different understanding of the question of choice. Overall, most women felt that though they could not choose their attractions, they could certainly choose whether or not to act on them:

> I think that when the idea of being with women was available to me as an option, as a real option, I chose to see it as a valid one, and I chose to actively ignore what I'd always been trained to think, and to really open my mind and say yes, in spite of the fact that you know, I had always been surrounded by friends and family that weren't nec-

essarily open to that. So in that sense, I think that I sort of chose it. (age twenty-seven, unlabeled)

Well, there's just a difference between feeling and acting. Anyone can control how they act, but how they feel, I don't think that's something that you can ever change. (age twenty-four, bisexual)

I feel like I have the choice of whether or not to act on it, because being bisexual, I could've just ignored my attraction for women. But I mean the fantasies would not have stopped. So you know, the attraction always would have been there. (age twenty-eight, bisexual)

Well, I guess because of how comfortable I've been able to feel about my sexuality, being with a woman feels comfortable for me because I've been accepted in that way. But I guess I can also see how if things were different, and I felt that I couldn't for some reason be comfortable with a woman, then it is certainly possible that I could be with a man. So, I don't know, I do feel like I've been able to make a choice for myself, even though these feelings are here anyway. (age twenty-six, unlabeled)

Interestingly, some women noted that the question of choice had different ramifications for bisexual women—who could, in theory, be happy with either men or women—than for lesbian women, who only wanted to be with women:

Certainly there are bisexual people who experience it like a choice, and I don't want to dismiss that, I don't want to dismiss bisexuality, but I would say for me, I would say it felt less like a choice, or at least the stakes of the choice seem pretty awful for me. It's like, I could be a lesbian or I could be an alcoholic. So, you know, those are both choices. But obviously one is a much more happy choice. (age twenty-nine, lesbian)

Other study participants had a strong sense that all women had some capacity for fluidity, and that they could choose to open themselves up to it or not:

When my heterosexual female friends say, "Oh, I wish I could be a lesbian, it's so much easier, but I just love men so much," I'm like, "That's bull, you could have sex with women and enjoy it, I could have sex with men and enjoy it, but you choose not to because of the way you see yourself in society." I think people place restrictions on themselves and they think, "Oh, I could never think that way," because they don't want to identify as that. (age twenty-one, lesbian)

I think that most people have it in them to be attracted to both men and women, and I think people choose whether or not to admit that, explore it, or give in to those feelings. I think some people are more on the side of being gay and some people are more on the side of being straight, but it's my belief that it's very rare that somebody is completely gay or completely straight, although I think that exists also. But I think it's a choice to follow through with it, and I think everyone has that choice. (age twenty-six, unlabeled)

These diverse responses suggest that there is no single answer to the question of how choice affects women's experiences of their same-sex sexuality, and especially changes in their sexual feelings over time. Some women feel that no matter what they choose to do, how they identify, or how they think about themselves, their attractions remain unchanged. Women who acknowledge a strong capacity for fluidity, and who have had the opportunity to observe their own attractions ebb and flow over time, appear more open to the question of choice. Yet even for them, choice is limited to the conscious decision about which attractions and opportunities to focus on and allow to flourish. As one woman put it, choice was the willingness to pursue one's attractions.

The Role of Relationships

Several women in my study experienced more dramatic changes in sexual attractions. Recall Karen, who went from near exclusive lesbianism to a happy heterosexual marriage (albeit to a bisexually identified man). Several bisexual women reported similarly dramatic changes in the opposite direction. Some became committed to women and lived as lesbians despite continuing to acknowledge attractions to men. Given that I have argued that sexual orientation itself does not generally undergo large-scale changes, how can we interpret the small number of cases in which it seems to do just that?

The context of these transformations provides the key: whenever these dramatic changes occurred, they were always precipitated by specific intimate relationships. Women's attractions did not fluctuate broadly without a powerful reason, and that reason was typically an unexpected love affair. This pattern became so reliable that whenever a woman reported that her percentage of same-sex attractions had changed by at least 20 percent from the previous interview, I began waiting for the magic phrase: "Well, then I met X. . . ."

These women (whom I describe more fully in the next chapter) do not represent cases of complete change in orientation. Rather, they represent a subset of women whose day-to-day erotic feelings are—at their core—as strongly shaped by their current partner as by their underlying predisposition.

In all the variability I observed in my study, one additional phenomenon has important implications for some of the political debates over choice and change in sexuality. Whereas many women felt that they could make active choices to allow certain attractions to flourish—whether same-sex attractions among predominantly heterosexual women or other-sex attractions among predominantly lesbian women—not a single woman reported being able to *extinguish* certain attractions by turning attention away from them.

This finding is consistent with the large-scale trend toward nonexclusivity. In short, women found it easier to add certain attractions to their repertoire than to eliminate them. Similar findings have emerged in studies of adult sexual minorities, in which some men and women report experiencing their capacity for bisexuality as something that developed as an adjunct to their existing orientation.[25]

Perhaps this is why women did not view changes in their sexuality as indicative of phases. The notion of a phase implies something that is temporary—for example, an attraction that suddenly springs out of nowhere, only to disappear just as quickly. Yet for the women in my study, even transient experiences of same-sex sexuality had long-term repercussions. As one currently heterosexual women stated, "You never know about the future. If it happened once, it could happen again." This, of course, does not bode well for advocates of reparative therapy. To the extent that therapists seek to eliminate attractions, they may be doomed to failure, and this likelihood is certainly consistent with the research findings on such therapies.

This is not to say that reparative therapy cannot teach individuals to distract themselves from unwanted feelings through cognitive-behavioral strategies such as "thought stopping," avoidance of situations that trigger same-sex attractions, and mobilization of social support. Such techniques can alter a person's subjective desires, just as attending Weight Watchers meetings and keeping "forbidden" foods out of the house can reduce a dieter's cravings for salty, fatty, calorie-dense foods. Furthermore, any reader of Shakespeare or Jane Austen will recognize that these cognitive and behavioral techniques have been used for hundreds of years by individuals who had the misfortune of becoming attracted to partners of the right sex but the wrong family, social class, or nation. But these techniques do not appear to alter the basic existence of those inconvenient attractions (a point on which both Shakespeare's and Austen's success depends).

In the final analysis, perhaps the most important characteristic of human sexual nature, and one that probably applies to men as well as to women, is its capacity for expansion, for broadening an individual's opportunities for joy and pleasure over the life course instead of cutting them off. Female sexual fluidity heightens this basic capacity, facilitating the development of unexpected, situation-specific desires that might not change a woman's overall sexual disposition, but just might change her life. In open, accepting environments, fluidity can create unprecedented opportunities for self-discovery and reflection. Not a single one of the women in my sample, not even those who have reidentified as heterosexual or made commitments to male partners, regrets her same-sex experiences. To the contrary, the vast majority were grateful for having had the opportunity to reflect deeply on their emotional and physical desires and to explore their own capacity for intimacy. Whether society chooses to support or punish such opportunities, of course, is up to us.

CHAPTER 6

Attractions to
"the Person, Not the Gender"

Imagine your ideal sexual partner, someone who possesses all the qualities you find arousing. Now take out a piece of paper and list these qualities, in no particular order. Your list probably contains a mix of different attributes, some of them physical (tall, husky voice, muscular chest), some personality-based (funny, confident, seductive), and some interpersonal (understanding, supportive, loving).

Most of the physical items on your list are probably *gender-linked,* meaning that they apply only to one gender. For example, large breasts are considered desirable only in women, whereas large muscular arms are usually considered desirable only in men. Of course, some physical traits are considered desirable in both genders, such as a fit body or a "pretty" face (think Leonardo DiCaprio).

Now consider the items on your list that focus on personality or emotional qualities. Are they gender-linked? Probably not. Characteristics like "funny," "kind," or "respectful" are gender-neutral; in other words, they could apply to men or women. The main point is that when we find someone sexually desirable, we are responding to a mix of gender-linked and gender-neutral traits.

Nonetheless, most people think that gender is the key starting point. In fact, the very notion of sexual orientation presumes that gender plays a fundamental role in determining whether we can become sexually attracted to someone. Numerous studies have tried to identify universal, cross-cultural differences between the features that spark men's versus women's sexual attractions.[1] The rationale underlying this research is that men and women may be genetically "wired" to find different traits attractive. Yet such studies have consistently found that both men and women place as much weight on gender-neutral traits such as intelligence and kindness as on gender-specific traits.[2]

Still, most researchers would argue that if another person is the wrong gender for your sexual orientation, then gender-neutral traits like "funny" might inspire liking but not sexual attraction. Consider the gender-neutral traits on your own list. If you are sexually oriented to women (that is, you are a heterosexual man or a lesbian woman), what happens when you imagine a *man* with these characteristics? Or if you are oriented to men (in other words, you are a heterosexual woman or a gay man), what happens when you imagine a *woman* with these traits? Would you find that person sexually attractive, despite the fact that he or she is the wrong gender for you? Perhaps you can appreciate the person's attractiveness (and maybe you would try to set him or her up with one of your single friends), but you are not likely to feel attracted yourself.

Some people claim that they can respond erotically to anyone with a desirable personality or with whom they have a strong personal connection, regardless of that person's gender. They typically describe being attracted to "the person, not the gender." I refer to such cases as *person-based attractions*. Person-based attractions challenge many assumptions underlying traditional models of sexual orientation, such as the notion that gender always matters when it comes to sexual desire. They are also critical to understanding female sexual fluidity, since such attractions are necessarily flexible. Yet they have received almost no systematic attention in previous research.

In this chapter I describe two cases in which a woman's person-based attractions radically changed her understanding of her sexuality, and one case in which a woman's flexibility regarding the gender of her partners actually led her to question her own gender identity. These women's experiences, and the broader phenomenon of person-based attractions, raise questions about the role of gender in structuring our basic experiences of desire.

What Does It Mean to Be Attracted to the Person, Not the Gender?

Although the notion of person-based attractions might be unfamiliar to most people, scattered accounts of this phenomenon have appeared in scientific and popular writings on sexual orientation.[3] In the late 1970s, Philip Blumstein and Pepper Schwartz pointed out that traditional models of homosexuality failed to account for individuals "whose fundamental sexual desire seems to be produced within the context of a relationship, rather than by an abstract preference for women or men."[4] They identified person-based attractions as a mainly female phenomenon, and noted that male-based models of sexuality, with their emphasis on physical acts and physical characteristics, had overlooked the fact that "women's sexuality is organized by other than physical cues. For modern Western women, the recognition of love or admiration for the pleasure in companionship or deep friendship most often leads to erotic attraction and response."[5]

In the 1980s, a group of researchers studying bisexuality in San Francisco interviewed numerous men and women with person-based attractions.[6] They described these individuals as possessing an "open gender schema," meaning that they had disconnected gender from sexual desire. As a result, they could respond sexually to a broad range of traits and characteristics, regardless of gender. Interestingly, these researchers found that men with open gender schemas were typically heterosexually identified individuals who sought periodic same-sex contact for purposes of sexual release. In women, by contrast, open gender schemas almost always entailed falling in love with a particular person, a finding that was consistent with virtually all other accounts of this phenomenon.

This was also the case for the respondents in my own study. As one woman remarked, "Deep down, it's just a matter of who I meet and fall in love with, and it's not their body, it's something behind the eyes, an emotional honesty, it's a form of kindness, a strength, an aura, the vibe that folks give off." Others emphasized the distinction between a person's "inside"—emotions, intellect, and personality—and the "outside," or physical, gendered body. As one woman said, "I'm attracted to a person's soul, and the packaging is incidental." Others noted that they had trouble becoming physically attracted to someone before they got to know that person inside. As one woman described:

> My feelings of physical attraction are always influenced by the interpersonal fit, you know, the connection between me and another person, and are we able to relate, are the same things important to us; does someone provide me with a lot of care and support, do they know what I need when . . . when I'm happy or when I'm upset and vice versa, do we laugh about the same sort of things, do we connect intellectually. . . . When I feel a connection on many of those, I tend to become more attracted to someone, regardless of their sex.

This sentiment was echoed by another respondent, who noted, "My attractions to people always happen after talking to them and getting to know them. I'm attracted to who a person is, and the physicality of it, like their appearance, and their physical sex, really doesn't mean much of anything." This is particularly interesting because it is the exact reverse of how we assume that the majority of intimate relationships develop. Most people believe that a relationship starts out with physical attraction and then deepens into a more significant emotional, intellectual, or spiritual bond.

How Common Is This Experience?

How widespread are person-based attractions? It is impossible to know for sure because they have never been systematically studied. Whenever they have turned up in the scientific literature, they have been treated as anomalies. In my own research, I attempted to estimate the prevalence of person-based attractions by asking each woman to rate, on a scale of 1 to 5, her agreement with the statement, "I'm the kind of person who becomes physically attracted to the person rather than their gender." I should point out that I added this question to my interview only in the last few years of the study. When I first started out, it never occurred to me to ask such a thing. But over the years, so many women spontaneously described person-based attractions that I realized I had to collect more information about them.

Overall, about one-fourth of the women reported the strongest possible agreement (that is, a rating of 5 on the 1-to-5 scale) with this statement. An additional one-fourth reported that they somewhat agreed (a rating of 4). Thus, fully half of the sample has had some experience with person-based attractions. So much for the phenomenon being an anomaly! Of course, we must consider the motives that women might have for describing their attractions as person-based. Perhaps some of them are trying to distance themselves from the stigma associated with same-sex sexuality. As one of the lesbian respondents in my study noted, "I've had some friends that are now with men. They say that before, they weren't really lesbians, they'd just fallen in love with the particular person, who happened to be a woman. I don't know, I just think they're scared."

This might be the case for some women, especially those living in particularly restrictive environments, or whose cultural or socioeconomic backgrounds make it dangerous for them to claim a lesbian or bisexual identity. Yet this does not appear to explain person-based attractions in my sample. Among the women who most strongly agreed that they were attracted to the person and not the gender, more than half were "out" to all their immediate family members and two-thirds were out to at least 90 percent of their friends. So claiming person-based attractions did not appear to be a strategy for denying their same-sex sexuality. Moreover, claiming person-based attractions was unrelated to a woman's current or childhood socioeconomic status, her educational level, or whether she had been raised in a religious household.

Another possibility is simply misperception. Some lesbian, gay, and bisexual individuals report that though they *initially* thought their same-sex attractions were restricted to one or two special people, they eventually realized that this was not so.[7] It is difficult to interpret such accounts because they come from the most self-selected samples possible: openly identified lesbian/gay/bisexual individuals who are thinking back on their previous experiences. What happens when we take women with person-based attractions and follow them forward? Do any of them eventually reject this notion and admit that they were always intrinsically oriented to women (or, alternatively, that they were never attracted to women at all)? And what about person-based attractions to men?

Two cases shed some light on these questions.

Sarah

Sarah was a white, middle-class eighteen-year-old with shoulder-length blond hair, a slight build, and a soft, halting voice. When she sat down for our first interview, she was visibly nervous. I began the interview, as usual, with the standard questions about how she currently thought about her sexual identity. After a long pause, she replied that she did not know. I proceeded to ask how she had first begun to question her sexuality. At that point, she took a deep breath and began her story:

Just last week I sort of became involved with my best friend, who I'm currently living with, and who I've known since I was twelve. We've always been really affectionate, but last Tuesday it just sort of . . . kept going. I stopped it at first—I was sort of freaked out. Finally we just let it happen. I don't know what we're doing—are we dating? We haven't even told anyone. Right now I only have these feelings for her, and I don't know if that'll change. I don't know if I'm a lesbian. I just know I want to be with her forever.

As the interview continued, I tried to understand the nature of this experience. Sarah seemed relieved to be talking about it openly. She and her friend were keeping the relationship secret, and in fact they would continue to do so for the duration of the study. I remain the only person besides the two of them who knows what actually happened—even Sarah's current husband has no idea that the "best friend" they periodically see for dinner was sexually involved with his wife.

According to Sarah, she and her friend (whom I will call Nadine) had always enjoyed an intense and exclusive friendship. When I asked Sarah how the friendship had evolved into a sexual relationship, she was not sure. She described the experience as an "overflow" of intimacy from the mental to the physical domain, but she did not know what triggered it. "Maybe it's the fact that we're roommates, and so we are spending so much time together right now," she guessed. Apparently the two women had spent considerable time discussing their feelings, trying to determine if they were doing the right thing and if physical attraction had been part of their relationship all along.

Both Sarah and Nadine found their relationship as physically and emotionally satisfying as any of their previous heterosexual relationships. Yet they were confused by the fact that neither of them was ever sexually attracted to any other women. As far as they knew, this was impossible. If they were really lesbian or bisexual, shouldn't they now be aware of long-suppressed attractions for women in general? They found themselves scrutinizing women on the street, asking each other, "What about her? Do you think you're attracted to *her?*" It did not make sense that they had these feelings only for each other. As we ended the interview, Sarah looked at me and asked, "Are we normal?"

I reassured her that this experience was not uncommon, but I was just as stumped as she was. According to the existing research on sexual orientation, people did not generally experience "just one" or "just a few" same-sex attractions. Heterosexuals might experiment with same-sex sexuality or settle for same-sex partners in atypical settings such as prisons, but they were thought to find such encounters unsatisfying compared with heterosexual relationships. Yet Sarah and Nadine were delighted with each other. The only other interpretation, according to conventional understandings of sexual orientation, was that despite their attempts at self-reflection and self-analysis, they were repressing their true lesbianism or bisexuality.

The only test, I concluded, was time. If Sarah were really lesbian or bisexual, then by the two-year follow-up interview she would probably have realized that her feelings were not restricted to Nadine, and she probably would have become aware of being attracted to women in general. Conversely, if she were really heterosexual, then by the two-year follow-up she would probably have realized that the relationship had not, in fact, been fundamentally satisfying, and that she had been confusing her emotional connection to Nadine with sexual feelings.

So which was it? Neither. Sarah's two-year follow-up proved that neither of those simplistic interpretations (that she was always attracted to women or had never really been attracted to women) was quite right. Her story's complexity speaks for itself:

Well, we both decided that it didn't feel like it was the right thing. It lasted about a year and a half. Neither one of us really identified as anything during that time, and we didn't tell anybody what was going on. It felt totally different than relationships with men, so close, and I was so happy with the relationship, but it just didn't feel right for some reason. . . . I never developed those sorts of feelings for other women, and that made me think that my feelings were about *her,* and not a big part of *me.* The same is true for her—she doesn't have those feelings for anybody else. . . . But she was ready to be open about the relationship anyway, and I wasn't.

Sarah's reluctance to openly identify as lesbian or bisexual is understandable. Given that she was attracted only to Nadine, taking on the stigma of a lesbian or bisexual identity must have felt like a huge risk. After all, what if this was the only same-sex relationship she ever had? Nadine, though, had grown frustrated with the secrecy. Eventually they decided it would be better for their friendship if they ended their sexual relationship. Yet their emotional bond remained intense. At the time of the two-year follow-up interview they were still living together, and in fact Sarah said that they were trying to work out the best way to maintain a primary, lifelong commitment to each other, something deeper and more serious than the average best friendship.

I was moved by the strength of their connection, the struggles they had undergone to understand their feelings, and their determination to maintain their unusual emotional bond. Sarah and Nadine embarked on this journey without any cultural landmarks to help them. Not only were there no terms to describe their sexual identities (heterosexual seemed as inappropriate as lesbian), but once they "broke up," there were also no words to describe their changed status: more than friends but no longer lovers. Yet they managed to maintain their powerful relationship over the ensuing years. By the ten-year point, enough time had passed that there was no trace of awkwardness between them. Sometimes they talked about their affair, but not often. It remained a sweet, secret part of their shared history. By 2005 Sarah had married, and she doubted that she would ever experience or act on same-sex attractions again. Nonetheless, she and Nadine had no regrets.

Megan

Megan's history provides a noteworthy contrast to Sarah's. Like Sarah, Megan is currently married to a man, yet her person-based attractions took her on a very different journey to this outcome. When I first interviewed Megan, she was twenty years old and had been strongly identified as lesbian for more than two years. She was a fair-skinned, middle-class woman with a round, freckled face and a surprisingly high-pitched voice that contrasted with her androgynous dress and short-cropped hair.

Growing up, Megan had always developed very close female friendships. She and one friend in particular spent so much time together and were so physically affectionate that many of their classmates spread rumors that they were lesbians. Megan and her friend laughed off the notion as ridiculous. As Megan got older, she noticed that she was never very interested in the boys she was dating. After becoming sexually active, she remembered wondering, "What's the big deal about this?" She finally began to question her sexual identity in college, when her attractions to women became strong and unmistakable. By the time of the first interview, she felt totally certain and comfortable with her lesbian identity. When asked whether she thought it might ever change, she answered, "No. I mean, I just really like women so much more than men, both physically and emotionally. It has been more of what I have always wanted and hoped for. I have more of an emotional bond with women; it's more satisfying sexually as well."

But at the next interview, two years later, her life had taken an abrupt turn. She had started graduate school, where she became close friends with a man. Soon their emotional connection evolved into a physical relationship. As Megan described it:

I was pretty surprised . . . I didn't think we'd end up dating, we'd talked about it a bit when we were becoming really emotionally close . . . and then we ended up together. I guess I'm still more inclined to date women. He's really the only man I have any attractions for. And I don't really have any women in my life that I'm emotionally close to. So I'm not sure how to think of my sexual identity right now. . . . Everything is more uncertain now. I guess I'd have to say I was bisexual, but I've never really felt that bisexual is a label that I really want. But I can't say I'm a lesbian dating a man. People just don't accept that, even though that's sort of what I feel like. . . . My feelings about women haven't really changed, it's just that I'm more open and accepting about my feelings for men, or at least to this man—I'm definitely more attracted to him than I've been to men before. . . . After we started dating, I had sort of a last fling, or incident, with my ex-girlfriend. . . . I think I was trying to figure out if I could really be attracted to *him* like I had been to *her*. And I guess I found out that it doesn't matter, you know, the sort of biological effects of the person, and their gender. It's more who they are and whether I'm attracted to them as a person.

Megan and her boyfriend were still together at the five-year follow-up interview, and she continued to express uncertainty about the most appropriate label for her sexual identity. As she said, "Well, I guess I'm in a heterosexual *relationship,* that's about as far as I go. I guess what happens in the future depends on what would happen with the relationship, because I don't intend to leave the relationship to change my identity, but if the relationship were to end, I'm not really sure what would happen." She continued to feel that her sexual attractions to women were largely unchanged, and in fact she admitted that her current relationship was more satisfying emotionally than physically. This led her to question periodically how important the physical versus emotional aspects were, and whether she might eventually want to end the relationship just to see if she might be more physically satisfied with someone else.

Two years later, they got married. In Megan's opinion, this transition "closed the door" on the issue of women, though she still regularly found herself "looking at hot women on the street." She continued to consider herself unlabeled, and she emphasized that for her, love revolved around the person as opposed to his or her biological sex. Furthermore, she was finding that as time went on, sex was less of a focus in her relationship with her husband; it was the emotional intensity of the bond that provided its foundation. She said she did not know whether she felt this way because he was a man, or whether it was just something that happens in long-term relationships.

Although Megan was happy, she admitted to feeling wistful about losing "the other side of my identity." She and her husband were living in an area without a strong lesbian community, and she felt that once people found out she was married, they just assumed she was heterosexual. Over time, this prompted her to discuss her same-sex attractions more openly, even though she knew she would probably never act on them again. By the ten-year point, she had switched from unlabeled to bisexual, claiming that the bisexual label "really sort of encompasses my history, and my current feelings toward people I'm attracted to. I think I just got more used to being in this relationship with a man and saying that I'm also attracted to women. But it's still surprising to me that the person I ended up marrying isn't the sort of person that I think I ever would have described as my ideal partner, physically, and in terms of physical attraction. I just never would have thought it would be this person."

Thus, whereas Sarah's person-based attraction diverted her only temporarily from an otherwise heterosexual pathway, Megan's person-based attraction turned her whole life upside down, to her own surprise and the surprise of her friends and family. These two cases demonstrate the power of person-based attractions. Even when they do not change an individual's underlying sexual orientation, they can completely change her identity and her life path.

Characteristics of Person-Based Attractions

Sarah and Megan might be considered extreme cases of person-based attractions because each of them became attracted to someone who was the wrong gender for her sexual orientation. Yet their experiences highlight a number of core themes that emerged in the reports of other women with this pattern of desire: *nonexclusivity and change* in attractions, *links* between emotional and physical feelings, and reluctance to *label* their sexual identity.

As we saw in Chapter 4, some bisexual-identified women (and some researchers) view bisexuality as a gender-neutral form of desire that is based on individual people rather than on gender categories. Does this mean that person-based attractions are simply bisexual attractions? Certainly, most of the women in my sample with person-based attractions fell squarely into a bisexual range, typically reporting that between 40 percent and 70 percent of their day-to-day physical attractions were directed toward women. Yet it is a mistake to equate person-based attractions with bisexuality. After all, not all bisexuals experience their attractions as gender-neutral. For some women with nonexclusive attractions, gender-linked characteristics play an important role in triggering their desires, even though they respond to both female-specific and male-specific traits. So the most accurate conclusion is that though all women with person-based attractions appear to have a capacity for nonexclusive attractions (by definition), not all women with nonexclusive attractions experience person-based desires.

Recall that when I asked respondents to describe the percentage of their day-to-day attractions that were directed to women, I asked them to separately estimate their physical and emotional attractions. These estimates did not always agree, especially among women with person-based attractions. But women with person-based attractions showed a greater connection between their physical and emotional attractions *from interview to interview* than was observed among the other women. When one type of attraction went up or down, the other did as well. Of course, this does not reveal which type changed first—were emotional attractions "leading" physical attractions, or vice versa? Nonetheless, the tight linkage between these women's physical and emotional feelings fits with their own descriptions.

This connection was confirmed by the fact that virtually all the women with person-based attractions agreed strongly with the statement, "When I'm really emotionally bonded to someone, I find myself becoming physically attracted to them." Overall, more women strongly agreed with this statement (one-third of the sample) than with the statement about being attracted to the person and not the gender (one-fourth of the sample). Thus, not all women whose emotional feelings influence their physical feelings think of themselves as having person-based desires. Rather, the latter group seems to be a subset of the former.

Consider the experience of Amy, a bisexual woman who does not think of herself as being attracted to the person, not the gender, but who does tend to become physically attracted to people with whom she has emotionally bonded: "There's this one woman at work, and she weighs 400 pounds, and in my sense of attractiveness, well . . . you know, it just wasn't there. When I first met her, I wasn't, like, wanting to grab her and take her into another room. But this woman is just amazing, she rocks, and now we're really, really close emotionally, so now I'm actually attracted to her. She's just wonderful but I had to get to know her." Thus it seems that a capacity to become physically attracted on the basis of emotional feelings is a necessary—but not sufficient—condition for having predominantly person-based attractions.

Given that there is no label to represent these gender-neutral, person-based attractions, how do women who experience them identify themselves? It should not be surprising that women with person-based attractions often considered themselves unlabeled. As one woman said, "I don't even identify as a bisexual, just because my definition of bisexuality is one who maybe craves both men and women . . . whereas with me I'm all about one person. I've gotten to the point now in my life where it's not even like a sexual or gender identification; I'm attracted to certain things about a . . . *whole person,* and if and when I find that, their sex doesn't really matter that much for me anymore." Another woman noted, "I still don't label my identity, because I'm not really attracted to either sex until I get to know the person, and there's no label that reflects that. I bet you probably hear that a lot."

She was right: I did. Some women had noticed that their attractions varied simply as a function of whom they happened to be around and whom they happened to connect with. As one woman noted, "I tend to get along with only 1 percent of the guys that I meet, and I get along with *way* more women. So it's much more likely that among the people that I meet, I end up being attracted to women, but it could totally change, I could imagine some day some guy delivers my pizza and he's like the perfect person for me. What are you going to do? I wouldn't send him away." This openness was also evident in a woman who had initially identified as a lesbian while attending an all-female college. Once she graduated and started developing more friendships with men, she began to experience more other-sex attractions:

> I found myself, not necessarily only attracted to both sexes, but also slightly more open-minded to the notion that maybe . . . maybe I can find something in just *a* person, that I don't necessarily have to be attracted to one sex versus the other. . . . Currently I'm in a long-term relationship with a man that I find very, very, very enjoyable and fulfilling, so it's hard for me to identify, so therefore I prefer to not iden-

tify or just kind of joke about it and say, "I'm not bisexual or homosexual, I'm just sexual."

Given these complexities, we can see why nearly 70 percent of the women with person-based attractions considered themselves unlabeled at some point during the ten years of the study (compared with about one-third of the other women). By 2005, more than half of the women with person-based attractions were currently identifying as bisexual, and more than one-third were unlabeled. Recall that these two groups have been systematically excluded from prior research on same-sex sexuality. This may be why researchers understand so little about the phenomenon of person-based attractions, despite the fact that women with such attractions have turned up in studies of same-sex sexuality for decades.[8] These women have probably always existed, and they might account for some of the notable contemporary cases (such as Anne Heche and Julie Cypher) in which women who have led otherwise heterosexual lives abruptly develop erotic ties to specific female partners. Their experiences deserve close attention, because they have important implications for how we understand sexual orientation.

A Different Type of Orientation?

How might we rethink sexual orientation in light of person-based attractions? I can imagine two possibilities. One is that the capacity for person-based attractions might actually be an independent form of sexual orientation.[9] In other words, whereas the present categories of heterosexual, lesbian/gay, and bisexual presume that gender is important to everyone, and that the key differences simply concern which gender a person desires, perhaps there is a fourth category of individuals for whom gender is irrelevant.

Such individuals would necessarily possess the capacity for attractions to either gender, though this does not necessarily mean that they would think of themselves as bisexual. Rather, like some of the women in my study, they might adopt alternative labels such as "queer," a term that is increasingly used to signify a form of sexuality that resists rigid categorization.[10] As one woman noted, "I used to identify as bisexual, and I wasn't sure whether or not I wanted to be with men or women. Now I feel like my sexuality is more fluid, and I call myself queer because it includes all genders. It's a better term; it pretty much conveys the fact that I'm not attracted to a man or woman based on their gender, but who they are."

Many women with person-based attractions reported that this was a longstanding pattern for them, which often first manifested itself in early adolescence as a persistent ambiguity between love and friendship. Their experiences support the notion of a gender-neutral orientation. As one woman noted, "I have a really blurry line between friendships and crushes—I always tend to like people and not distinguish whether I like them as a friend or more than a friend." As we will see in the next chapter, many people develop passionate attachments to childhood friends that appear to disregard gender. As we grow older, we typically come to distinguish between liking somebody "as a friend" and liking that person as a potential lover. Perhaps part of the uniqueness of having person-based attractions is not just that you are insensitive to gender as a basis for attraction, but also that you have more fluid boundaries between love and friendship.

This raises the inevitable question of how the rest of us come to acquire and internalize such distinctions. The psychologist Laura Brown, reflecting on the tendency for many women to develop passionate relationships with other women, has remarked that instead of asking why certain women eroticize these bonds and become lesbians, perhaps we should ask why other women *don't*.[11] How do we begin to draw boundaries around certain types of emotional intimacy? Developmental timing may play a role. Since Kinsey, many researchers have argued that not until late adolescence do we fully integrate a sense of gender into our sexual desires.[12] As John Gagnon argued, "It is quite clear that during the ages of 12 to 17 the gender aspects of the 'who' in the sexual scripts that are being formed are not fixed. . . . A deeper complication is that it is not obvious whether it is the gender aspects of the 'who' that have provoked the nascent desire or even if the desire is linked to a 'who' at all."[13] Perhaps, then, an orientation toward person-based attractions represents a deeper form of this gender-neutrality, in which our sexual scripts remain fundamentally open with regard to the sex of the person to whom we are attracted.

Another possibility is that a capacity for person-based attractions is not a fourth form of sexual orientation but rather an independent characteristic that all individuals possess, in greater or lesser degrees. To understand how this might work, consider sex drive as an analogy. Among heterosexual and lesbian/gay/bisexual individuals, there are those with strong sex drives and those with weaker sex drives. Having a strong or a weak sex drive is not a separate type of orientation; nor does it reveal anything about a person's orientation—it is simply an additional source of variation among people.

Perhaps the capacity for person-based attractions operates in the same way. In other words, maybe there are different types of heterosexual, bisexual, and lesbian/gay individuals—some for whom gender is extremely important, and some for whom it is not. So, for example, a lesbian woman like Megan might generally be attracted only to women, but her person-based attractions might periodically trigger attractions to men. Other lesbians might not possess such a capacity, in which case even their closest, most wonderful male friends would do nothing for them sexually.

This last scenario was described by a number of the lesbians in my study; in fact, some women reported that it was their lack of sexual attraction to their best male friends that helped convince them that they were lesbians! This was true of Lori, who reported, "My best friend in high school was a guy. He was perfect for me in every way. I totally loved him, and we ended up dating for a couple of years. But when I was around sixteen I had this total realization that I really wasn't attracted to him, no matter how much I loved him. But he was so great, and so I really really tried to be attracted to him, but I just couldn't do it. He was actually the one who told me that I might be a lesbian."

We can imagine the same distinction among heterosexual women. Sarah, described earlier, would represent a heterosexual woman with a tendency to form person-based attractions. For such women, the development of a robust emotional bond to a female friend can spark unexpected feelings of physical desire that are specific to that friend. Other heterosexual women might never have such an experience, no matter how deep their same-sex friendships. For example, one respondent who initially identified as unlabeled but eventually reidentified as heterosexual realized over time that even though she felt extremely close emotionally to her female friends, she would never experience the same sort of desire for them that she experienced for men:

> I used to think that you fell in love with the person, and *then* you would be sexually attracted. I always thought that I could be with women because I did find women attractive, and it seems like I love some of my female friends so much, but now I realize there's something there that I don't understand that makes it so that the friends I become sexually attracted to happen to be men, and I don't know why that is, and why it's not true with my best female friends.

Of the two possibilities I have outlined—person-based attractions as a fourth orientation or as an additional aspect of sexual variability—which seems most likely? We simply do not have enough information to make definitive conclusions at the present time, but my data suggest evidence for both views. Consider the following: if a capacity for person-based attractions were an additional aspect of sexual variability that could exist among all women, then we should find women with this capacity sprinkled throughout my entire sample—some in the lesbian group, some in the bisexual group, some in the unlabeled group, and some in the heterosexual group.

But this is not the case. I was surprised to find that none of the women who identified as lesbian at the ten-year point strongly felt that they were attracted to the person and not the gender. Although some women who wholeheartedly agreed with this statement had identified as lesbian *in the past,* all those women had switched to bisexual or unlabeled identities by 2005. So a capacity for person-based attractions does not appear to be totally independent of the degree of a person's same-sex attractions. Instead, it seems to apply only to women with fairly nonexclusive patterns of attraction.

With that in mind, what about the comparison group of open-minded heterosexuals? Did they experience this capacity as well? About half said that they did, and half said that they did not (accordingly, they had an average rating of 3.4 on the 1–5 scale rating the degree to which they became attracted to the person rather than to the gender—right about at the midpoint). One of the heterosexual women who strongly endorsed the idea of being attracted to the person and not the gender described her female friendships as unusually close though not explicitly sexual:

The only uncertainty that I have ever felt about my sexual identity is when I think about some of the close friendships that I have had with women. It's like we are more than just friends, but they're not sexual. It's like there's this nebulous level between friendship and intimacy. . . . Normally it's not something that I talk about, but there is one friend where we have talked about it, we both know we are heterosexual, but it's like we are both aware that the potential for more intimacy is there, and acknowledging that we are that close to one another is all that's important, we don't need to go further. We've never really talked about the actual possibility of being sexual with each other. We talk about it on a more abstract level, like, "Everybody has the potential to love women and men," and "Look at that woman, if I was going to be a lesbian, I would want to go out with her."

Another heterosexual respondent similarly emphasized that her only potential for same-sex eroticism was in her close friendships. At the first interview, though, she was aware of a clear distinction between physical and emotional intimacy: "I have always had really strong emotional bonds to women, but I have never felt funny about it because society expects strong emotional bonds between women, so I never thought that I shouldn't pursue such strong emotional relationships. I'm rarely physically attracted to women, although sometimes when I meet a really great woman it's like I have a strong urge to get to know her better." Yet as the years went by, she was more willing to consider actual same-sex intimacy, and she became more aware of actual fantasies and attractions to women:

I guess when I first started thinking of sexual orientation in more political, or social political terms, I started questioning, "Could I be attracted to women?" And at that point, it was a very intellectual, "Yes, I could." I had fantasized about it, but I've never really wanted to or had the urge to. I've never met anyone that I would do that with. Now, it's a little different, I can picture myself, I can see myself exploring that with some of my female friends. You know, I can see myself spooning with them, or sleeping nonsexually with them. So, I guess it could veer into something more sexual, but I haven't allowed myself to go that far. It would be more an expression of love towards the women that are in my life.

By the 2005 interview she was happily married, and for that reason she found herself "cutting off" potential attractions to both women and men other than her husband because, as she reasoned, "why look if you can't touch?" Nonetheless, at this point she was even more certain about her own potential for same-sex intimacy: "If at any time in the future my marital status ever changes, I can see myself not with another man but with another woman. Whether it's living together, sexual or nonsexual. I can imagine I would find another woman more compatible, or have some sort of chemistry and then we would have a long-term relationship."

Some heterosexual women echoed this sentiment but said that they were unlikely to pursue same-sex attractions because of the social stigma attached to them:

> I am very much a believer in the continuum . . . and on the whole I think that women are more, I guess, open to being curious about both sexes and about having relationships with both sexes. But it is certainly easier to follow the path of least resistance, at least as far as social norms go, which for the moment is heterosexuality. But you know, as I'm getting older and still not meeting people that I want to be with, it seems even sillier to only consider men when I bond more easily with women.

The fact that some of the heterosexual respondents so strongly endorsed the notion of same-sex person-based attractions despite being mainly attracted to men supports the notion that a capacity for person-based attractions is a separate form of sexual orientation, perhaps a variant of bisexuality. Yet this characterization does not quite tell the whole story, either. If a capacity for person-based attractions were truly a separate orientation, then we might expect individuals to either have it or not. But it is not quite this clear-cut—women had a wide range of responses to the question about being attracted to the person and not the gender. Although some gave it a 5 on the 1–5 scale ranging from total disagreement to total agreement, some gave it a 4, others a 3, and so on. In other words, some women experience person-based attractions to *some* degree, *some* of the time, for reasons that are not clear. As noted in Chapter 4, it is difficult to interpret such variation without knowing more about how gender gets "coded" into our experiences of desire to begin with, and which aspects of gender are most important.

How Far Does Fluidity Go?

The gaps in our knowledge about the specific links between gender and desire raise a broader and even more perplexing question: If you are someone who responds to the person and not his or her gender, then where does your own gender fit in? In other words, does fluidity in sexual desire ever extend to fluidity in gender identity?

Gender identity is defined as an individual's internal psychological experience of being male or female, regardless of how masculine or feminine he or she might appear to other people. The association between sexual orientation and gender identity is a complex and controversial one.[14] As noted earlier, historical understandings of homosexuality assumed that it was a disorder of "gender inversion," as if the only way a man could desire another man was if he thought or felt like a woman (and vice versa for women desiring other women). We now know that this is not the case; lesbian/gay/bisexual individuals generally have completely normal gender identities, even if some are gender atypical in dress, behavior, or appearance. In other words, the average "butch lesbian" might have extremely short hair and a very masculine mode of dress, but she will still express certainty about her status as a woman. Individuals whose gender identities are discordant with their biological sex—that is, women who feel that they are really male, or men who feel that they are really female—are transsexuals, not homosexuals. In recent years, the broader term "transgender" has been increasingly used to denote the total spectrum of individuals who experience their gender identity as somewhat fluid, or who experience various degrees of discordance between their gender identities and their physical bodies.[15]

When I began this project, I was not expecting to deal with issues of gender identity. I was familiar with the research showing that though some gay and bisexual men are (or were as children) more gender-atypical in dress, behavior, and appearance than heterosexual men, this is less often the case for lesbian and bisexual women.[16] Few of my respondents spontaneously discussed issues related to gender identity, though over time some women did note changes in the degree of femininity and masculinity that they found attractive in potential partners.

Imagine my surprise in the summer of 2000, then, when I discovered that the reason I had been having so much difficulty tracking down one of my respondents was that she had changed her name from Cynthia to Mark. "Oh goodness," I remember thinking. "This is going to be *some* interview." In all, four study participants started identifying as transgendered over the next few years. They have all been patient with my questions and have forthrightly shared with me their complex, fascinating journeys. I present two of their stories below. Each raises questions about the role of fluidity in sexual identity, sexual desire, and gender itself.

Cynthia

Cynthia was a perfect example of the early-developing lesbian prototype. She was a tomboy growing up and very much enjoyed boys' company and games. Her working-class family tried to get her to dress and act more feminine, to no avail. At age twelve, she developed a strong crush on one of her female classmates. She did not spend a lot of time analyzing or reflecting on it; she simply did the only thing that seemed reasonable: she wrote the girl a love poem. She sent it to her anonymously, but soon everyone at school found out who wrote it. For the next year and a half, Cynthia was mercilessly taunted and ostracized. The other kids ganged up on her, sent her hate mail, and defaced her locker (this was how she first encountered the word "lesbian," which she had to look up in the dictionary). Eventually she became good friends with a group of other "misfits," most of them boys, and things settled down. She came out as bisexual at fourteen and then as lesbian at fifteen, when she began a romance with her best female friend. By the time I met her, it was clear that she had managed to flourish in the face of adversity. She was enrolled in an all-women's college, had a vibrant network of supportive lesbian friends, and was a confident activist. She was warm, forthright, and happily in love with her current girlfriend. Several years later, they married, though their union had no legal standing. Life was going well—Cynthia had a stable job in the computer field, and her wife was in graduate school.

That's when things got tricky. Almost all of Cynthia's colleagues at work were men, and the working environment was pretty macho. Women did not garner any respect, and Cynthia (who since her elementary and high school days was accustomed to spending a lot of time with males) found herself adopting an increasingly masculine "stance" in her interactions at work. She soon found that she was largely relating to her colleagues as a man, which perplexed her. She started doing research on transgender issues and began considering taking on a male gender identity. Her wife, already stressed out with her graduate studies, was against it. "I'm a lesbian," she told Cynthia. "I want to be with a woman, not a man." By this point they were already growing apart, and Cynthia's questioning of her gender identity only made matters worse. Eventually she made her decision. Although she did not take any hormones or otherwise alter her body, Cynthia began dressing and presenting herself as male much of the time, and she changed her name to Mark. Her wife left her.

This was the point at which I interviewed her—I say "her" because at the time Mark was not consistently identifying as male or female, and instead was comfortable with a more ambiguous gender identity. I asked her to try to describe the changes that she had experienced in her sense of self, and whether they affected her sexual desires:

> I guess right now my gender identity would be masculine. My biological—whatever—is female. I can't even tackle the pronoun thing because it's too confusing. I find that "none of the above" is pretty much how I tend to label myself. And my sexual orientation is bisexual. . . . After I got divorced I started dating lots of people of both genders. It was an eye-opening experience for myself because for so long I pretty much lived in lesbian space. And so now here I am in this very fluid gender space, and my sexuality kind of went the same way. I was surprised to find that I started looking at men again. It was odd; guys would flirt with me and I would be like, "Hey, I don't mind that. That doesn't turn me off or make me angry or whatever." Because it used to really annoy me, and it doesn't anymore. I've dated gay men, bisexual men, heterosexual men. Most of them tend to be, well, very open-minded.

Mark was forthright about the fact that she was still actively questioning her gender identity. Her colleagues at work knew that she was biologically female, but they also knew that she now identified as Mark. I asked whether she expected to identify as male full-time in the future, and she replied, "You know, I really just don't know."

Two years later, at the age of twenty-six, Mark was fully identified as male. He thought about experimenting with testosterone and getting a double mastectomy, but he did not have enough money at the time. He had, however, met and fallen in love with a wonderful woman. She had previously identified as heterosexual but accepted Mark's liminal status, and the two planned to marry. I asked Mark if anything about his sexual attractions had continued to change. He remarked that he continued to be unusually attracted to gay men, though virtually 100 percent of his current attractions were directed toward his fiancée. Another change he noticed concerned the gender dynamic between him and his girlfriend, which was more fluid and flexible than he had experienced in the past:

> In general it's a pretty heterosexual dynamic between myself and my fiancée, you know, me being the guy, her being the woman, but there are many times when it changes, you know, and all of a sudden she's the solid, steady, more masculine partner and I'm the one that's hysterical and stereotypically feminine, and sometimes we're just like two children together with no gender, you know, just giggling, and being silly, and having a good time with each other, and it's like there's no awareness of gender at all. It's just—this is a person.

At the ten-year follow-up interview, Mark and his fiancée (who now identified as bisexual) were happily married, and Mark felt that "queer" was probably the best overall representation of his complicated gender and sexual identity. He continued to find himself attracted to gay men, and in fact the more settled and secure he became with his male gender identity, the more he noticed such attractions. But he did not plan to act on them, since he was committed to his new wife. Mark seemed truly at peace. Even his family, after much reflection, had come to accept his choices. His journey had been unbearable at times, but he was very happy now:

> Well, growing up I really believed that because I was gay, I was doomed to an unhappy, painful existence, and I would die alone and unloved and in pain. And today I really don't believe that at all. I fully and wholly believe that I have a God that loves me and wants me to be happy, and that I was made just the right way, and that there's a purpose for me to be this way, and I just have to figure out why, and go from there.

Lori

Lori represents a very different but equally compelling case. Unlike Cynthia, who had been strongly identified as lesbian for many years, Lori considered herself bisexual, and she could remember being attracted to both men and women from a very early age. She even remembers having a collage on her bedroom wall with pictures of attractive female *and* male body parts! She first started identifying as bisexual in college, when she actively dated both men and women, though her most substantive emotional ties were formed with women.

In college Lori started reading about transgender issues and meeting transsexual people. As a result, she began thinking more about her own sense of gender. She had always been fairly "butch" in appearance and demeanor, but now she started to imagine pushing the boundaries of her own gender expression. The transgender literature gave her concrete ways of thinking about some of the gender-identity issues she had been quietly wrestling with for years. By the time of our third interview, when she was twenty-seven years old, she had started identifying as transgendered. For her, an important part of this identification was a rejection of the notion of "two and only two" genders:

> I still identify as bisexual, but it's been interesting because I also identify as transgendered. So it's kind of tricky: if people just generally don't have much of a sense of trans, then I just say bisexual, but since bisexual relies on two genders, and I don't really believe in that anymore, it makes it very problematic. I mean, yeah, for the sake of the whole homosexual-heterosexual-bisexual-whatever scale, it's bisexual, in my mind. But in a sense of believing in two genders and the whole box theory of categorization of gender, that just doesn't really fly for me anymore.

Unlike Cynthia, who found that her sexual attractions became more fluid once she adopted a more fluid gender identity, Lori had already started out with fairly fluid sexual attractions, and this did not change when she began to identify as transgendered. By the fourth interview, when she was twenty-nine years old, she had started to think of herself as "pansexual":

> For me pansexual is looking past the two genders. I don't know if it originated from the trans community, but that's where I think a good portion of it is. . . . I mean, if I'm trans and I'm dating someone, what does that make me? Or what if I'm dating someone who is trans and doesn't identify as male or female? What is my sexual orientation? So I think it's more about saying it doesn't really make a difference what their gender is; it's more about who you're attracted to.

At this point, Lori had had a double mastectomy and was taking testosterone, so her outward appearance was convincingly male. Yet she insisted on keeping her female-typical name and, unlike Mark, did not identify as male on a day-to-day basis. For her, this choice was consistent with her fundamentally fluid sense of gender, though it was a constant source of confusion for the people around her:

> People have a really hard time with categorizing me because I don't categorize as male or female. I don't want to be a guy, I certainly don't want to be seen as a heterosexual white man in our society because there are all these implications with that. And you know, I like my name, my mom gave it to me, it means a lot to me, everything I've done was under that name, my degrees, my transcripts, and I've seen what guys go through when they change their name, their identities, and I really have no desire for that at this point in my life. And so I identify as gender queer and people just get really crazed about it because they feel this need to constantly see things in two boxes, and if you switch the boxes, then you can be a boy who wants to be a girl or a girl who wants to be a boy, but you can't ever be outside the boxes or change the boxes constantly or anything like that. But I kind of blur or fall outside of those gender dichotomies.

Although Lori had not initially noticed any major changes in her attractions when she first started to identify as transgendered, after she started taking testosterone she found herself more attracted to men than before. She attributed this to the fact that she was living in a neighborhood with a lot of attractive gay men and not very many women. Overall, she continued to find that her most intense, passionate connections were formed with women: "I've never fallen in love with a guy. It doesn't make me weak in the knees, it doesn't take my breath away. So, if I'm looking for some fun, then my actions are very strong towards boys. But if that's not what I'm looking for in that instant and it's between a girl and a boy, then I'll always pick the girl over the boy. It's not like an even choice. It's like, 'Do I want a gourmet meal, or do I want a sundae?'"

At the ten-year interview, Lori had developed a satisfying, stable relationship with a female partner, and she was considering going off the testosterone in the future so that they could have children. That's right—*Lori* wanted to bear them. She was fully aware that the notion of a "trans guy who actually wants to give birth" might be startling for some, but children had always been important to her, and as she was getting older they were becoming more of a priority. Her biggest hurdle, however, remained her family. Her mother, surprisingly, had no idea about Lori's transition. The last time she saw her daughter was at a family wedding, and Lori had worn "female drag" to avoid upsetting anyone. She shaved the beard she had grown, wore a dress and make-up, and did her best not to rock the boat. She knew she could not do that again, but she was deeply worried about how her mother and her extended family would react:

> I haven't seen my family since that wedding, and I don't know where I stand, which is a very uncomfortable place to be, to not be connected physically to your family, not see them, not be able to talk to them, not to be real with them. And then know that your Mom without a doubt is going to have a very horrific time with this, and maybe

many of your family members will, and my fear is that my grandma is going to pass away in the next couple of years, and I'm going to be stuck. Because I can't imagine not going to the funeral, and *I can't be a girl*. I physically can't do it. I just can't pull it off. So I'm trying to get my stuff together, tell my Mom, and she can have her little heart attack over it for a couple years before . . . God forbid, my grandma dies. So, that's where, I mean, that's really the biggest concern. I have no concern with lovers, bodies, jobs, and none of that, just my family.

Lori articulates the dilemma that fluidity—with respect to both gender and sexuality—raises for all people, female, male, and otherwise. Namely, how do you live a noncategorical life in a rigidly categorical world? As Lori stated, no matter how much you might resist putting your identity and your desires into neat and tidy boxes, society still wants you to do so. It is more acceptable to be a man trapped in the body of a woman than to be neither male nor female, neither gay nor straight. Transgendered people shine a spotlight on our culture's ongoing, slavish adherence to rigid sexual and gender categories. People like Lori and Mark, who challenge those categories every time they step outside the front door, pay a dear price for their insistence on a different path and a different truth. But they would have it no other way. When I asked Lori what was the most satisfying thing about her life right now, she said without hesitation, "I'm becoming myself."

For Lori and other women with person-based attractions, the process of "becoming" is deeply connected to their experiences in intimate relationships. Their questions about orientation and identity are not about isolated selves; rather, they concern feelings for and relationships with other people. In the next chapter we will see why this is the case.

CHAPTER 7

How Does Fluidity Work?

If female sexual desires are, in fact, sensitive to situation and context, how exactly does this work? What psychological or biological processes are involved? What role does romantic love play, given that fluidity is often triggered by strong emotional bonds? And why is fluidity more characteristic of women than of men? Too little research has been conducted on this topic to yield definitive answers. But I do have my own hypotheses about the "how" and "why" of sexual fluidity.

Specifically, my research suggests that female sexual fluidity is made possible by three interrelated phenomena. The first involves the distinction between two different types of sexual desire, which scientists call *proceptivity* and *arousability*. Despite the technical-sounding terms, the basic ideas are easy to grasp. Proceptivity refers to what we might call "lust" or "libido." It is a relatively automatic, intense, hormone-driven form of sexual motivation. Arousability, in contrast, refers to a person's capacity to become aroused once certain triggers, cues, or situations are encountered. I will argue that sexual orientation is only "coded" into proceptivity, whereas arousability is an intrinsically more flexible system. I will also show that arousability has a greater day-to-day influence on female sexual desire than on male sexual desire, for reasons having to do with women's hormonal cycles. When considered together, these factors suggest that women's day-to-day sexual desires should be more flexible and fluid than men's.

The second phenomenon involved in female sexual fluidity is the "unorientation" of romantic love. Although we commonly assume that sexual orientation directs people's romantic feelings along the same lines as their sexual desires, this is not the case. Rather, what we know about the evolutionary origins and neurobiological mechanisms of romantic love suggests that it (1) functions independent of sexual desire, with different biological underpinnings; (2) can develop even in the absence of sexual desire; and (3) does not have an "orientation" in the same way that sexuality does. As a result of these features, we can fall in love with someone without being attracted to him or her, even if that person is the wrong gender for our sexual orientation.

The third phenomenon involved in female sexual fluidity is the connection between romantic love and sexual desire. This connection makes it possible to start out with strong platonic (that is, nonsexual) feelings of love for another person, and sometimes develop new and unexpected sexual desires for that person as a result. This occurs because love and desire, despite being separate processes, nonetheless have strong cultural, psychological, and neurobiological links between them. One experience can facilitate the other. We are all aware that sexual desire can develop into romantic love, but the opposite can also occur: romantic love can lead to sexual desire.

Given this two-way connection between love and desire, we can develop sexual desire for a person of the "wrong gender," just as we can fall in love with someone of the wrong gender. Such atypical desires might be restricted to one special relationship. This type of experience may be more common among women than among men because there is substantial evidence that the cultural, biological, and psychological pathways leading from love to desire are more robust among women.

Taken together, these three phenomena provide a possible explanation for the fascinating twists and turns experienced by the women in my sample over the past ten years: the changes they have undergone in their sexual thoughts and feelings across different environments, situations, and life stages; the sensitivity of their sexual desires to specific relationships; their ability to fall in love with "the person and not the gender"; the diversity and ambiguity in their self-reported experiences of sexual desire; and the fact that lesbians sometimes have one-time-only affairs with men while heterosexual women sometimes have one-time-only affairs with women. In this chapter, I review each of these building blocks of fluidity, explain how they operate, and discuss their implications for our understanding of female sexuality.

Sexual Desire: Two Types Are Better Than One

Most people would probably concur with the definition of sexual desire put forth by the psychologists Pamela Regan and Ellen Berscheid: "an interest in sexual objects or activities or a wish, need, or drive to seek out sexual objects or to engage in sexual activities."[1] Yet this seemingly straightforward definition actually lumps together two experiences that are not quite the same: an *interest* in sexual objects and activity and a drive to *seek out* sexual objects and activity.

This distinction plays an important role in our understanding of the sexual behavior of nonhuman primates and has been studied extensively in that context.[2] Yet it also applies to humans.[3] Primate researchers have called these two different types of sexual desire *proceptivity* and *receptivity* (or *arousability*). Proceptivity, or lust, can emerge spontaneously across a variety of environments and so can be thought of as situation independent. A straightforward example of proceptive desire would be a general feeling of "horniness" that might emerge for no particular reason. The defining characteristic of proceptive desire is that it is highly motivating and often prompts individuals to seek sexual gratification. Arousability is quite different. It represents a person's capacity to become interested in sex as a result of encountering certain situations or stimuli (such as the sexual advances of an attractive partner), even if the individual did not initially feel sexually motivated. The defining characteristic of arousability is that it is triggered by external cues or situations. As such, it can be thought of as situation-dependent.

The distinction between proceptivity and arousability was initially made to represent the different types of sexual behaviors that female mammals pursue during fertile versus infertile periods of their menstrual cycles.[4] Many mammalian species pursue sexual behavior only when the female is ovulating and therefore capable of conceiving. In other species, females might respond to a male's sexual advances at any point in their menstrual cycle, though they are not likely to initiate sex unless they are ovulating. To represent this distinction, researchers used the label "proceptivity" whenever a female initiated sexual activity and "receptivity" whenever she responded to sexual advances.

Nearly everything we know about proceptivity and arousability is based on studies of animal behavior. Because we cannot ask animals about their subjective sexual feelings, different types of observable sexual behaviors (or signs of arousal, such as erections) are treated as markers of different sexual states. Hence, animal researchers generally talk not about proceptive *desire* but rather about proceptive *behaviors* such as following a potential sexual partner, displaying one's genitals to the potential partner, and directly attempting to mate with him or her. Behavioral markers of arousability typically include participating in sexual activity once it is initiated by a partner.

The link between sexual desire and sexual behavior is obviously less direct for humans. Unlike monkeys or rodents, humans often initiate sex when they do not really want it, or refrain from initiating sex even when they *do* want it. Thus in the human context, it makes more sense to speak about proceptivity and arousability with respect to desires rather than to observable behaviors. Furthermore, in humans the distinction between proceptivity and arousability is relevant for both females and males. Because of the significant role of social and cultural factors in structuring human sexual desires, the notion that internally motivated sexual desires are different from those that are triggered externally by a person, stimulus, or situation applies to both men and women. It also bears noting that proceptivity and arousability are not mutually exclusive. In other words, we can experience them at the same time, to different degrees. In fact, any particular instance of sexual desire probably involves some degree of each. A sudden, automatic feeling of lust might be primarily driven by proceptivity, whereas a gradual increase in sexual arousal while watching a romantic movie might be primarily driven by arousability. Most experiences fall somewhere between these two extremes.

One of the most important things to understand about proceptivity and arousability is that they are governed by different mechanisms. Proceptivity is driven by sex hormones: androgens in men (most famously, testosterone) and both androgens and estrogen in women.[5] Most people are familiar with the notion that testosterone facilitates sexual desire, and numerous studies have found that when men or women are given testosterone, they show corresponding increases in sex drive, though the results are much more consistent for men.[6] With all the focus on testosterone, the role of estrogen in facilitating female sexual desire receives less attention. Yet studies in which women keep daily diaries of their sexual feelings and behaviors, accompanied by daily blood samples, show that changes in estrogen levels over the course of the menstrual cycle are associated with changes in sexual motivation. When estrogen levels are highest, around ovulation, women report stronger desires for sex.[7]

In contrast, variability in arousability is not related to either estrogen or testosterone. Administering either of these sex hormones to men or women does not increase their ability to become aroused when presented with sexual stimuli.[8] In fact, even men who have had their testicles removed, and therefore have the lowest possible levels of testosterone, can still become aroused when presented with erotic stimuli. Notably, however, such men lack proceptive desire: they do not report spontaneous sexual urges nor seek out sexual stimuli or activity.[9]

If arousability is not dependent on sex hormones, then what does it depend on? Because of its situation-specific nature, we can think about arousability as being driven by an individual's exposure to the right sexual cues. These could be almost anything—different images, environments, smells, or ideas—and they will vary not only from culture to culture but from individual to individual, as a function of someone's particular pattern of sexual experiences, expectations, memories, and attitudes.

Cues for arousability might also include interpersonal experiences and emotions. As discussed, the process of forming an intense emotional bond with another person can spark feelings of sexual desire, even for individuals who would not otherwise be considered appropriate sexual partners. This is a perfect example of arousability in action because most women in these cases did not initially experience strong, spontaneous (that is, proceptive) sexual urges for these individuals.

Because arousability is situation-dependent, some people will experience it more than others, simply because they encounter more day-to-day sexual cues than other people. Similarly, changes in a person's environment or relationships can bring about changes in sexual cues, and hence changes in arousability. Some individuals are especially *reactive* to sexual cues, perhaps because of differences in their sexual norms or attitudes, different degrees of comfort and self-acceptance regarding sexuality, or different levels of sexual experience.

Now that we have a clear picture of the different causes of proceptivity and arousability, we are in a position to understand some important gender differences in these two types of desire. Proceptivity is driven by sex hormones—androgens for men and both androgens and estrogen for women. Adult women, of course, have dramatic changes in their estrogen levels over the course of a month, owing to their menstrual cycles. Estrogen levels are highest the few days around ovulation and notably lower the rest of the month. Men, in contrast, have constant, high levels of androgens.

Consider what this means for day-to-day experiences of proceptivity: men's proceptive desires (that is, their situation-independent sexual urges) should be fairly constant. But women's proceptive desires should peak around the time of ovulation and then decrease the rest of the month. This is just what studies have shown. It is also consistent with research showing that though women and men are equally capable of intense sexual desire, women report fewer day-to-day sexual urges than do men, as well as fewer sexual fantasies and less motivation to seek or initiate sexual activity.[10]

Some researchers have interpreted these findings to indicate that women have fundamentally weaker sex drives than men, but others have cautioned that it is more accurate to characterize women's sex drives as fundamentally periodic—that is, characterized by regular highs and lows.[11] After all, studies have shown that when women *do* experience strong urges for sex, the intensity of those urges is as strong as those of men.[12] Yet because these peak levels are not constant, men's sexual motivation frequently exceeds women's on a day-to-day level.

Women also face considerable social pressure to deny or dismiss their sexual urges, especially urges to initiate sexual activity (since that is the role that most cultures grant to men). Many women receive strong messages, beginning at an early age, that men are more sexual than women, and that it is unusual or inappropriate for women to experience intense sexual desires. Over time, such messages can significantly dampen women's experiences of both proceptivity and arousability.[13]

Yet the most important point about the cyclical nature of female proceptivity is how it determines the relative role of proceptivity and arousability in women's day-to-day sexual desires. Consider the following: if female proceptivity peaks for only a few days per month, then during the rest of the time, a woman's sexual desires will be driven primarily by arousability and therefore will be dependent on her exposure to various situational cues. These cues should have comparatively less influence on men's day-to-day sexual desires because men have such consistent levels of hormonally driven proceptivity. This is not to say that men's sexuality is not influenced by situational factors and cues—it most certainly is! Yet the balance of influences is different for men versus women in that situational factors play a bigger role for women.

This difference has been confirmed in scores of studies looking at different aspects of female and male sexual thoughts and behaviors.[14] It is also consistent with lay people's commonsense notions about differences between female and male sexuality. For example, Regan and Berscheid asked a group of college students what they thought caused female and male sexual desire. Approximately two-thirds of respondents (both women and men) thought that male sexual desire was caused by internal, automatic processes such as "physical need" or "maleness." Only about 15 percent listed interpersonal or environmental factors as important causes of male sexual desire. The proportions were almost completely reversed when it came to female sexual desire: approximately two-thirds of respondents listed interpersonal or environmental factors as causes of female sexual desire, and only one-third listed internal, automatic processes. These findings are exactly what we would expect if, in fact, women's day-to-day desires are more consistently influenced by arousability than is the case for men.

Implications for Same-Sex Desire

Now we are ready to consider how all these factors might help explain female sexual fluidity. Let us start with the different evolutionary functions of proceptivity versus arousability. The evolutionary function of proceptivity is fairly straightforward: it facilitates sexual reproduction by motivating sexual activity. For women, it makes perfect sense for proceptivity to peak during ovulation because this ensures that sexual activity will likely result in conception. For the same reasons, it also makes sense for proceptivity to be intrinsically targeted toward other-sex partners, to ensure that these desires result not simply in sexual activity but in *reproductive* sexual activity. In this model, homosexual and bisexual orientations represent (at least in some cases) intrinsic deviations from this program.

But what about arousability? Is it also intrinsically oriented? In all likelihood, no. As long as our ancestors' proceptive desires were directed toward reproductive (that is, other-sex) partners, there would be little adaptive benefit to orienting arousability as well. After all, the cues for arousability that our ancestors most frequently encountered were undoubtedly other-sex cues, given that humans in preindustrial societies were typically steered toward other-sex relationships very soon after sexual maturation.[15] Accordingly, there would be little need for arousability to be "gender targeted" in the same manner as proceptivity.

If this is the case, then it is reasonable to expect that sexual orientation may be programmed only into proceptivity. Arousability, in contrast, should be more open to a wide range of cultural, situational, and interpersonal cues. This means, of course, that an individual does not need to possess a same-sex orientation to experience same-sex arousability. With the right set of circumstances and triggers, people who might never otherwise seek out same-sex activity could nonetheless find themselves aroused by it.

This is certainly consistent with extensive anthropological data indicating that in many cultures, it is considered normal for heterosexual individuals to periodically pursue same-sex sexual activity in specific social situations or developmental periods.[16] Importantly, these behaviors have no discernible long-term effects on the individuals' sexual identities or orientations. In our own culture, a relevant analogy might be same-sex activity pursued by individuals who are temporarily living in sex-segregated environments. Research suggests that many people in these circumstances temporarily engage in same-sex activity but return to other-sex activity as soon as their sex segregation ends. This phenomenon has been called "facultative" or "opportunistic" same-sex sexuality, and it has been observed in correctional institutions, military environments, and boarding schools.[17]

Thus the correct response to the longstanding question, "Is homosexuality genetic or environmental?" is not "yes" or "no" but rather, "Which kind?" Whereas consistent desires to seek out and initiate same-sex activity probably stem, at least in part, from an alteration in the intrinsic gender coding of proceptive desires, same-sex arousability needs no such programming, and depends instead on environmental and situational factors. This does not mean that sexual-minority individuals can be neatly divided into two groups: those with (biologically based) same-sex proceptivity and those with (environmentally based) same-sex arousability. Rather, different combinations of these two factors probably come into play for different people. This is exactly what researchers investigating the potential biological underpinnings of same-sex sexuality have increasingly concluded: both biological and environmental factors operate together to shape same-sex sexuality.

Yet there is one thing we can conclude for certain: more women than men should have arousability that triggers desires, behaviors, and relationships that "contradict" the gender coding of their proceptive desires. If the majority of women's day-to-day desires are governed by arousability, and if arousability is a "gender-neutral" system, then in certain circumstances heterosexual women should be capable of experiencing same-sex desires and lesbian women should be capable of experiencing other-sex desires. Men, in contrast, should be less likely to have such "cross-orientation" desires, since their gender-neutral arousability has a less predominant influence on their day-to-day sexual feelings.

If this scenario is true, then we should expect to observe a number of additional differences between male and female same-sex sexuality. In particular, women should be more likely than men to report nonexclusive attractions, since such attractions probably result from combinations of gender-coded proceptivity and gender-neutral arousability.[18] We would also expect more women than men to report that chance, circumstance, and specific intimate relationships influenced their same-sex desires; more women than men to report abrupt disjunctures in their desires and behaviors as a result of changes in their environments and relationships; and more women than men to report that their same-sex desires are linked to a specific individual—one of the most potent and common cues for same-sex arousability.

It should be obvious by now that this is exactly what has been found in extensive research on female sexuality conducted by myself and many others. Traditionally, such phenomena have been dismissed as inexplicable or exceptional. They have been attributed to the longstanding social and cultural repression of female sexuality, which likely blunts women's awareness of their desires. These repressive influences certainly exist, but they do not rule out the possibility that female sexuality is also more situation-dependent than men's.

Rethinking Sexual Categories

This perspective offers new ways to think about different subtypes of same-sex sexuality. Until now, the only subtype that has received substantial attention is bisexuality, as if the single most interesting and important characteristic of same-sex desire is whether it is exclusive or nonexclusive. What if, instead, we focused on whether an individual's same-sex desires were generally driven more by proceptivity than by arousability? I say "generally" because any single experience of desire has its own mix of proceptivity and arousability, and this mix might change across different times and situations. For example, during ovulation a woman's desires might have more of a proceptive component than during other times of the month. Yet it makes sense that for some women, same-sex desires involve *some* proceptive element, whereas for other women, same-sex desires usually involve arousability alone.

Both same-sex proceptivity and same-sex arousability vary from low to high: variations in proceptivity represent different sexual orientations, whereas variations in same-sex arousability stem from differences in environmental factors, specific relationships, cultural norms, and so on. By considering different combinations of same-sex proceptivity and same-sex arousability, we have a new way to understand diverse manifestations of sexuality. For example, imagine that someone with high same-sex proceptivity (for example, a lesbian) is immersed in a restrictive environment that offers few opportunities for same-sex arousability. She might not become aware of—or act on—her predisposition for same-sex attractions unless she moves to a more permissive environment. In contrast, imagine that someone with low same-sex proceptivity (for example, a heterosexual) happens to live in an environment with heightened opportunities for same-sex arousability, or becomes involved in an emotionally intimate relationship that gives rise to this arousability. She might experience *only* same-sex desire in such contexts. This would explain the experiences of women who fall in love with "just one person"; those who first begin to experience same-sex attractions after meeting or reading about lesbian/gay/bisexual individuals; those who claim that they fall in love with "the person, not the gender"; and those who describe their same-sex attractions as predominantly emotional.

Considering different combinations of proceptivity and arousability also helps to explain why the evidence for biological contributions to same-sex sexuality is stronger for men than for women. If there are a larger number of women than men whose same-sex sexuality is more attributable to situation-dependant arousability than to biologically based proceptivity, then these gender differences regarding the biological evidence make perfect sense. Consider, for example, the genetic data. The sexuality of women with low same-sex proceptivity but high same-sex arousability should have a minimal or nonexistent genetic component. If genetic researchers inadvertently include such women in their samples, then estimates of heritability will be dampened, since only same-sex proceptivity should have a genetic component.

Note that heterosexuals with high same-sex arousability have historically been portrayed as suffering from "false consciousness" concerning their true desires, on the assumption that situation-dependent same-sex desires are somehow less authentic than situation-independent desires.[19] Yet according to this logic, any individual who needs a certain combination of situational cues to facilitate sexual desire (specific music, a particular partner, certain clothing, a conducive mindset, a long "warm-up" period) is not experiencing authentic desire. This is clearly not the case, and no sex researcher has ever suggested that the only authentic type of sexual desire is automatic, spontaneous, uncontrollable lust. Furthermore, through repeated experience, positive reinforcement, and selective attention, some people's situation-dependent same-sex desires might eventually show as much stability and resistance to conscious control as same-sex proceptivity.[20] Thus distinctions among individuals regarding the contexts in which they most often experience same-sex desires do not necessarily predict past or future desires, behaviors, and identifications.

Once we abandon the notion that people must fall into neat categories when it comes to sexual desire and orientation, we might imagine hundreds of different subcategories representing different mixes of same-sex proceptivity and same-sex arousability. Importantly, individuals with predominantly heterosexual orientations but extremely high same-sex arousability are probably pretty rare, because very few social environments would be expected to provide so much access and positive reinforcement of same-sex cues as to completely override an otherwise heterosexual orientation. Rather, such environments are probably more influential on individuals whose proceptive desires already lean in a same-sex direction, even if only slightly.

This raises another important point, which is that nonexclusive attractions can occur among many different types of people, for a variety of reasons. Some women might have intrinsically nonexclusive desires but never become aware of these desires because they are immersed in restrictive environments that stigmatize same-sex sexuality. Other women might be primarily lesbian but possess *just enough* other-sex arousability to generate consistently nonexclusive attractions. The fact that there are so many different types and sources of nonexclusivity might help to explain why researchers and laypeople continue to debate the very existence of nonexclusivity. Yet one thing we can conclude for certain is that the relatively greater role of arousability in women's day-do-day desires should create more opportunities for women to experience nonexclusive desires than for men to experience them. And this, of course, is exactly what researchers have found.

What about Love?

Throughout this book, the link—sometimes the missing link—between romantic love and sexual desire has come up repeatedly. Some of the women in my study reported that feelings of love triggered their first, or only, feelings of same-sex attraction. Other women lamented that sometimes their emotional and physical feelings did not match. What should we make of these reports? How do love and desire function together to shape female sexuality? This question has been an undercurrent of this entire book, and we are now in a position to address it head on.

Everyone agrees that though romantic love and sexual desire are not the same thing, they are somehow related. Many people assume that sexual orientation governs both sexual desire and romantic feelings. Accordingly, when researchers administer the 7-point Kinsey Scale to assess the degree to which individuals are oriented toward people of the other sex versus people of the same sex, one of the dimensions they typically assess is "romantic affection."[21] It is expected that if you are predisposed to experience sexual desires for same-sex partners, then you are also predisposed to fall in love with same-sex partners. And, in fact, the majority of heterosexual individuals do tend to fall in love with other-sex partners, whereas the majority of lesbian and bisexual individuals fall in love with same-sex partners.

But not always, and the exceptions are instructive. Although we might imagine that feelings of love and desire are closely related, they are actually governed by independent brain systems with different functions and neurobiological bases. This has profound implications for sexual orientation and sexual fluidity.

First, though, let us back up and define "romantic love." This term is typically used to describe powerful feelings of emotional infatuation and attachment between romantic partners. Yet this definition is a bit too general: most researchers acknowledge a difference between the earliest stage of love, sometimes called passionate love, infatuation, or "limerence," and the later-developing, deeper stage of long-term love, called companionate love, attachment, or "pairbonding."[22] Passionate love appears to be a temporary state of heightened interest and preoccupation with a specific or potential partner. Individuals experiencing passionate love typically report strong desires for closeness and physical contact with the love object, frequent and intrusive thoughts about him or her, intense resistance to separation, and extreme excitement and euphoria when receiving his or her affection and attention. This intense state typically characterizes the first one to two years of a new relationship, after which it gradually transforms into companionate love. Companionate love is also characterized by desires for closeness to the partner and resistance to separation, but it does not have the same intensity and urgency as passionate love. Instead, this stage of love is characterized by feelings of security, care, and comfort. Sexual desire is highly relevant to the distinction between passionate and companionate love. After all, most people can easily imagine (or have experienced firsthand!) long-term companionate relationships in which sexual desire has gradually waned; yet it might be more difficult to imagine experiencing the early, passionate stage of frenzied infatuation without sexual desire. Does this ever actually occur?

In fact, it does. In her exhaustive study of infatuation, the psychologist Dorothy Tennov found that 61 percent of women and 35 percent of men reported experiencing infatuation without feeling any need for sex.[23] Even stronger evidence is provided by a study that investigated experiences of infatuation among more than two hundred youths between the ages of four and eighteen.[24] The researchers reasoned that if sexual desire were a necessary component of infatuation, then prepubertal children should have the *weakest* reports of infatuation and postpubertal adolescents should have the *strongest*. Why? Because the hormonal changes of puberty increase the frequency and intensity of sexual desires.[25] So the researchers had the respondents fill out a "Passionate Love Scale," which asked them to think about a boyfriend or girlfriend for whom they had intense feelings. They had to rate their agreement with statements such as "I am always thinking about X," or "When X hugs me my body feels warm all over." Each respondent ended up with a passionate love score representing the intensity of his or her infatuation. The researchers then tested whether these scores were higher among young people with more advanced pubertal maturation.

They were not: youths of all ages were capable of maximally in-

tense infatuations, regardless of their degree of pubertal maturation. Some of the strongest experiences of infatuation were reported
by younger children, and some of the weakest were reported by
older children. Although the authors cautioned that their results
could not reveal whether the subjective experience of infatuation
was really the same for seven-year-olds as for eighteen-year-olds,
their findings nonetheless show that sexual desire is not the driving
force behind infatuation.

This finding is consistent with a growing body of research showing that the basic brain systems underlying love and desire are
fundamentally different. As noted, sexual desire is strongly influenced by levels of androgens and estrogens, and the study described
above shows that these hormones do not influence passionate love.
Rather, love has a "brain circuitry" entirely different from that of
sexual desire, involving neurochemicals such as dopamine,
corticosterone, nerve growth factor, oxytocin, and vasopressin,
which are related to experiences of reward, pleasure, and security.[26]
The neurochemical oxytocin is of particular interest and will be discussed in more detail below.

In recent years, researchers have also devoted increasing attention to mapping the neurobiological "signatures" of love and desire
using brain-imaging techniques such as functional magnetic reso-
nance imaging (fMRI). This technique maps blood flow in the brain
in order to pinpoint regions of the brain that are active during different types of thoughts and experiences. One preliminary study
used this method to examine the brain activity of heterosexual individuals who reported being "truly, deeply, and madly in love."
The study measured brain activity under two conditions: when the
subjects were viewing pictures of their beloved and when they were
viewing pictures of other-sex friends.[27] Compared with viewing
friends, viewing pictures of loved ones was associated with heightened activation in the middle insula and the anterior cingulate cor-
tex. These regions are associated with positive emotion, attention

to one's own emotional states, attention to the emotional states of social partners, and even opioid-induced euphoria! This study also found that viewing pictures of loved ones was associated with *deactivation* in the posterior cingulate gyrus, the amygdala, and the right prefrontal, parietal, and middle temporal cortices—the regions of the brain associated with sadness, fear, aggression, and depression.

A more recent fMRI study conducted by a team of researchers led by the psychologist Art Aron and the anthropologist Helen Fisher focused specifically on individuals who were in the earliest stage of passionate love.[28] This study found that when viewing a photograph of a loved one, individuals showed specific activation in the right ventral tegmental area, the dorsal caudate body, and the caudate tail. Consistent with the neurochemical findings noted above, these dopamine-rich brain regions play major roles in reward and motivation. The caudate, for example, plays an important role in detecting and anticipating rewards, mentally representing goals, and integrating sensory information in order to prepare for action. Thus, love-related activation in this region is consistent with the widespread view that romantic love is a strong motivational force. Notably, both of these studies found that the brain regions showing love-specific activation do *not* overlap with regions that have been shown to be associated with sexual arousal.[29]

Additional evidence for the independence of love and desire comes from the fact that heterosexuals form powerful, nonsexual infatuations with same-sex friends. Anthropologists and historians have collected many accounts of these unusually intense friendships, which contain all the feelings typically associated with romantic infatuation, such as extreme preoccupation, inseparability, impassioned expressions of devotion and commitment, and heightened physical affection.[30] These bonds are common enough that they have inspired their own unique terms in different cultures and historical periods, such as "romantic friendships," "smashes,"

"Tom-Dee relationships," "camaradia," and "mummy-baby friendships." Importantly, such relationships have been observed among men as well as among women. The anthropologist Walter Williams documented similarly intense but nonsexual bonds between North American Indian men, and noted that early Western explorers were surprised by how these men seemed to "fall in love" with one another.[31] Similarly passionate friendships have also been documented between young Bangwa men in Cameroon, Melanesia, Samoa, the Polynesian islands, and Guatemala.[32] According to these accounts, such relationships involve "affection of an extreme kind which . . . resembles more the passion of heterosexual lovers than the calm friendship of equals."[33]

It is tempting for modern Western observers to conclude that these relationships were not, in fact, platonic friendships but rather repressed and subverted sexual liaisons. Note, for example, the continuing debate over whether Eleanor Roosevelt and Lorena Hickok, who exchanged intensely affectionate and emotional letters, were "really" lovers or just very close friends who were passionately attached to each other.[34] Consider, for example, this quotation from one of Roosevelt's letters to Hickok: "Hick darling, all day I've thought of you and another birthday [when] I *will* be with you, and yet to-night you sounded so far away and formal, oh! I want to put my arms around you, I ache to hold you close. . . . [Today I] took a party to the concert. There I thought only of you and wanted you even more than I do as a rule."[35] Does Roosevelt's "ache" to hold and embrace Hickok signal sexual desire? Or are we making an inappropriate assumption that passionate attachments are *necessarily* erotic?

Similarly, the public has long wondered about the true nature of Oprah Winfrey's friendship with Gayle King. Commenting on the never-ending rumors that the two are lovers, Oprah reflected, "I understand why people think we're gay. There isn't a definition in our culture for this kind of bond between women. So I get why people have to label it—how can you be this close without it being sexual?" Gayle concurred, then added, "But that said, I have to admit, if Oprah were a man, I would marry her!"[36]

Oprah is (as always!) absolutely right. Whereas other cultures have created words and categories to represent such powerful friendships, ours has not, and so the only way we seem able to make sense of these emotional connections is to assume that they are infused with secret sexual ardor. This suspicion reflects the widespread assumption that infatuation and sexual desire are cut from the same cloth.[37] Yet those who study passionate friendships throughout history have emphasized that though some of these relationships may have involved sexual attraction or activity, most did not, and a sexual component was rarely even suspected in the cultures and historical periods during which such bonds have been most prevalent.[38]

For example, in nineteenth-century America, passionate attachments between women (like that between Roosevelt and Hickok) were actually considered healthy outlets for adolescent intimacy because they were nonsexual.[39] The diaries of young girls during this period frequently contained fervent proclamations of love and devotion for female friends, and such relationships were considered safe and age-appropriate forms of "rehearsal" for later marital intimacy.[40] They were particularly prevalent at the women's colleges that dotted New England at this time: one nineteenth-century schoolmistress described them as "an extraordinary habit which they have of falling violently in love with each other, and suffering all the pangs of unrequited attachment, desperate jealousy etc. etc., with as much energy as if one of them were a man. . . . If the 'smash' is mutual, they monopolize each other and 'spoon' continually, and sleep together and lie awake all night talking instead of going to sleep."[41]

Yet as women's changing roles began to threaten the prevailing social order, these relationships began to invite suspicion. The historian Lillian Faderman pinpoints 1920 as a critical moment, after which we no longer find a public discourse on women's romantic friendships; instead, discussion turns to the problem of lesbianism (brought to light by the publication in 1928 of Radclyffe Hall's lesbian novel, *The Well of Loneliness*). As a result, "women who could not accept the stigmatizing label of 'lesbian' had to deny themselves the possibility of intense same-sex emotional involvement that females had enjoyed for centuries. If only lesbians loved other women, and they themselves were not lesbians, then they had to repress an intense feeling they might experience for another female."[42] Not much has changed: ironically, the dramatic and beneficial increases in societal awareness of lesbianism and bisexuality have unfortunately created a situation where heterosexual women may avoid "too much" intimacy with female friends, lest they be mistaken for lesbians.[43]

Although Western culture still lacks a defined category for platonic same-sex infatuations, they continue to occur and have been most frequently documented between women.[44] If such relationships were simply repressed lesbian affairs, then we would expect women in the most permissive and gay-positive environments (such as liberal-minded universities with active sexual-minority and feminist communities) to freely admit that these relationships were driven by sexual desire. Yet they do not.[45] In fact, friendship researchers have increasingly acknowledged that ties between women are often as intense as new love affairs, such that heterosexual women often describe the beginning of a same-sex best friendship in terms of "excitement, heightened energies, frequent thought about the other, invigorated self-regard—in short, in terms of the ardent sensibilities of romantic love."[46] In one study of older German women, numerous respondents (none of whom described themselves as being sexually attracted to women) spoke of adolescent same-sex friendships akin to smashes, typically involving kissing, cuddling, dancing together, or sleeping in the same bed. One woman remarked, "My first love was a girl. . . . It was wonderful," despite noting that she found the notion of same-sex *sexual* relationships disgusting and unnatural.[47] The psychologist Olivia Espín cites anecdotal examples of single aunts in Latin American communities "whose 'intimate' women friends were always invited to family gatherings. . . . I can assert with reasonable assurance that they were never sexual with each other. . . . Yet they saw each other every day and also spent endless hours talking to each other."[48] Even the *New York Times* recently discussed the widespread phenomenon of the "girl crush," concluding that it was *not* an indicator of same-sex sexual desire.[49]

What about men? As noted above, data indicate that men are also capable of forming intense, nonsexual friendships. But do they continue to do so? Probably not with as much frequency as women, since our culture has more restrictive expectations surrounding male-male than female-female friendships.[50] Specifically, society's view of heterosexual masculinity forbids open displays of affection between men, while permitting them between women. As a result, highly intimate and affectionate same-sex friendships are more likely to create suspicion of homosexuality when they occur between men than when they occur between women.[51]

The Unorientation of Love

Even those who grant that sexual desire is not a necessary component of romantic love might still suspect that sexual orientation directs romantic love. In other words, perhaps we possess sexual orientations *and* matching affectional or "bonding" orientations. This might make evolutionary sense because it would ensure that individuals formed intense emotional bonds with partners with whom they were having children. These bonds might then enhance reproductive success by keeping partners together and thereby giving children two parents instead of one.[52]

But there is one problem with this idea: it assumes that the basic psychological mechanisms underlying romantic love evolved specifically for the purpose of bonding reproductive mates together, and this does not appear to be the case. Rather, numerous psychologists, anthropologists, ethologists, and evolutionary biologists have argued that the emotions associated with reproductive pairbonding (in our commonsense terms, the emotions of romantic love) originally evolved, not in the context of mating, but in the context of *infant-caregiver attachment,* a biologically based bonding program that evolved to ensure that highly vulnerable mammalian infants stayed close to their caregivers to improve their odds of survival.[53] Animal researchers had long noted that mammalian infant-caregiver attachment and adult pairbonding were characterized by the same core behaviors and neurobiological mechanisms. On the basis of such evidence, the psychologists Cindy Hazan and Philip Shaver argued in the late 1980s that human romantic love was actually an adult version of infant-caregiver attachment.[54] It is safe to say that this argument revolutionized research on adult love and is now a tenet of this field of study.

The implications of this observation for the study of sexual orientation, however, have largely gone unappreciated. In order to make them clear, we need to review infant-caregiver attachment and its link to adult love.

The psychoanalyst John Bowlby developed his influential theory of attachment to explain his observation that children required a secure, enduring bond with a specific caregiver in order to develop normally.[55] He argued that infant-caregiver attachment is an emotion-driven mammalian motivational system that evolved to ensure that infants stayed in close proximity to their caregivers during the first few years of life. This system was critical to survival because relative to other species, mammalian infants—especially those of primates and humans—are born in an extremely vulnerable state, unable to feed or care for themselves. Human infants, for example, cannot even move around independently in order to flee from danger. Accordingly, their only chance for survival is to have intensive parental care. This is where attachment comes in. The system operates on the basis of emotional signals. When infants are separated from their caregivers, they experience distress and signal the caregiver for attention by crying or reaching out. Once the caregiver is sufficiently close, the infant feels calmed.

Although attachment is a biologically based, somewhat automatic process, Bowlby observed that it is not instantaneous. Rather, it takes approximately six months of regular contact for infants to attach fully to their caregivers.[56] During this period, the infant displays an increasingly intense fixation on the caregiver and greater and greater distress upon being separated from that person. The infant starts to selectively prefer the caregiver over all others as a source of comfort and security and seeks regular physical contact with him or her. These basic features have been observed not only in humans but across a wide variety of mammalian and primate species.[57]

Take another look at those signs of attachment—intense fixation, separation distress, extensive physical contact—do they seem familiar? If we look back to the classic characteristics of passionate love described earlier, we find the exact same set of features. It was on the basis of such similarities that Hazan and Shaver first proposed that adult romantic love and infant-caregiver attachment are governed by the same basic psychological system. But why should this be so? Evolutionary theorists have argued that natural selection is a stingy process: it does not tend to create new structures and mechanisms if perfectly good ones are already available.[58] In the case of pairbonding, the basic "problem" to be solved—motivating two individuals to stay together—is really no different from the "problem" that was solved with the attachment system. So the psychological process of attachment was gradually adapted to this new context.[59] In technical terms, this means that adult pairbonding is an "exaptation"—a system that originally evolved for one reason but came to serve another.[60]

Some of the strongest evidence for the view that adult pair-bonding and infant-caregiver attachment are governed by the same psychological program comes from neurobiological research, most of it conducted on animals. This research shows that the related neuropeptides oxytocin and vasopressin play critical roles. These two neuropeptides are chemically quite similar; their genes appear on the same chromosome and appear to have evolved from a common "ancestor" gene.[61] Here I focus on oxytocin because it plays a more functionally important role for females whereas vasopressin appears more relevant for males.[62] Oxytocin is a neuropeptide hormone unique to mammals. It is synthesized in the hypothalamus and released into the bloodstream through the pituitary gland. Oxytocin is best known for stimulating the contractions of labor and facilitating milk let-down in nursing mothers, but it is also involved in multiple aspects of attachment and bonding in mammals. Studies of animals (typically rats and prairie voles) have identified direct effects of oxytocin on maternal feeding behavior, maternal-infant bonding, and kin recognition.[63] Importantly, some of these effects may operate through oxytocin's role in regulating the release of other important neurochemicals, such as noradrenaline, dopamine, prolactin, and opiates, which are also involved in affiliative behavior.[64] Oxytocin also facilitates the formation of preferences for certain places and social partners, as well as the soothing, stress-alleviating effects that occur when animals maintain contact with their preferred partners.[65] Oxytocin has well-documented antistress effects.[66] In addition, some studies have suggested that it may be responsible for the fact that socially supportive relationships—particularly family and marital relationships—protect people from the negative effects of stress and promote both physical and mental well-being.[67]

Researchers now believe that oxytocin plays a key role in the psychobiological process through which mammals form stable, intrinsically rewarding bonds to specific social partners, most importantly the mother. Researchers have actually been able to facilitate infant-caregiver attachment in animals by administering oxytocin directly into their brains, and to prevent bond formation by administering chemicals that block the effects of oxytocin.[68] Physical contact and closeness may be important for these bonding processes. Oxytocin release in rats is facilitated by closeness and touch, and may be responsible for the comforting effects typically associated with such contact.[69] On the basis of these findings, researchers have suggested that as we develop a bond with another person, we pursue increasing closeness and contact with him or her. This triggers oxytocin release, and over time, we come to associate the other person with the soothing, rewarding effects of oxytocin.[70]

If romantic love is an adult version of infant-caregiver attachment, then does oxytocin also facilitate adult reproductive pair-bonding? In fact, it does. Much of the research in this area has focused on the prairie vole, a rodent that looks like a guinea pig and is distinguished by the fact that it is one of the few rodent species to form enduring pairbonds. Just as we saw with infant-caregiver attachment, infusing oxytocin into the brain of a prairie vole can speed up the bonding process with a new reproductive partner, whereas blocking the actions of oxytocin in the brain can prevent pairbonding.[71] Moreover, as with infant-caregiver relationships, physical contact facilitates bonding by triggering oxytocin release.

On the basis of such findings, researchers have concluded that adult pairbonding and infant-caregiver attachment are governed by the same evolved psychological "program" and driven by the same neurobiological pathways. This fact also helps to explain the independence between love and desire. After all, sexual desire is obviously not necessary for infant-caregiver attachment. Since romantic bonding and infant-caregiver bonding are governed by the same biological mechanisms, it is not necessary for romantic bonding either.

Before moving on, it bears repeating that most of what we know about oxytocin's role in bonding is based on animal research. Although studies increasingly indicate that oxytocin has similar functions in humans, the relevant processes are probably not exactly the same.[72] As yet we have no direct evidence to suggest that pair-bonding in voles and humans shares the same underlying physiological mechanisms.[73] We are only beginning to understand the full range of emotional and physical phenomena (other than nursing and labor) associated with oxytocin release in humans, and the consequences for subjective feelings.[74] Future research on such questions is critical for charting the basic nature and functioning of love versus desire. Also, a number of other brain chemicals including serotonin, dopamine, prolactin, vasopressin, and norepinephrine influence mammalian social behavior and deserve more attention for their potential role in mammalian bonding.[75]

Perhaps the most important implication of the correspondence between infant-caregiver attachment and adult romantic love concerns questions of "orientation." Earlier, I mentioned that "affectional orientations" might exist to steer adults into pairbond relationships with potential reproductive partners, thereby enhancing the survival of their offspring. But how would such orientations become part of the pairbonding system? If the neurobiological mechanisms underlying adult romantic love are the same as those that underlie infant-caregiver attachment, then affectional orientations—if they exist—must have evolved in the context of infant-caregiver attachment.

Yet obviously, such orientations make no sense in that context. Infants do not become selectively attached to other-sex versus same-sex caregivers, and it would be maladaptive if they did. Rather, the cues that trigger attachment formation in infants are the caregiver's familiarity and responsiveness. Notably, these cues also trigger the development of close bonds to both friends and romantic partners.[76] So when it comes down to it, there is really no plausible evolutionary basis for other-sex *or* same-sex orientations to be coded into the basic psychological and biological processes of pairbonding.

This means that though individuals might report stable tendencies to fall in love with one gender or the other, such tendencies have no intrinsic basis. But how then do we explain the fact that most lesbian and gay individuals do, in fact, consistently fall in love with same-sex partners, whereas most heterosexual individuals fall in love with other-sex partners? Part of the reason is probably cultural. Society expects romantic love and sexual desire to be linked, and we grow up internalizing those expectations. Yet another piece of the puzzle might be physical proximity and contact. Physical closeness and contact facilitate attachment formation, not only between infants and caregivers but also between adult reproductive partners. In our culture, children have plenty of this closeness and contact with their parents, but adults typically have this sort of physical intimacy only with potential or actual sexual partners. Thus the average friendship—no matter how emotionally close—is unlikely to develop the intensity of full-fledged romantic love in the absence of such regular physical affection.

Accordingly, perhaps one of the factors that transforms a close friendship into a passionate affair as in the historical and cross-cultural examples I discussed earlier, is heightened physical closeness and contact. In fact, evidence suggests that this might be the case. Descriptions of passionate same-sex friendships across different cultures and historical periods frequently make reference to partners' "inseparability" and their physical displays of affection.[77] This might also explain why passionate same-sex friendships are particularly likely to develop in sex-segregated environments like boarding schools.[78] Such environments heighten the opportunities for same-sex friends to develop "inseparable," physically affectionate bonds. They also restrict individuals' contact with people of the other sex, whose sexual desirability (at least to heterosexuals) might draw attention and energy away from same-sex friends. Supporting this view, one respondent in an interview study noted that the same-sex "crushes" that she and her girlfriends routinely developed "stopped when we started noticing the boys."[79]

If extensive physical contact does, in fact, play such an important role in bond formation—strong enough to trigger the formation of same-sex romantic attachment among otherwise heterosexual individuals—then we might expect to see an analogous phenomenon in animals. Sure enough, we do. Although only a small number of studies speak directly to this question, they all indicate that nonsexual, same-sex pairbonds are observed in (presumably heterosexual) mammals, though such bonds are not generally as exclusive or enduring as typical heterosexual pairbonds.

Notable examples include "female-bonded" primate species in which bonds between females are of great importance for communal infant care.[80] Female-female bonds in such systems provide security and protection, and they are characterized by the same physical contact and closeness that characterize male-female pairbonds.[81] Although the psychobiological mechanisms underlying female-female bonds in such species have not been studied extensively, researchers have once again pinpointed oxytocin as playing a potentially pivotal role.[82] One striking piece of evidence for this point comes from a study that specifically examined same-sex pairbonding in prairie voles.[83] The researchers found that they could initiate bond formation between two female voles simply by having them live together. However, later introduction of a male prairie vole tended to disrupt these female-female pairbonds, bringing to mind the aforementioned observation that some young women stop developing same-sex infatuations once they start "noticing the boys." Interestingly, a subsequent study detected gender differences in voles' propensities to form same-sex pairbonds. Specifically, female voles formed same-sex pairbonds more quickly than did males, and the females' preferences for their same-sex partners were more robust over time. The authors hypothesized that this may reflect the fact that female-female affiliative bonding is more important for female than male survival and reproductive success.[84]

These studies strongly suggest that the basic mechanisms underlying pairbonding are not oriented according to the same-sex/other-sex status of one's partner. Thus instead of thinking about love as being "oriented," we might instead conclude that though we are born with complex neurobiological circuitry that prepares us to form emotional bonds, this program is fundamentally flexible when it comes to the target of bond formation, and it is ready to adjust to whatever the environment affords.[85]

Getting from Love to Desire

Until now I have emphasized the distinctions between love and desire. But a recurring theme throughout this book has been the tendency for some women to begin experiencing same-sex attractions as a direct result of falling in love with a same-sex friend. How can we understand this process, given what we now understand about the "unorientation" of love and its independence from sexual desire? Certainly, though love and desire are separate systems, individuals undeniably perceive and experience powerful links between them. These links are sustained by psychological, cultural, and biological processes. For example, adolescents may come to *associate* love with desire as they become increasingly likely to pursue intimate and affectionate relationships with romantic partners rather than with platonic friends. Cultural norms and practices may further reinforce such associations. Finally, neurobiological pathways may play an additional role, as I will discuss further below.

Yet interestingly, though most laypeople and scientists readily acknowledge that there are active pathways between love and desire, they typically presume that these pathways run in one direction only: from sexual desire to love, but not the other way around. But there is actually no basis for this presumption. In fact, we have every reason to believe that the cultural, psychological, and bio-behavioral pathways linking love and desire are *bidirectional,* such that individuals can "get to" sexual desire from love, just as they "get to" love from desire. If so, then it makes sense that when individuals form unexpected attachments to people who are the wrong gender for their sexual orientation, they might also end up developing sexual desires for these individuals. Because these "cross-orientation" desires should be dependent on the emotional and biological processes of attachment formation, they should be specific to the relationship in question. This is, of course, exactly what so many women have described, in my own study as well as in many others. It certainly fits with the notion of being attracted to the person and not the gender. The feeling of becoming attracted to "the person" may, in fact, be the psychological experience of attachment formation, with its associated experiences of preoccupation, fixation, separation distress, possessiveness, and so on.

But how exactly might those feelings lead to actual sexual desire? Yet again, oxytocin might play a key role. In addition to its role in attachment, oxytocin also appears to influence sexual arousability and satisfaction.[86] Thus attachment-related increases in oxytocin levels, experienced in the context of an intense emotional bond, might trigger associations to oxytocin-related sexual arousability. This might be more likely among women than among men, for both cultural and biological reasons. On a cultural level, keep in mind that many societies actively constrain women's sexual activity to marital ties or socialize women to believe that sexual activity is acceptable only when pursued within a committed, long-term, affectional relationship.[87] Furthermore, many women do, in fact, have their first sexual experiences in the context of heterosexual dating relationships (whereas many young boys have their first sexual experiences in the context of solitary masturbation).[88] Altogether, these factors should serve to strengthen the psychological associations that women develop between love and desire. It is not surprising, then, that many sexual-minority women report that their first experience of same-sex attractions occurred in the context of an emotional attachment.

On a biological level, animal research demonstrates that oxytocin's effects on attachment and sexual behavior are estrogen-dependent and therefore highly gender-specific, suggesting potential biologically based differences in the pathways from love to desire.[89] For example, research on rats has detected more extensive oxytocin circuits in female brains than in male brains, perhaps to facilitate oxytocin-dependent mothering behavior, and some oxytocin receptors have been found to differ between male and female animals.[90] We do not yet know if the same is true for humans, but if so, it is possible that in addition to the strong cultural and psychological associations that women develop between love and desire, they might have particularly robust *neurobiological* connections between these experiences as well. Altogether, this may render the pathways between these experiences more pronounced among women than among men.

Thus maybe the fact that women tend to place more emphasis than men on the relationship aspect of sexuality, and the fact that women often fall in love with one specific person and develop novel sexual desires for that person, are both connected to oxytocin's joint, gender-specific role in sexual arousability and attachment. I do not mean to discount the influence of culture and socialization on sexual feelings. They obviously play critical roles and have been widely and comprehensively documented by psychologists and anthropologists.[91] I simply argue that these effects might actually be amplified by gender-specific biological processes.[92] Keep in mind, for example, that women generally have greater cultural permission to develop intense, affectionate bonds with same-sex friends than is the case for men. This, too, might make women more likely than men to develop attachment-based sexual desires.

Consider, finally, the gender differences discussed at the beginning of this chapter regarding proceptivity and arousability. An "attachment-based" sexual desire would certainly qualify as an example of arousability rather than proceptivity. So not only might gender-specific oxytocin pathways make it likely for women to develop novel sexual desires on the basis of forming strong emotional bonds, but the role of arousability in women's overall sexual feelings might make them more reactive to such novel desires.

At this point in time, sex researchers have not yet directly studied the mechanisms that potentially underlie sexual fluidity. This is partly due to the fact that female sexual fluidity has only recently been widely acknowledged as a real phenomenon. Although I hope to have demonstrated that there is considerable evidence for a number of psychological and biological processes through which female sexual fluidity might operate, we cannot make firm conclusions about such processes without additional research. This is especially true given that so much of the existing research on the biological underpinnings of attachment is based on animals. We need to determine the true extent to which the research findings that I have mentioned apply to humans.

Yet undoubtedly, there is no longer any excuse for dismissing female sexual fluidity as an anomaly attributable to women's repression, disingenuousness, confusion, or immaturity. After all, uncovering the psychological and biological processes that potentially underlie female sexual fluidity has the potential to radically reshape our understanding of the basic workings of sex, love, and sexual orientation. That alone makes it worth pursuing.

CHAPTER 8

Implications of
Female Sexual Fluidity

As a society we have made tremendous strides in fostering tolerance and acceptance of sexual diversity. It was approximately forty years ago that the Stonewall riots in New York City launched the modern gay rights movement; at that time, the stigma attached to same-sex sexuality and the denial of legal protections for same-sex relationships were taken for granted.[1] Growing up, a typical teenager encountered no information about same-sex sexuality in the mainstream media, in school textbooks, or in newspapers, and people with same-sex attractions often suffered years of intense shame, feeling that they were the only ones with such deviant and depraved feelings.[2]

Now, of course, things are radically different. Attitudes toward same-sex sexuality have improved dramatically over the past decade.[3] Although legal recognition of same-sex marriage has had a rocky road, with a number of states granting such recognition while Congress seeks federal laws to deny it, in general legal protections for lesbian/gay/bisexual individuals and their relationships have increased.[4] The same is true of public visibility. Sexual minorities populate television shows, movies, magazines, and books. Teenagers can readily find unbiased information that treats same-sex orientations as normal variations of human sexuality rather than as illness or spiritual failings.

Yet much of this information—positive and well intentioned as it is—still conveys an overly rigid model of same-sex sexuality that does not represent the true diversity of this phenomenon, especially in women. In textbooks and the popular media alike, sexual orientation is typically portrayed as developing early in life, though we know that for many women, it can emerge in mid- to late adulthood. It is described as strictly biological, and yet we know that environmental and interpersonal factors interact with biological influences. It is assumed to be rigidly fixed over the life course, and yet we know that women's sexual feelings can change either abruptly or gradually over time. It is viewed as governing both sexual and emotional feelings, though we know that some women experience significant differences in feelings of romantic passion, emotional intimacy, and sexual desire.

My voice is one of many calling for an expanded understanding of same-sex sexuality—and especially female sexuality—that better represents its diversity.[5] For decades scientists have questioned the rigid, categorical models of sexual orientation that continue to dominate both lay and scientific opinion. Yet the old models die hard. Why?

Perhaps we are reluctant to accept the notion of sexual fluidity because of the social and scientific implications of the phenomenon. Shifting away from sexual determinism and toward a more flexible understanding of sexuality, in which same-sex attractions might be possible for any woman, entails notable changes in the way we think about sexuality. Some people will embrace such changes because they involve more expansive understandings of all individuals' sexual possibilities. Others will reject them out of fear that they might trigger a conservative backlash against lesbian/gay/bisexual individuals and jeopardize hard-won progress toward social acceptance.

The key, I think, is in communicating exactly what sexual fluidity does and does not mean and heading off misconceptions before they have a chance to develop. Toward that end, in this chapter I directly address the implications of female sexual fluidity for our scientific models of sexuality as well as its current social and political meanings. I begin by suggesting a new framework for studying same-sex sexuality. This framework does a better job of representing and explaining variability not only in female sexuality but in human sexuality more generally. I then tackle some of the most common, controversial, and pressing questions regarding the notion of sexual fluidity: What does it mean with respect to the issue of "choosing" one's sexuality or seeking to change it? Is sexual fluidity a dangerous idea, given antigay efforts to portray same-sex sexuality as an immoral lifestyle instead of a basic human characteristic?

A Dynamical Systems Approach to Sexuality

Sexual fluidity does not imply that the long-term course of a woman's sexuality is random, unpredictable, and scientifically unexplainable. Indeed, though traditional models of sexuality fail to describe women's experiences over time, they are not completely useless. Rather, we require an altogether new type of model, one that systematically explains both stability and variability in sexuality; places equal emphasis on intrinsic orientations and the capacity for fluidity; emphasizes the ongoing interactions between women and the diverse contexts within which sexuality is expressed; makes sense of the complex links between love and desire; takes seriously the capacity for novel forms of sexual and emotional experience that emerge unexpectedly over the life course; and makes no assumptions about authentic sexual types or normal developmental pathways.

This might sound like a tall order, but the framework for such a model already exists. It is called *dynamical systems theory,* and it is changing the way researchers conceptualize a wide range of human phenomena, from infant motor development to adult personality. Dynamical systems models explain how complex phenomena (such as cognition, language, gender identity, or, in this case, same-sex sexuality) emerge, stabilize, change, and restabilize over time, through individuals' ongoing interactions with their changing environments. Dynamical systems theory is ideally suited to representing female sexual fluidity because its primary focus is change. Whereas traditional models of sexuality have implicitly assumed that an individual's sexuality is set during adolescence and then remains fixed, a dynamical systems approach *expects* change to occur. In fact, it places processes of change at the center of our analyses instead of at the margins.

Dynamical systems models were originally developed by mathematicians and physicists to explain physical phenomena whose states varied over time, for example, swinging pendulums or cloud formations in the atmosphere. They analyze the multiple factors that determine the state of the system, to predict its pattern of change over time, which otherwise might seem random, arbitrary, and abrupt. In the late 1980s, a number of forward-thinking psychologists observed that the development of many complex human phenomena during infancy and childhood—such as language and motor skills—resembled dynamical systems. Specifically, they were characterized by periodic, abrupt, unpredictable spurts in skills and behaviors, contrary to classic developmental models of gradual, step-by-step growth "programmed" by genetic factors.[6]

The psychologists began applying dynamical systems models to these complex patterns of development. They were able to show that such patterns arose as a direct result of interactions among "internal" elements (such as genes, skills, thoughts, and feelings) and "external" elements (such as relationships, experiences, and cultural norms). Some dynamical systems theorists go further to argue that because of these complex interactions, it is meaningless to differentiate between biological and environmental-cultural-social processes.[7] Dynamical systems approaches have since been applied to a wide range of psychological and social phenomena, amounting to a quiet revolution transforming multiple branches of social science. Thus far such models have been used to describe perception, emotion, language, children's play behavior, personality, coping, cognition, organizational decision-making, and even antisocial behavior.[8]

The feminist biologist Anne Fausto-Sterling has made a case for applying this approach to the study of gender development.[9] I would argue that it is also particularly well suited to helping us understand the development and expression of same-sex sexuality. After all, sexual feelings and behaviors are structured by complex interactions among individual and contextual factors, including genes, hormones, maturational state, personality traits, situational factors, interpersonal influences, and cultural norms.[10] Furthermore, research on same-sex sexuality among women has detected precisely the forms of variability that are classic hallmarks of dynamical systems: abrupt transitions in attractions, identity, and behavior over time; the sudden emergence of novel patterns of attraction and behavior; extreme sensitivity to fluctuations in situations, environments, or close relationships; and the fact that early milestones often fail to predict later outcomes.

In other words, the forms of variability in female same-sex sexuality that have historically been brushed aside as atypical and unexplainable are exactly the types of variability that dynamical systems models were developed to explain. Below I outline some of the characteristics that make this approach so flexible.

Scientific models that emphasize person-environment interactions instead of biological determinism are certainly nothing new, and they are becoming increasingly dominant within developmental psychology.[11] Yet even sex researchers who acknowledge that early-developing biological factors such as genes or perinatal hormones have only partial influences on adult sexuality insist on identifying *just how much* influence they have compared with environmental factors: Is it 30 percent, 50 percent, or 80 percent? This approach, unfortunately, is ultimately just as reductionistic as genetic determinism. It presumes that biological influences can always be neatly disentangled from contextual factors and analyzed on their own.

Dynamical systems models reject this idea, emphasizing instead that a person's initial traits and subsequent environments are in constant, mutually influential interaction with one another, and that they come to progressively influence one another over time.[12] As a result, you enter into each person-context interaction a slightly different person from the one you were at the last interaction. All your experiences are fundamentally shaped by what preceded them and set the stage for what follows. As the psychologist Esther Thelen summarized with respect to child development,

> How a child behaves depends not only on the immediate current situation but also on his or her continuous short and longer-term history of acting, the social situation, and the biological constraints he or she was born with. Every action has within it the traces of previous behavior. The child's behavior, in turn, sculpts his or her environment, creating new opportunities and constraints.[13]

Thus whereas classical approaches to development typically take complex behaviors and break them down into different components (for example, genes, hormones, nutrition, parental warmth, and peer pressure), dynamical systems approaches emphasize the transformational interrelationships among components. According to this perspective, trying to identify the specific percentage of genetic versus environmental determinants of any complex phenomenon—such as same-sex sexuality—is as futile as trying to pull apart a chocolate cake into the flour, sugar, eggs, and butter that went into it.

Dynamical systems theories are particularly valuable when it comes to nonlinear or discontinuous variability—in other words, abrupt and seemingly inexplicable changes in thought and behavior. Most psychological models focus on consistent patterns of thought and behavior: the tendencies for anxious people to worry, for achievement-minded individuals to succeed, for outgoing people to make friends. Yet when someone departs from his or her regular pattern (for example, taking a sudden career detour or abruptly changing political philosophies), these models can only ascribe such change to random error or "noise." *Oh well*, we say. *We can't predict everything.*

This is exactly how discontinuities in female sexuality have been treated. Yet from a dynamical systems perspective, such unexpected variability is not "noise" or "random error." Rather, the potential for such variability is a fundamental characteristic of the system, and the goal is to specify when and how it is most likely to occur. This means that we need to change the whole way we approach female same-sex sexuality. Instead of asking, "What makes some women lesbians?" we need to ask, "What factors create both stability and change in women's same-sex and other-sex sexuality?"

Because the long-range development of a dynamic system is continuously tweaked by ongoing experiences and interactions, it is impossible to definitively predict its final endpoint. Similarly, its development cannot be traced back to any single cause. Rather, multiple factors could have given rise to the system's present pattern, and multiple endpoints are always possible. The technical terms for these two related concepts are *equifinality* and *multifinality.* Equifinality means that two individuals can reach the same outcome through different routes, whereas multifinality means that two individuals with the same initial starting point might end up on completely different pathways.

This is precisely the case with respect to female same-sex sexuality: three different women might have similar patterns of same-sex attraction, fantasy, and behavior, and yet one might have been influenced by genetics, another by perinatal hormones, and another by altogether different factors. Consider identical twins: they share 100 percent of their genes and often have similar environments. Yet as reviewed in Chapter 2, they end up with the same sexual orientation only about 30 percent of the time. If same-sex sexuality were programmed by a straightforward genetic blueprint, this would be impossible. A dynamical systems perspective suggests that this sort of variability is an inevitable result of the fact that despite their identical genes, twins embark on distinct pathways, shaped by their own unique histories of relationships, experiences, feelings, cognitions, and situations.

Throughout my research I noticed the spontaneous development of "uncharacteristic" or cross-orientation attractions, often as the result of a close emotional bond. These experiences are virtually impossible to explain from a traditional developmental perspective, which contends that same-sex attractions (as well as other-sex attractions) must have existed all along, deep within the individual. If same-sex orientation is established by infancy, then new attractions cannot develop in adulthood.

A dynamical systems approach challenges this view, suggesting that development is never truly complete, and hence additional transformations are always possible, whether at age sixteen or age sixty. Such transformation is called *emergence*. This term refers to the coming-into-being of novel behaviors or experiences as a result of dynamic interactions between people and their environments. The notion of emergence stands in direct contrast to deterministic models of development, which presume that complex behaviors unfold during childhood according to a rigid, preset program.

As noted, deterministic models have dominated prior research on same-sex sexuality, and yet the increasing evidence for variability in the timing of key developmental milestones and abrupt discontinuities in experience directly challenges this view. The notion of emergence helps to explain these phenomena because it suggests that various events and experiences have the potential to "reorganize" a woman's sexual thoughts and feelings, sometimes producing altogether new desires.

This certainly helps to explain cases in which women fall in love with one specific person and experience new and unexpected desires as a result. The suddenness of such transitions is exactly what has led researchers and laypeople to doubt their authenticity. After all, sexual desires cannot come out of nowhere, right? They must have existed all along. Yet from a dynamical systems perspective, it makes perfect sense that a powerful experience such as falling in love could trigger an abrupt and massive reorganization of a woman's sexuality. So whereas proponents of traditional, deterministic models of sexuality have been skeptical when women report that an emotional attachment suddenly developed into sexual desire, a dynamical systems approach would treat this experience as a classic example of emergence.

Because emergence can take place at any point in the life course, dynamical systems theory would maintain that we can never definitively identify the end state of a woman's sexuality. Yet this does not mean that all forms of sexuality are equally likely for every single woman. Rather, they depend upon a woman's particular combination of inborn traits (including biological predispositions), environments, experiences, and relationships. Hence, though we might never be able to predict whom a thirteen-year-old girl or a thirty-five-year-old woman will find desirable at fifty, we can understand how changes in certain areas—intimate relationships, social norms, family conflict—might make some pathways more likely than others. I have argued that one of the factors we need to consider is a woman's specific degree of sexual fluidity. Not all women will have the same capacity to experience emergent sexual desires as a result of falling in love. Two heterosexual women might each have a same-sex passionate friendship in high school, yet one of them will eventually develop sexual attractions for her friend whereas the other will not.

It might seem from the discussion so far that dynamical systems always produce increasing variability over time. Yet this is not the case. One particularly important contribution of the dynamical systems approach is its capacity to reconcile both stability and change by distinguishing between short-term variability and long-term regularity. Specifically, the diverse contexts faced by a particular woman might produce considerable change in her thoughts and feelings during a particular period of time (for example, the changes in same-sex attractions and behaviors described in Chapter 5). Over the long term, however, a variety of constraining influences ranging from genes to cultural norms to simple habits will channel her into a relatively stable pattern.[14] Thus despite abrupt bursts of variability at particular moments in time, individuals tend toward consistency and regularity over the long term. This is why the existence of sexual fluidity does not mean that women's sexuality is utterly random and unpredictable.

In fact, this combination of short-term variability and long-term regularity provides a way to interpret one of the notable findings of my longitudinal study—the fact that though two-thirds of the participants underwent at least one "post–coming-out" identity change, their self-reported sexual attractions generally stayed in the same range throughout the study. Although they might report changes in their attractions of 10–15 percentage points in one direction or the other, women with predominant or near-exclusive same-sex attractions in 1995 tended to report predominant or near-exclusive same-sex attractions in 2005. Women with attractions in a bisexual range in 1995 tended to show the same pattern in 2005.

Thus women showed long-term regularity in their overall heterosexual, bisexual, or lesbian pattern of feelings and behavior, but they demonstrated substantial variability around those prototypical patterns at any one assessment. According to a traditional deterministic model of sexual orientation, such variability represents "falsehood"—denying or hiding one's true identity. From a dynamical systems perspective, this variability is perfectly understandable, since "true," enduring patterns of thought and behavior never rule out short-term fluctuations. Women themselves seemed to become increasingly aware of this fact over time—as one thirty-three-year-old lesbian said at the ten-year follow-up interview, "It doesn't freak me out anymore. I know that I can totally be a lesbian and still have the occasional attraction to a man."

It bears noting that though my discussion of dynamical systems theory has remained fairly general, applications of dynamical systems models usually involve fairly technical mathematical models of nonlinear change and development.[15] You will not be seeing any such equations here—my goal is to set forth dynamical systems theory not as the final answer to female sexuality but as an investigative approach that treats processes of change as fundamentally important. Hence, perhaps the most important contribution of a dynamical systems approach would be to alter how researchers think about and conduct research on sexual development, and what types of data are considered most relevant. It is no longer sufficient to collect isolated snapshots of sexuality at a single moment in time. If sexual development does, in fact, emerge and transform over time, we must observe these changes as they occur. This new perspective would contribute not only to our understanding of female sexual fluidity but also to sexuality more generally. Perhaps our first priority, then, should be to study sexual-minority men over as long a period of time, and in as much detail, as I have followed women.

With such goals in mind for the future, what about the present? If female sexuality really is fluid and our existing models of sexual orientation profoundly shortsighted, then what does this mean for the way society currently views and treats lesbian/gay/bisexual individuals? Might the notion of sexual fluidity introduce dangerous, poorly thought-out assumptions regarding choice and change that could jeopardize efforts to secure civil rights and social acceptance for sexual minorities? This controversial topic has been a continuing source of concern to me as I have studied sexual fluidity over the years. Hence, I conclude my discussion of sexual fluidity by dismantling some of the most common misinterpretations of this phenomenon, in the hope of clearing a path for more forward-thinking approaches to sexuality.

The Politics of Fluidity

Many advocates for lesbian/gay/bisexual rights have argued that sexual orientation is akin to ethnicity—a basic, stable trait that people are born with and over which they have no control. The logic goes something like this: If it is impossible—and perhaps even harmful—for sexual minorities to repress their same-sex desires and live duplicitous "heterosexual" lives, then society must accommodate their experiences and relationships. Lesbian/gay/bisexual individuals would then deserve systematic protection from discrimination, harassment, and victimization, as well as legal recognition of their intimate relationships. The antigay counter-argument is that sexual orientation is nothing like ethnicity, but rather a depraved lifestyle choice unworthy of legal protection or validation. After all, if someone chooses a spiritually bereft life of stigma and discrimination, then why should the government intervene? That person should simply make a different choice.

So the familiar battle lines are drawn: *fixed* = *biological* = *deserving of acceptance and protection*, whereas *variable* = *chosen* = *fair game for stigma and discrimination*. It does not seem to matter that the crude equations of "fixed = biological" and "variable = chosen" are scientifically false. This particular version of "Sexual Orientation for Dummies" continues to hold sway over popular opinion, falsely conveying the impression that debates about the legal status of lesbian/gay/bisexual individuals are scientific rather than political matters. In this distorted framework, the notion of sexual fluidity is unavoidably controversial. If sexuality is fluid, then the analogy to ethnicity breaks down and sexual minorities are launched into the treacherous "variable/chosen" side of the equation, where there is no need for civil rights protections. If you made this choice, you can unmake it.

Such arguments have resulted in the persistent denunciation of sexual minorities and their families. Conservative organizations such as Focus on the Family and Concerned Women for America have placed a high priority on blocking legal recognition of same-sex relationships and preventing same-sex couples from becoming parents. Sadly, their outreach efforts have succeeded in influencing some Americans' attitudes on these issues. A recent poll by the Pew Research Center found that more than 50 percent of Americans oppose same-sex marriage, and nearly as many oppose same-sex adoptions.[16] This is despite the many studies showing that the children of same-sex couples are no different from the children of heterosexual couples when it comes to gender roles, psychological adjustment, play behavior, social development, personality, or general well-being.[17] Thus while the overall visibility of lesbian/gay/bisexual issues suggests increasing acceptance of same-sex sexuality, there remains a deep reservoir of antigay sentiment in America that has stark legal implications.

It also has implications for basic health and safety. According to the FBI, approximately one-sixth of documented hate crimes are targeted at sexual minorities, and thousands of children each year are subjected to antigay harassment in elementary school, middle school, and high school.[18] Compared with their heterosexual counterparts, sexual-minority teenagers are more likely to be threatened or assaulted with weapons at school, more likely to have their property stolen or damaged, and (not surprisingly) less likely to feel safe at school.

In such a climate, perhaps it is too dangerous to introduce the notion of sexual fluidity. Couldn't it be misused by antigay activists?

Actually, it already has. I will never forget the day that a colleague told me that my research had been favorably cited on the website for the Concerned Women for America, a conservative organization opposed to civil rights for lesbian/gay/bisexual individuals. Sure enough, I found one of my publications cited in an online article entitled "Born or Bred? Science Does Not Support the Claim That Homosexuality Is Genetic."[19] The article argued that Americans "have been pummeled with the idea that people are 'born gay,'" leading sexual minorities to "mistakenly believe they have no chance themselves for change." The author went on to charge that the "born gay" argument hampers efforts to protect young people from dangerous "homosexual influences," most notably seduction into the gay lifestyle.

Adding to my dismay, I soon found that my work had also been cited on the website for NARTH, the National Association for Research and Therapy of Homosexuality, a group that advocates reparative therapy aimed at eliminating homosexuality and reestablishing heterosexual desires.[20] This article maintained that "the essentialist argument that homosexuality is biologically determined, and is therefore not amenable to change, continues to find little support in science." My work was referenced in support of this false claim.

Oh no, here we go, I thought to myself. From the very beginning, I knew that my research on female sexual fluidity could—and probably would—be misinterpreted and misappropriated by antigay activists. Accordingly, over the years I have taken pains to point out, in my published work and in public presentations, that experiencing one's sexuality as fluid and variable is *not* the same thing as choosing a particular lifestyle. Recall that my respondents typically felt that they had no control over their own sexual changes over the years and could neither predict nor control them. But of course such subtleties are overlooked by antigay activists bent on undermining lesbian/gay/bisexual rights.

This dilemma still wakes me up at night, and I do not know how to resolve it. Over the years many of my colleagues (usually those who do not study controversial topics!) have advised me not to worry about such matters. *Your job is to do the science,* they tell me. *What happens then is beyond your control, so let it go.* I respect that position, but I cannot abide it. Perhaps in an ideal world, I would be able to pursue my scientific work on sexual fluidity without a thought to its social implications, but this is simply not the case: the political consequences of misunderstanding fluidity are too significant to ignore. So I remain determined to challenge these misunderstandings and to advance a thoughtful, scientifically grounded consideration of fluidity's social and political implications.

Does Fluidity Mean That People Choose Their Sexuality?

The question of choice comes up almost every time I present my research findings. It is certainly a reasonable inquiry—after all, we are accustomed to thinking about the capacity for change as a matter of control and influence. But when it comes to sexuality, it does not work this way. The experiences of the women I have followed over the past ten years consistently demonstrate that sexual fluidity does *not* mean that women simply choose to feel same-sex attractions, that they can undo same-sex attractions with enough time and effort, or that any single experience can seduce someone into a lifetime of same-sex sexuality. Rather, sexual fluidity appears to be constrained by a complex array of intrinsic and extrinsic factors, many of which we have yet to discover. Variability typically occurs only within a certain range, and it appears unrelated to any conscious attempts to control it.

At the same time, this does not mean that we are randomly pushed to and fro, with no agency whatsoever. To the contrary, we make hundreds of decisions every day that indirectly influence our sexual and emotional experiences. One decision—for example, becoming roommates with your best friend during a particular time of your life—might shift your life path in directions that could lead to the emergence of novel, unexpected desires. Yet this does not mean that such an outcome was strategic, conscious, or "undoable." Consider, for example, dynamic systems other than sexuality. When one baby starts crawling three months earlier than another, do we conclude that they made different choices about getting across the room? Does an adolescent who suddenly "gets" trigonometry choose this insight? As for the question of change, how might we induce an infant to "unlearn" crawling, or make the adolescent forget his or her new insight and perceive trigonometry as a set of unrelated, unorganized, unfamiliar concepts and symbols?

These notions are obviously implausible, as they should be in the domain of sexuality. Sexual and emotional feelings—like all complex patterns of human experience—develop as the result of dynamic interchanges among innate, environmental, and cultural factors. It would be impossible to identify the specific moment at which unorganized impulses become stabilized into regular tendencies, or to pinpoint which particular factor (a gene? a hormone? a book? a kiss?) played the pivotal role. We might be able to change some of the input—for example, we might decide not to associate with certain people, not to read certain material, or not to permit ourselves to think certain thoughts—but such crude modifications could not "unorganize" a pattern of experience that became organized through a long, untraceable chain of psychological, biological, and cultural processes. Even if we tried to tweak as many of these elements as possible, how would we know which were the right ones, especially given that the particular mix might be different from person to person?

Consider the experiences of my study participants, who perceived little control over their own changes. Kerri was one of the women who described herself as attracted to the person and not the gender. After a period of sexual questioning in her early twenties, she eventually found that her sexual attractions consistently crystallized around men, despite her notable distaste for heterosexual culture. As she concluded, "I was never interested in being straight, but unfortunately I didn't actually get to pick." Other women, when asked about the issue of choice, spoke of choosing how to think about or act on their feelings rather than choosing the feelings themselves. Sexual fluidity may have given them a wider range of possibilities:

> For me it goes back to the choice of the kind of experiences that you allow yourself to have. If you meet someone that you connect with, you choose whether you want to express that part of yourself. But I don't know how you could choose it arbitrarily. I think it has to be something that you feel. (age twenty-five, unlabeled)

> For me sexuality encompasses how you choose to act on certain things, and it seems to me that there is quite a bit of choice in that. But I think that at least my experience has been that even a change in sexual identity among people that I know has come as a surprise and hasn't come as something they felt they were choosing. (age twenty-nine, unlabeled)

> I've kind of been surprised at how intense [the attraction to women] is. I mean, when it's happening. Whoa, how can you see? Or, I don't know . . . every now and then, I'll sit down and talk with one of my friends, and be like, "I don't understand . . . it's got to be biological, because I don't have any control over this!" It's so strong, and then it just reminds me, "Wow! I'm so gay!" (age thirty, lesbian)

Keep in mind the principles of dynamical systems theory outlined above: all of our experiences and interactions have a cumulative effect, so that the particular set of factors influencing our same-sex and other-sex desires are different today than they were ten years ago, and will be different tomorrow. Consequently, it is impossible to return to a previous state. This is consistent with respondents' patterns of change over the ten years of my study—the tendency was toward expansion rather than contraction, toward adding attractions and behaviors rather than eliminating them, even if the likelihood of acting on such attractions was minimal.

The overall tendency toward expansion in attractions concords with the fact that reparative therapy—also known as "conversion" or "reorientation" therapy—has been reliably unsuccessful in eliminating same-sex attractions, though it has been able to teach people cognitive skills and strategies for disattending to these attractions.[21] Does sexual fluidity imply that some people will be able to make such modifications more easily than others? After all, if fluid individuals are more sensitive to contextual factors, they might respond more readily to attempts to channel their attractions in one direction rather than another. This is certainly possible, and actually some data on gender differences in "successful" responses to reparative therapy support this possibility.[22] Yet in general, we need to treat reparative therapy success stories with a good deal of skepticism, since they generally do not support the notion that individuals' underlying sexual predispositions have been altered. As the psychologist Lee Beckstead observed from his interviews with clients of reparative therapy:

> [They] reported that, at the end of therapy, they could still be aroused erotically by the body shape of same-sex individuals. . . . Participants reported that therapy helped them change their thinking about and expression of homosexuality and sexuality but not their actual sexual orientation. As well, even those participants who reported having an increase in heterosexual attraction described those attractions as oriented only to their spouse and different from their homosexual arousal.[23]

Similar qualifications apply when interpreting the experiences of the many women in my study who had their first—and sometimes only—same-sex attractions in the context of an emotionally intense bond to one specific woman. As discussed, traditional understandings of sexual orientation allow only two possible interpretations of such experiences: either the women had same-sex attractions all along but had repressed them, or they did not really have them now; they were simply misinterpreting their feelings. Both these conclusions are wrong. As we now know, it is possible for specific relationships to spark the emergence of authentic—and authentically novel—sexual attractions that might contradict a person's sexual orientation.

Does this mean that it is possible to seduce someone into same-sex sexuality by drawing them into an intense emotional bond? The word *seduce,* of course, implies that one person is intentionally luring the other, which certainly does not characterize the cases I observed. In fact, it was the mutual trust, intimacy, vulnerability, and devotion that women experienced in their intimate friendships that appeared to give rise to their unique intensity, and to trigger each woman's sexual fluidity. It is hard to imagine that such a transition could be actively engineered. Moreover, the experiences of the women in my study suggest that relationship-based attractions tend to dissipate if the relationship itself dissipates, showing that fluidity always operates within constraints. Thus the notion of seducing another person into a long-term change in sexual orientation is unlikely.

In short, fluidity does not imply that individuals can mold either their sexuality or someone else's into a pattern of their choosing. Variability does not equal choice any more than stability equals genetics. As we have seen, the nature of same-sex sexuality is far more complicated: wholly biological and wholly cultural, 100 percent genetic *and* 100 percent environmental, stable over the long term and variable over the short term. The more we learn about the complexities of same-sex and other-sex sexuality, the more ridiculous it seems that we could ever imagine possessing the power to turn on or off *any* of our desires like a faucet.

What Would Change if Our Models of Sexuality Changed?

Beyond the issue of change and choice, other implications of sexual fluidity bear noting. In particular, we must acknowledge that one of the reasons for the persistence of our current, overly categorical model of sexual orientation is that it is more than just a scientific model. Indeed, it functions as a larger worldview about sexuality that serves the interests of heterosexually identified individuals by reassuring them of their permanent heterosexual status.

After all, if there are rigid and permanent boundaries between heterosexuals and sexual-minority individuals, then anyone who is fairly certain of his or her current heterosexual status now can be reassured that he or she will never be part of that strange and unsettling "homosexual" group. Such clear divisions allow mainstream society to treat the basic social and political issues of sexual-minority individuals as "special interests" that affect only a small number of people and have no broader implications for questions of privacy, family, and human dignity.

But to acknowledge that sexuality is fluid means to acknowledge that no matter how certain you feel about your sexuality at the moment, you might have an experience tomorrow or ten years from now that will place you squarely in sexual-minority territory. This, of course, is not exactly welcome information. I remember once speaking about my research at a meeting of parents and high school teachers who were serious about creating a supportive and accepting environment for lesbian/gay/bisexual students. After my presentation, one of the teachers asked me, "At what age can we be pretty sure that if a student is really lesbian/gay/bisexual, it would have shown up by that point?" Her question was well-meaning—who can blame parents or teachers for wanting to have a certain "cutoff" to guide them in making sense of adolescents' complex feelings and relationships? "Well, Sally must not be a lesbian because we would have known by now"; "Johnny made it to eighteen and he's still heterosexual, so we're home-free!"

I told the teacher the truth—that there was no survey or test any researcher could give to reassure someone, at any age, that they would never find themselves desiring or falling in love with a person of the same sex. As I have argued, there is no point at which sexuality completely finishes developing, neatly tying off loose ends and therefore ruling out the prospect of unexpected future transitions. Because of fluidity, same-sex sexuality remains an unpredictable possibility for all women throughout the life course, albeit an unlikely one (though this is due more to culture than to biology).[24]

What could be more unsettling? We all want to believe that we know ourselves fairly well, have a good grasp of our motives and goals, and can make reasonable predictions about our future. Therefore, it is understandably alarming and unsettling to acknowledge that one of the most deeply personal aspects of selfhood—sexuality—is neither as known nor as knowable as we may have thought. The average heterosexual would probably think it impossible that somewhere in the future, an unexpected confluence of emotions, habits, relationships, events, and environments could jar him or her from a thirty-year pattern of exclusive heterosexuality into an altogether unexpected same-sex love affair. If something like that is beyond self-knowledge, then what else might be?

Of course, in the process of coming out, most sexual minorities have already reckoned with the discomforting unpredictability of their own sexual development. For such individuals—including the women in my own sample—it is not as much of a leap to acknowledge the fluidity of sexuality and the attendant uncertainty about one's own sexual future. As one of the unlabeled participants responded when I asked her what sorts of relationships and desires she expected to pursue in the future, "Considering my sexuality hasn't held steady in any point in the past, for like eight years, I don't see any reason why it would continue to hold steady. I didn't anticipate in what direction it would change. I have no reason to think that I'll be able to anticipate it in the future."

This uncertainty has caused many sexual minorities to cast off traditional labels to avoid misrepresenting the fluid and multidimensional nature of their erotic and emotional lives. Yet though this approach to sexual identification is increasingly popular among contemporary sexual-minority youths, who are more critical of categorical notions of sexuality than have been previous cohorts of lesbian/gay/bisexual individuals, it nonetheless remains outside the mainstream.[25]

This is somewhat ironic, given that "anticategorical" models of orientation that make allowances for fluidity date back to Kinsey himself. When he first developed his famous scale representing a continuum of other-sex to same-sex experience, he sought to capture variability in erotic and emotional experiences, not only across different individuals, but also within the same individual over time. Obviously, this particular usage never caught on. Nor, of course, did Kinsey's anticategorical approach to sexuality. Researchers have long been taking the Kinsey Scale and chopping it up into "lesbian/gay," "bisexual," and "heterosexual" sections, thereby subverting Kinsey's intent. So despite Kinsey's famous assertion that "the world is not to be divided into sheep and goats," we seem bound and determined to maintain discrete categories.[26] Clearly, categorical models of sexuality—on both personal and scientific levels—will not be easily dismantled.

Nor should they, at least not entirely. After all, there is plenty of evidence that people do, in fact, possess a core sexual predisposition that plays a role in channeling their sexual interest toward one sex, the other sex, or both. The variability introduced by sexual fluidity is variability around this "malleable core."[27] Hence, it is still useful to speak of sexual orientations, their multiple determinants, and their developmental trajectories. We simply need to shift from treating these orientations as rigidly fixed to viewing them as multidimensional and dynamic.

Some activists feel that the climate is not yet right for such a shift in our thinking about sexual freedom. Given the recent resurgence of conservative antigay activism (much of it focused on banning same-sex marriage), it may well be that for now, the safest way to advocate for lesbian/gay/bisexual rights is to keep propagating a deterministic model: sexual minorities are born that way and can never be otherwise. If this is an easier route to acceptance (which may in fact be the case), is it really so bad that it is inaccurate?[28]

Over the long term, *yes,* particularly because women are systematically disenfranchised by this approach. For hundreds of years scientists and politicians have treated men's experiences as normative and have marginalized women.[29] This approach, of course, has always produced bad science and bad public policy, and this is as much the case for sexuality as for any other domain. For too long, women with discontinuous, changing patterns of same-sex and other-sex desire have been written off as atypical and inauthentic, not only by researchers, but also by many subsets of the gay/lesbian/bisexual community. In my interviews, I repeatedly found that participants seemed slightly embarrassed by the ways their sexual histories deviated from conventional models—they had no idea how common fluidity was.

Nor do most other women. Almost every time that I have spoken about my research to lesbian/gay/bisexual audiences, women have lined up afterward to confess to me, in hushed tones, that their own life history has paralleled the fluid trajectories of the women in my sample. Until that point, they thought there was something wrong with them. I have also had parents, friends, and siblings of lesbian and bisexual women express profound relief at the knowledge that their loved one was not the only person to undergo periodic shifts in sexual identity. As with so many other areas of psychology, feeling different can be a powerful motive for self-silencing.

This silencing effect is ironic, given that part of the genesis of the modern lesbian/gay/bisexual rights movement was a widespread acknowledgment that silence was both personally and politically damaging. Just as the first generation of activists emphasized the importance of speaking up about simply having same-sex attractions, the current generation should give voice to the true diversity of these experiences. To some extent, this is already happening. While adults continue to argue about the meaning and prevalence of sexual fluidity, sexual-minority adolescents appear to have gotten this message. Having grown up with more accurate, positive, and diverse models of same-sex sexuality than the generation that preceded them, they not only have more positive attitudes about same-sex sexuality but also more flexible definitions of sexual identity and orientation.[30]

Accordingly, they do not place nearly as much emphasis on adopting a clear and consistent lesbian/gay/bisexual identity as did previous generations. It used to be that simply claiming "I'm gay" constituted a radical political act (and, of course, in certain repressive environments, this is still very much the case). Yet this is less so today, with the increased visibility of same-sex sexuality. In a recent issue of *In Style* magazine, the married heterosexual actress Kate Winslet gushed about meeting her idol, Meryl Streep, at an awards ceremony: "I went up to her and said, 'Omigod, I love you so much I would happily tongue-kiss you right now!'"[31] The fact that such a remark carries no negative consequences (at least not for someone who is unambiguously heterosexual) shows how much things have changed. The idea of a heterosexual woman being so impressed and bedazzled by another woman that her response verges on the erotic is no longer altogether shocking.

Teenagers today increasingly perceive same-sex sexuality as a personal rather than a political matter, and they place greater emphasis on personal exploration than on rigid identification. As the psychologist Ritch Savin-Williams noted, "Teenagers are increasingly redefining, reinterpreting, and renegotiating their sexuality so that possessing a gay, lesbian, or bisexual identity is practically meaningless. Their sexuality is not something that can be easily described, categorized, or understood apart from being part of their life in general."[32] Hence the tendencies toward unlabeled identities and more fluid understandings of sexuality might reach fruition sooner than we think. From the perspective of the next generation of activists working on behalf of acceptance and social legitimation of same-sex sexuality, hand-wringing over the implications of sexual fluidity might, in time, prove to be a nonissue.

Looking Ahead: The Future of Female Sexuality

The fluidity of female sexuality has not been entirely unnamed or hidden from view; it has not been threatened by total erasure. And yet it remains beneath the radar, so to speak—hidden in plain sight. Which is worse? For one's experiences to be silenced and made invisible, or for those experiences to be voiced and visible yet dismissed—by scientists, politicians, family members, friends, perhaps even lovers—as inauthentic, unusual, exceptional, and trivial?

Our slavish adherence to a rigid and obviously ill-fitting model of sexuality makes a certain amount of sense, on personal, scientific, and psychological levels. The conventional, categorical model is easy to understand; it generates nice, clean predictions; it is politically expedient; it provides psychological comfort. In the final analysis, however, none of these factors are acceptable substitutes for truth. Our ability to understand the complex phenomenon of sexual orientation and its multiple manifestations in men and women at different ages and in different cultures and contexts depends directly on our willingness to confront those aspects of orientation that most confound us. Female sexual fluidity should be at the top of this list. Untold numbers of women have surely found that our current sexual theories leave their own experiences unexplained: a person they inexplicably loved and cannot forget; a summer when everything changed; dreams and fantasies that do not fit; memories of a different self, long ago; expectations of a different self in the future. We cannot allow such experiences to collapse and disappear for want of clear, creative language. Our task is to *create* this language and to start listening.

REFERENCES

NOTES

ACKNOWLEDGMENTS

INDEX

References

Abramson, P. R., C. A. Repczynski, and L. R. Merrill. (1976). The menstrual cycle and response to erotic literature. *Journal of Consulting and Clinical Psychology*, 44, 1018–1019.

Adams, D. B., A. R. Gold, and A. D. Burt. (1978). Rise in female-initiated sexual activity at ovulation and its suppression by oral contraceptives. *New England Journal of Medicine*, 299, 1145–1150.

Ainsworth, M. D. S., M. C. Blehar, E. Waters, and S. Wall. (1978). *Patterns of attachment: A psychological study of the Strange Situation.* Hillsdale, NJ: Lawrence Erlbaum Associates.

Alexander, G. M., and B. B. Sherwin. (1993). Sex steroids, sexual behavior, and selection attention for erotic stimuli in women using oral contraceptives. *Psychoneuroendocrinology*, 18, 91–102.

Amaro, H. (1978). Coming out: Hispanic lesbians, their families and communities. Paper presented at the National Coalition of Hispanic Mental Health and Human Services Organizations, Austin, TX.

Anderson-Hunt, M., and L. Dennerstein. (1995). Oxytocin and female sexuality. *Gynecologic and Obstetric Investigation*, 40, 217–221.

Argiolas, A., M. R. Melis, A. Mauri, and G. L. Gessa. (1987). Paraventricular nucleus lesion prevents yawning and penile erection induced by apomorphine and oxytocin but not by ACTH in rats. *Brain Research*, 421, 349–352.

Arletti, R., and A. Bertolini. (1985). Oxytocin stimulates lordosis behavior in female rats. *Neuropeptides*, 6, 247–253.

Arnow, B. A., J. E. Desmond, L. L. Banner, G. H. Glover, A. Solomon, M. L. Polan, T. F. Lue, and S. W. Atlas. (2002). Brain activation and sexual arousal in healthy, heterosexual males. *Brain: A Journal of Neurology*, 125, 1014–1023.

Aron, A. P., D. G. Dutton, E. N. Aron, and A. Iverson. (1989). Experiences of falling in love. *Journal of Social and Personal Relationships,* 6, 243–257.

Aron, A., H. Fisher, D. J. Mashek, G. Strong, H. Li, and L. L. Brown. (2005). Reward, motivation, and emotion systems associated with early-stage intense romantic love. *Journal of Neurophysiology,* 94, 327–337.

Arver, S., A. S. Dobs, A. W. Meikle, R. P. Allen, S. W. Sanders, and N. A. Mazer. (1996). Improvement of sexual function in testosterone deficient men treated for one year with a permeation enhanced testosterone transdermal system. *Journal of Urology,* 155, 1604–1608.

Bagdy, G., and M. Arato. (1998). Gender-dependent dissociation between oxytocin but not ACTH, cortisol or TSH responses to m-chlorophenylpiperazine in healthy subjects. *Psychopharmacology,* 136, 342–348.

Bailey, J. M. (1995). Sexual orientation revolution. *Nature Genetics,* 11, 353–354.

———. (1996). Gender Identity. In R. C. Savin-Williams and K. M. Cohen, eds., *The lives of lesbians, gays, and bisexuals: Children to adults.* (pp. 71–93). Fort Worth, TX: Harcourt Brace.

———. (2003). Biological perspectives on sexual orientation. In L. D. Garnets and D. C. Kimmel, eds., *Psychological perspectives on lesbian, gay, and bisexual experiences,* 2nd ed. (pp. 50–85). New York: Columbia University Press.

Bailey, J. M., and A. P. Bell. (1993). Familiality of female and male homosexuality. *Behavioral Genetics,* 23, 313–322.

Bailey, J. M., and B. A. Benishay. (1993). Familial aggregation of female sexual orientation. *American Journal of Psychiatry,* 150, 272–277.

Bailey, J. M., and K. Darwood. (1998). Behavioral genetics, sexual orientation, and the family. In C. Patterson and A. R. D'Augelli, eds., *Lesbian, gay, and bisexual identities in families: Psychological perspectives* (pp. 3–18). New York: Oxford University Press.

Bailey, J. M., M. P. Dunne, and N. G. Martin. (2000). Genetic and environmental influences on sexual orientation and its correlates in an Australian twin sample. *Journal of Personality and Social Psychology,* 78, 524–536.

Bailey, J. M., J. Nothnagel, and B. A. Wolfe. (1995). Retrospectively measured individual differences in childhood sex-typed behavior among gay men: A correspondence between self and maternal reports. *Archives of Sexual Behavior,* 24, 613–622.

Bailey, J. M., and M. Oberschneider. (1997). Sexual orientation and professional dance. *Archives of Sexual Behavior,* 26, 433–444.

Bailey, J. M., and R. C. Pillard. (1991). A genetic study of male sexual orientation. *Archives of General Psychiatry,* 48, 1089–1096.

———. (1995). Genetics of human sexual orientation. *Annual Review of Sex Research,* 6, 126–150.

Bailey, J. M., R. C. Pillard, M. C. Neale, and Y. Agyei. (1993). Heritable factors influence sexual orientation in women. *Archives of General Psychiatry,* 50, 217–223.

Bailey, J. M., L. Willerman, and C. Parks. (1991). A test of the maternal stress theory of human male homosexuality. *Archives of Sexual Behavior,* 20, 277–293.

Bailey, J. M., and K. J. Zucker. (1995). Childhood sex-typed behavior and sexual orientation: A conceptual analysis and quantitative review. *Developmental Psychology,* 31, 43–55.

Baldwin, J. D. (1985). The behavior of squirrel monkeys (Saimiri) in natural environments. In L. A. Rosenblum and C. L. Coe, eds., *Handbook of squirrel monkey research* (pp. 33–53). New York: Plenum.

Bancroft, J. H. (1978). The relationships between hormones and sexual behavior in humans. In J. B. Hutchison, ed., *Biological determinants of sexual behavior* (pp. 493–519). Chicester, England: John Wiley.

———. (1989). Sexual desire and the brain. *Sexual and Marital Therapy,* 3, 11–27.

Bancroft, J. H., G. Tennent, K. Loucas, and J. Cass. (1974). The control of deviant sexual behaviour by drugs. I. Behavioural changes following oestrogens and anti-androgens. *British Journal of Psychiatry,* 125, 310–315.

Bartels, A., and S. Zeki. (2000). The neural basis of romantic love. *Neuroreport: For Rapid Communication of Neuroscience Research,* 11, 3829–3834.

Bartz, J. A., and E. Hollander. (2006). The neuroscience of affiliation: Forging links between basic and clinical research on neuropeptides and social behavior. *Hormones and Behavior,* 50, 518–528.

Baum, M. J. (2006). Mammalian animal models of psychosexual differentiation: When is "translation" to the human situation possible? *Hormones and Behavior,* 50, 579–588.

Baumeister, R. F. (2000). Gender differences in erotic plasticity: The female sex drive as socially flexible and responsive. *Psychological Bulletin,* 126, 247–374.

Baumeister, R. F., K. R. Catanese, and K. D. Vohs. (2001). Is there a gender difference in strength of sex drive? Theoretical views, conceptual distinctions, and a review of relevant evidence. *Personality and Social Psychology Review,* 5, 242–273.

Baumeister, R. F., and J. M. Twenge. (2002). Cultural suppression of female sexuality. *Review of General Psychology,* 6, 166–203.

Beach, F. A. (1976). Sexual attractivity, proceptivity, and receptivity in female mammals. *Hormones and Behavior,* 7, 105–138.

Beck, J. G., A. W. Bozman, and T. Qualtrough. (1991). The experience of sexual desire: Psychological correlates in a college sample. *Journal of Sex Research,* 28, 443–456.

Beckett, L. A., B. Rosner, A. F. Roche, and S. Guo. (1992). Serial changes in blood pressure from adolescence into adulthood. *American Journal of Epidemiology,* 135, 1166–1177.

Beckstead, A. L. (2006). Understanding the self-reports of reparative therapy "successes." In J. Drescher and K. J. Zucker, eds., *Ex-gay research: Analyzing the Spitzer study and its relation to science, religion, politics, and culture* (pp. 75–81). Binghamton, NY: Haworth Press.

Bell, A. P., and M. S. Weinberg. (1978). *Homosexualities: A study of diversity among men and women.* Bloomington: Indiana University Press.

Bell, A. P., M. S. Weinberg, and S. K. Hammersmith. (1981). *Sexual preference: Its development in men and women.* Bloomington: Indiana University Press.

Bem, D. J. (1993). *The lenses of gender: Transforming the debate on sexual inequality.* New Haven: Yale University Press.

———. (1996). Exotic becomes erotic: A developmental theory of sexual orientation. *Psychological Review,* 103, 320–335.

Berenbaum, S. A., and M. Hines. (1992). Early androgens are related to childhood sex-typed toy preferences. *Psychological Science,* 3, 203–206.

Berenbaum, S. A., and S. M. Resnick. (1997). Early androgen effects on aggression in children and adults with congenital adrenal hyperplasia. *Psychoneuroendocrinology,* 22, 505–515.

Bergler, E. (1954). Spurious homosexuality. *Psychiatric Quarterly Supplement,* 28, 68–77.

Blackwood, E. (1985). Breaking the mirror: The construction of lesbianism and the anthropological discourse on homosexuality. *Journal of Homosexuality,* 11, 1–17.

———. (2000). Culture and women's sexualities. *Journal of Social Issues,* 56, 223–238.

Blackwood, E., and S. E. Wieringa. (2003). Sapphic shadows: Challenging the silence in the study of sexuality. In L. D. Garnets and D. C. Kimmel, eds., *Psychological perspectives on lesbian, gay, and bisexual experiences,* 2nd ed. (pp. 410–434). New York: Columbia University Press.

Blanchard, R. (1997). Birth order and sibling sex ratio in homosexual versus heterosexual males and females. *Annual Review of Sex Research,* 8, 27–67.

———. (2001). Fraternal birth order and the maternal immune hypothesis of male homosexuality. *Hormones and Behavior,* 40, 105–114.

Blanchard, R., and L. Ellis. (2001). Birth weight, sexual orientation and the sex of preceding siblings. *Journal of Biosocial Science,* 33, 451–467.

Blanchard, R., K. J. Zucker, A. Cavacas, S. Allin, S. J. Bradley, and D. C. Schachter. (2002). Fraternal birth order and birth weight in probably prehomosexual feminine boys. *Hormones and Behavior,* 41, 321–327.

Block, I. (1909). *The sexual life of our time.* London: Heinemann.

Blumstein, P., and P. Schwartz. (1977). Bisexuality: Some social psychological issues. *Journal of Social Issues,* 33, 30–45.

———. (1983). *American couples: Money, work, sex.* New York: Morrow.

———. (1990). Intimate relationships and the creation of sexuality. In D. P. McWhirter, S. A. Sanders, and J. M. Reinisch, eds., *Homosexuality/heterosexuality: Concepts of sexual orientation* (pp. 307–320). New York: Oxford University Press.

Bode, J. (1976). *View from another closet: Exploring bisexuality in women.* New York: Hawthorne.

Bogaert, A. F. (2005). Sibling sex ratio and sexual orientation in men and women: New tests in two national probability samples. *Archives of Sexual Behavior,* 34, 111–116.

268 · References

Bornstein, K. (1994). *Gender outlaw: Men, women, and the rest of us.*
New York: Routledge.
Boswell, J. (1990a). Categories, experience, and sexuality. In E. Stein, ed.,
*Forms of desire: Sexual orientation and the social constructionist
controversy* (pp. 133–173). New York: Garland Publishing.
———. (1990b). Sexual and ethical categories in premodern Europe. In
D. S. McWhirter, S. A. Sanders, and J. M. Reinisch, eds., *Homosexu-
ality/heterosexuality: Concepts of sexual orientation* (pp. 15–31).
New York: Oxford University Press.
Bowlby, J. (1958). The nature of the child's tie to his mother. *International
Journal of Psychoanalysis, 39,* 350–373.
———. (1973a). Affectional bonds: Their nature and origin. In R. W.
Weiss, ed., *Loneliness: The experience of emotional and social isolation* (pp. 38–52). Cambridge, MA: MIT Press.
———. (1973b). *Attachment and loss,* vol. 2: *Separation: Anxiety and an-
ger.* New York: Basic Books.
———. (1973c). *Separation.* New York: Basic Books.
———. (1979). *The making and breaking of affectional bonds.* London:
Tavistock.
———. (1980). *Attachment and loss,* vol. 3: *Loss: Sadness and depression.* New York: Basic Books.
———. (1982). *Attachment and loss,* vol. 1: *Attachment,* 2nd ed. New
York: Basic Books.
Boxer, A., and B. Cohler. (1989). The life course of gay and lesbian youth:
An immodest proposal for the study of lives. *Journal of Homosexuality, 17,* 315–355.
Bradley, S. J., and K. J. Zucker. (1990). Gender identity disorder and
psychosexual problems in children and adolescents. *Canadian Journal of Psychiatry, 35,* 477–486.
———. (1997). Gender identity disorder: A review of the past ten years.
*Journal of the American Academy of Child and Adolescent Psychia-
try, 36,* 872–880.
Brain, R. (1976). *Friends and lovers.* New York: Basic Books.
Breedlove, S. M., B. M. Cooke, and C. L. Jordan. (1999). The orthodox
view of brain sexual differentiation. *Brain, Behavior and Evolution,
54,* 8–14.
Bright, C. (2004). Deconstructing reparative therapy: An examination of
the processes involved when attempting to change sexual orientation.
Clinical Social Work Journal, 32, 471–481.

Brookey, R. A. (2000). Saints or sinners: Sociobiological theories of male homosexuality. *International Journal of Sexuality and Gender Studies, 5,* 37–58.

Brown, L. (1995). Lesbian identities: Concepts and issues. In A. R. D'Augelli and C. Patterson, eds., *Lesbian, gay, and bisexual identities over the lifespan* (pp. 3–23). New York: Oxford University Press.

Brown, W. M., C. J. Finn, B. M. Cooke, and S. M. Breedlove. (2002). Differences in finger length ratios between self-identified "butch" and "femme" lesbians. *Archives of Sexual Behavior, 31,* 123–127.

Brown, W. M., M. Hines, B. A. Fane, and S. M. Breedlove. (2002). Masculinized finger length patterns in human males and females with congenital adrenal hyperplasia. *Hormones and Behavior, 42,* 380–386.

Burch, B. (1993). *On intimate terms: The psychology of difference in lesbian relationships.* Chicago: University of Illinois Press.

Burr, C. (1996). *A separate creation: The search for the biological origins of sexual orientation.* New York: Hyperion.

Buss, D. M. (1989). Sex differences in human mate preferences: Evolutionary hypotheses tested in thirty-seven cultures. *Behavioral and Brain Sciences, 12,* 1–49.

Buss, D. M., and D. P. Schmitt. (1993). Sexual strategies theory: A contextual evolutionary analysis of human mating. *Psychological Review, 100,* 204–232.

Butler, J. P. (1990). *Gender trouble: Feminism and the subversion of identity.* London: Routledge.

Byers, E. S., and L. Heinlein. (1989). Predicting initiations and refusals of sexual activities in married and cohabiting heterosexual couples. *Journal of Sex Research, 26,* 210–231.

Byrd, A. D. (2006). *Homosexuality: The essentialist argument continues to erode.* Retrieved May 11, 2006, from http://www.narth.com/docs/essentialist.html.

Caldwell, J. D. (2002). A sexual arousability model involving steroid effects at the plasma membrane. *Neuroscience and Biobehavioral Reviews, 26,* 13–30.

Caldwell, J. D., A. J. J. Prange, and C. A. Pedersen. (1986). Oxytocin facilitates the sexual receptivity of estrogen-treated female rats. *Neuropeptides, 7,* 175–189.

Caldwell, J. D., C. H. Walker, C. A. Pedersen, A. S. Barakat, and G. A. Mason. (1994). Estrogen increases affinity of oxytocin receptors in the medial preoptic area anterior hypothalamus. *Peptides,* 15, 1079–1084.

Caplan, P. J., M. Crawford, J. S. Hyde, and J. T. R. Richardson. (1997). *Gender differences in human cognition.* New York: Oxford University Press.

Carballo-Dieguez, A. (1989). Hispanic culture, gay male culture, and AIDS: Counseling implications. *Journal of Counseling and Development,* 68, 26–30.

Carballo-Dieguez, A., and C. Dolezal. (1994). Contrasting types of Puerto Rican men who have sex with men (MSM). *Journal of Psychology and Human Sexuality,* 6, 41–67.

Carey, B. (July 5, 2005). *Straight, gay or lying? Bisexuality revisited. New York Times,* p. 1.

Carmichael, M. S., V. L. Warburton, J. Dixen, and J. M. Davidson. (1994). Relationships among cardiovascular, muscular, and oxytocin responses during human sexual activity. *Archives of Sexual Behavior,* 23, 59–79.

Carrier, J. M. (1989). Gay liberation and coming out in Mexico. *Journal of Homosexuality,* 17, 225–252.

Carter, C. S. (1992). Oxytocin and sexual behavior. *Neuroscience and Biobehavioral Reviews,* 16, 131–144.

———. (1998). Neuroendocrine perspectives on social attachment and love. *Psychoneuroendocrinology,* 23, 779–818.

Carter, C. S., and M. Altemus. (1997). Integrative functions of lactational hormones in social behavior and stress management. *Annals of the New York Academy of Science,* 807, 164–174.

Carter, C. S., and A. C. DeVries. (1999). Stress and soothing: An endocrine perspective. In M. Lewis and D. Ramsay, eds., *Soothing and stress* (pp. 3–18). Mahway, NJ: Lawrence Erlbaum Associates.

Carter, C. S., and E. B. Keverne. (2002). The neurobiology of social affiliation and pair bonding. In J. Pfaff, A. P. Arnold, A. E. Etgen, and S. E. Fahrbach, eds., *Hormones, brain and behavior,* vol. 1 (pp. 299–377). New York: Academic Press.

Carter, C. S., I. I. Lederhendler, and B. Kirkpatrick, eds. (1999). *The integrative neurobiology of affiliation.* Cambridge, MA: MIT Press.

Carter, D. (2005). *Stonewall: The riots that sparked the gay revolution.* New York: St. Martin's.

Cass, V. (1979). Homosexual identity formation: A theoretical model. *Journal of Homosexuality, 4*, 219–235.

———. (1990). The implications of homosexual identity formation for the Kinsey model and scale of sexual preference. In D. P. McWhirter, S. A. Sanders, and J. M. Reinisch, eds., *Homosexuality/heterosexuality: Concepts of sexual orientation* (pp. 239–266). New York: Oxford University Press.

Cassingham, B. J., and S. M. O'Neil. (1993). *And then I met this woman: Previously married women's journeys into lesbian relationships.* Freeland, WA: Soaring Eagle Publishing.

Chan, C. S. (1992). Cultural considerations in counseling Asian American lesbians and gay men. In S. H. Dworkin and F. J. Gutierrez, eds., *Counseling gay men and lesbians: Journey to the end of the rainbow* (pp. 115–124). Alexandria, VA: American Association for Counseling and Development.

Chapman, B. E., and J. C. Brannock. (1987). Proposed models of lesbian identity development: An empirical examination. *Journal of Homosexuality, 14*, 69–80.

Charbonneau, C., and P. S. Lander. (1991). Redefining sexuality: Women becoming lesbian in midlife. In B. Sang, J. Warshow, and A. J. Smith, eds., *Lesbians at midlife: The creative transition* (pp. 35–43). San Francisco: Spinsters.

Chivers, M. L., G. Rieger, E. Latty, and J. M. Bailey. (2005). A sex difference in the specificity of sexual arousal. *Psychological Science, 15*, 736–744.

Cho, M. M., A. C. DeVries, J. R. Williams, and C. S. Carter. (1999). The effects of oxytocin and vasopressin on partner preferences in male and female prairie voles (Microtus ochrogaster). *Behavioral Neuroscience, 113*, 1071–1079.

Christman, S. S. (2002). Dynamic systems theory: Application to language development and acquired aphasia. In R. G. Daniloff, ed., *Connectionist approaches to clinical problems in speech and language: Therapeutic and scientific applications.* (pp. 111–146). Hillsdale, NJ: Lawrence Erlbaum Associates.

Clarke, C. (1983). The failure to transform: Homophobia in the black community. In B. Smith, ed., *Home girls: A black feminist anthology* (pp. 197–208). New York: Kitchen Table Press.

Clausen, J. (1999). *Apples and oranges: My journey through sexual identity.* Boston: Houghton Mifflin.

Cochran, S. D., and V. M. Mays. (1988). Disclosure of sexual preferences to physicians by black lesbians and bisexual women. *Western Journal of Medicine,* 149, 616–619.

Cohen-Bendahan, C. C. C., C. van de Beek, and S. A. Berenbaum. (2005). Prenatal sex hormone effects on child and adult sex-typed behavior: Methods and findings. *Neuroscience and Biobehavioral Reviews,* 29, 353–384.

Colapinto, J. (2000). *As nature made him: The boy who was raised as a girl.* New York: HarperCollins Publishers.

Cole, S. S., D. Denny, A. E. Eyler, and S. L. Samons. (2000). Issues of transgender. In L. T. Szuchman and F. Muscarella, eds., *Psychological perspectives on human sexuality.* (pp. 149–195). New York: John Wiley and Sons.

Coleman, E. (1981/1982). Developmental stages of the coming out process. *Journal of Homosexuality,* 7, 31–43.

Coleman, P., and A. Watson. (2000). Infant attachment as a dynamic system. *Human Development,* 43, 295–313.

Collaer, M. L., and M. Hines. (1995). Human behavioral sex differences: A role for gonadal hormones during early development? *Psychological Bulletin,* 118, 55–107.

Collins, P. H. (1990). Homophobia and black lesbians. In P. H. Collins, ed., *Black feminist thought: Knowledge, consciousness, and the politics of empowerment* (pp. 192–196). New York: Routledge.

Coons, F. W. (1972). Ambisexuality as an alternative adaptation. *Journal of the American College Health Association,* 21, 142–144.

Coontz, S., and P. Henderson. (1986). *Women's work, men's property: The origins of gender and class.* London: Verso.

Cooper, M. (1990). Rejecting "femininity": Some research notes on gender identity development in lesbians. *Deviant Behavior,* 11, 371–380.

Corbett, K. (1998). Cross-gendered identifications and homosexual boyhood: Toward a more complex theory of gender. *American Journal of Orthopsychiatry,* 68, 352–360.

———. (1999). Homosexual boyhood: Notes on girlyboys. In M. Rottnek, ed., *Sissies and tomboys: Gender nonconformity and homosexual childhood* (pp. 107–139). New York: New York University Press.

Crumpacker, L., and E. M. Vander Haegen. (1993). Pedagogy and prejudice: Strategies for confronting homophobia in the classroom. *Women's Studies Quarterly,* 21, 94–106.

Curtis, T. J., and Z. Wang. (2003). The neurochemistry of pair bonding. *Current Directions in Psychological Science, 12,* 49–53.

Curtis, W., ed. (1988). *Revelations: A collection of gay male coming out stories.* Boston: Alyson.

Davidson, J. M., C. A. Camargo, and E. R. Smith. (1979). Effects of androgen on sexual behavior in hypogonadal men. *Journal of Clinical Endocrinology* and *Metabolism, 48,* 955–958.

Davis, A. (1999). *Confessions of a LUG.* Flagpole Magazine Online, October 25, 1999.

DeCecco, J. P., and M. Shively. (1984). From sexual identity to sexual relationships: A contractual shift. *Journal of Homosexuality, 9,* 1–26.

Defries, Z. (1976). Pseudohomosexuality in feminist students. *American Journal of Psychiatry, 133,* 400–404.

D'Emilio, J. (1983). Capitalism and gay identity. In D. Morton, ed., *The material queer: A lesbigay cultural studies reader* (pp. 467–475). Boulder, CO: Westview Press.

———. (1983). *Sexual politics, sexual communities.* Chicago: University of Chicago Press.

D'Emilio, J., and E. B. Freedman. (1988). *Intimate matters: A history of sexuality in America.* New York: Harper and Row.

De Monteflores, C. (1986). Notes on the management of difference. In T. Stein and C. Cohen, eds., *Contemporary perspectives on psychotherapy with lesbians and gay men* (pp. 73–101). New York: Plenum.

Depue, R. A., and J. V. Morrone-Strupinsky. (2005). A neurobehavioral model of affiliative bonding: Implications for conceptualizing a human trait of affiliation. *Behavioral and Brain Sciences, 28,* 313–395.

Derlega, V. J., R. J. Lewis, S. Harrison, B. Winstead, and R. Constanza. (1989). Gender differences in the initiation and attribution of tactile intimacy. *Journal of Nonverbal Behavior, 13,* 83–96.

DeVries, A. C., and C. S. Carter. (1999). Sex differences in temporal parameters of partner preference in prairie voles *(Microtus ochrogaster). Canadian Journal of Zoology, 77,* 885–889.

DeVries, A. C., C. L. Johnson, and C. S. Carter. (1997). Familiarity and gender influence social preferences in prairie voles *(Microtus ochrogaster). Canadian Journal of Zoology, 75,* 295–301.

De Wied, D., M. Diamant, and M. Fodor. (1993). Central nervous system effects of the neurohypophyseal hormones and related peptides. *Frontiers in Neuroendocrinology, 14,* 251–302.

Diamond, L. M. (1998). Development of sexual orientation among adolescent and young adult women. *Developmental Psychology,* 34, 1085–1095.

———. (2000a). Passionate friendships among adolescent sexual-minority women. *Journal of Research on Adolescence,* 10, 191–209.

———. (2000b). Sexual identity, attractions, and behavior among young sexual-minority women over a two-year period. *Developmental Psychology,* 36, 241–250.

———. (2002). "Having a girlfriend without knowing it": The relationships of adolescent lesbian and bisexual women. *Journal of Lesbian Studies,* 6, 5–16.

———. (2003a). Was it a phase? Young women's relinquishment of lesbian/bisexual identities over a five-year period. *Journal of Personality and Social Psychology,* 84, 352–364.

———. (2003b). What does sexual orientation orient? A biobehavioral model distinguishing romantic love and sexual desire. *Psychological Review,* 110, 173–192.

———. (2005a). From the heart or the gut? Sexual-minority women's experiences of desire for same-sex and other-sex partners. *Feminism and Psychology,* 15, 10–14.

———. (2005b). A new view of lesbian subtypes: Stable vs. fluid identity trajectories over an eight-year period. *Psychology of Women Quarterly,* 29, 119–128.

———. (2005c). What we got wrong about sexual identity development: Unexpected findings from a longitudinal study of young women. In A. Omoto and H. Kurtzman, eds., *Sexual orientation and mental health: Examining identity and development in lesbian, gay, and bisexual people* (pp. 73–94). Washington, D.C.: American Psychological Association Press.

———. (2006). How do I love thee? Implications of attachment theory for understanding same-sex love and desire. In M. Mikulincer and G. Goodman, eds., *Dynamics of romantic love: Attachment, caregiving, and sex* (pp. 275–292). New York: Guilford.

Diamond, L. M., and R. C. Savin-Williams. (2000). Explaining diversity in the development of same-sex sexuality among young women. *Journal of Social Issues,* 56, 297–313.

Diamond, M. (1993). Homosexuality and bisexuality in different populations. *Archives of Sexual Behavior,* 22, 291–310.

———. (1995). Biological aspects of sexual orientation and identity. In L.

Diamant and R. D. McAnulty, eds., *The psychology of sexual orientation, behavior, and identity: A handbook* (pp. 45–80). Westport, CT: Greenwood Press.

———. (1998). Bisexuality: A biological perspective. In E. J. Haeberle and R. Gindorf, eds., *Bisexualities: The ideology and practice of sexual contact with both men and women* (pp. 53–80). New York: Continuum.

———. (2002). Sex and gender are different: Sexual identity and gender identity are different. *Clinical Child Psychology and Psychiatry, 7,* 320–334.

Dick, D. M., R. J. Rose, R. J. Viken, J. Kaprio, and M. Koskenvuo. (2001). Exploring gene-environment interactions: Socioregional moderation of alcohol use. *Journal of Abnormal Psychology,* 110, 625–632.

Dickerson, S. S., and M. E. Kemeny. (2004). Acute stressors and cortisol responses: A theoretical integration and synthesis of laboratory research. *Psychological Bulletin,* 130, 355–391.

Dittmann, R. W. (1997). Sexual behavior and sexual orientation in females with congenital adrenal hyperplasia. In L. Ellis and L. Ebertz, eds., *Sexual orientation: Toward biological understanding* (pp. 53–69). Westport, CT: Praeger Publishers.

Dixon, J. K. (1984). The commencement of bisexual activity in swinging married women over age thirty. *Journal of Sex Research,* 20, 71–90.

———. (1985). Sexuality and relationship changes in married females following the commencement of bisexual activity. *Journal of Homosexuality,* 11, 115–133.

Dörner, G. (1976). *Hormones and brain differentiation.* Amsterdam: Elsevier.

Downey, J. I., and R. C. Friedman. (1998). Female homosexuality: Classical psychoanalytic theory reconsidered. *Journal of the American Psychoanalytic Association,* 46, 471–506.

Drescher, J. (2002). Sexual conversion ("reparative") therapies: History and update. In B. E. Jones and M. J. Hill, eds., *Mental health issues in lesbian, gay, bisexual, and transgender communities* (pp. 71–91). Arlington, VA: American Psychiatric Publishing.

Drescher, J., and K. J. Zucker, eds. (2006). *Ex-gay research: Analyzing the Spitzer study and its relation to science, religion, politics, and culture.* Binghamton, NY: Haworth Press.

Dunbar, R. (1996). *Grooming, gossip, and the evolution of language.* Cambridge, MA: Harvard University Press.

Ehrhardt, A. A. (1985). Sexual orientation after prenatal exposure to exogenous estrogen. *Archives of Sexual Behavior,* 14, 57–77.

———. (2000). Gender, sexuality, and human development. In J. H. Bancroft, ed., *The role of theory in sex research* (pp. 3–16). Bloomington, IN: Indiana University Press.

Ehrhardt, A. A., H. F. Meyer-Bahlburg, L. R. Rosen, and J. F. Feldman. (1989). The development of gender-related behavior in females following prenatal exposure to diethylstilbestrol (DES). *Hormones and Behavior,* 23, 526–541.

Elise, D. (1997). Primary femininity, bisexuality, and the female ego ideal: A re-examination of female developmental theory. *Psychoanalytic Quarterly,* 66, 489–517.

———. (1998). Gender repertoire: Body, mind, and bisexuality. *Psychoanalytic Dialogues,* 8, 353–371.

Ellis, B. J., and D. Symons. (1990). Sex differences in sexual fantasy: An evolutionary psychological approach. *Journal of Sex Research,* 27, 527–555.

Ellis, H. (1933/1978). *Psychology of sex,* 2nd ed. New York: Harvest/ HBJ.

Ellis, L. (1996). The role of perinatal factors in determining sexual orientation. In R. C. Savin-Williams and K. M. Cohen, eds., *The lives of lesbians, gays, and bisexuals: Children to adults* (pp. 35–70). Fort Worth, TX: Harcourt Brace.

Ellis, L., and M. A. Ames. (1987). Neurohormonal functioning and sexual orientation: A theory of homosexuality-heterosexuality. *Psychological Bulletin,* 101, 233–258.

Ellis, L., and S. Cole-Harding. (2001). The effects of prenatal stress, and of prenatal alcohol and nicotine exposure, on human sexual orientation. *Physiology and Behavior,* 73, 213–226.

Elman, J. L. (1995). Language as a dynamical system. In R. F. Port and T. van Gelder, eds., *Mind as motion: Explorations in the dynamics of cognition* (pp. 195–225). Cambridge, MA: MIT Press.

Emanuele, E., P. Politi, M. Bianchi, P. Minoretti, M. Bertone, and D. Geroldi. (2006). Raised plasma nerve growth factor levels associated with early-stage romantic love. *Psychoneuroendocrinology,* 31, 288–294.

Epstein, S. (1987). Gay politics, ethnic identity: The limits of social constructionism. *Socialist Review, 17,* 9–53.

Erlhagen, W., and G. Schöner. (2002). Dynamic field theory of movement preparation. *Psychological Review,* 109, 545–572.

Espin, O. M. (1984). Cultural and historical influences on sexuality in Hispanic/Latina women: Implications for psychotherapy. In C. Vance, ed., *Pleasure and danger: Exploring female sexuality* (pp. 149–163). London: Routledge and Kegan Paul.

———. (1987). Issues of identity in the psychology of Latina lesbians. In Boston Lesbian Psychologies Collective, ed., *Lesbian psychologies: Explorations and challenges* (pp. 35–51). Urbana: University of Illinois Press.

———. (1993). So, what is a "Boston marriage" anyway? In E. D. Rothblum and A. D. Brehony, eds., *Boston marriages* (pp. 202–207). Amherst: University of Massachusetts Press.

———. (1997). Crossing borders and boundaries: The life narratives of immigrant lesbians. In B. Greene, ed., *Ethnic and cultural diversity among lesbians and gay men* (pp. 191–215). Thousand Oaks, CA: Sage.

Esterberg, K. G. (1994). Being a lesbian and being in love: Constructing identities through relationships. *Journal of Gay and Lesbian Social Services,* 1, 57–82.

Ettore, E. M. (1980). *Lesbians, women, and society.* London: Routledge.

Faderman, L. (1981). *Surpassing the love of men.* New York: William Morrow.

———. (1991). *Odd girls and twilight lovers.* New York: Penguin.

———. (1993). Nineteenth-century Boston marriage as a possible lesson for today. In E. D. Rothblum and K. A. Brehony, eds., *Boston marriages* (pp. 29–42). Amherst: University of Massachusetts Press.

Fausto-Sterling, A. (2000). *Sexing the body: Gender politics and the construction of sexuality.* New York: Basic Books.

Federal Bureau of Investigation. (2004). *Hate Crime Statistics 2004.* Retrieved May 15, 2006, from http://www.fbi.gov/ucr/hc2004/section1.htm.

Feinberg, L. (1996). *Transgender warriors: Making history from Joan of Arc to Dennis Rodman.* Boston: Beacon Press.

Field, T. M. (1998). Massage therapy effects. *American Psychologist, 53,* 1270–1281.

Finder, A., P. D. Healy, and Z. Zernike. (February 22, 2006). President of Harvard resigns, ending stormy five-year tenure. *New York Times*, p. 1.

Fine, M. (1988). Sexuality, schooling, and adolescent females: The missing discourse of desire. *Harvard Educational Review, 58*, 29–53.

Firestein, B. A., ed. (1996). *Bisexuality: The psychology and politics of an invisible minority.* Thousand Oaks, CA: Sage.

Firth, R. W. (1967). *Tikopia ritual and belief.* Boston: Allen and Unwin.

Fisher, H. E. (1998). Lust, attraction, and attachment in mammalian reproduction. *Human Nature, 9*, 23–52.

Floody, O. R., T. T. Cooper, and H. E. Albers. (1998). Injection of oxytocin into the medial preoptic-anterior hypothalamus increases ultrasound production by female hamsters. *Peptides, 19*, 833–839.

Fogel, A. (1993). *Developing through relationships.* Chicago: University of Chicago Press.

Fogel, A., E. Nwokah, J. Y. Dedo, and D. Messinger. (1992). Social process theory of emotion: A dynamic systems approach. *Social Development, 1*, 122–142.

Fogel, A., and E. Thelen. (1987). Development of early expressive and communicative action: Reinterpreting the evidence from a dynamic systems perspective. *Developmental Psychology, 23*, 747–761.

Forel, A. (1908). *The sexual question: A scientific, psychological, hygienic and sociological study,* C. F. Marshall, trans. New York: Physicians and Surgeons Book Company.

Foucault, M. (1980). *The history of sexuality,* vol. I. New York: Vintage.

Fox, R. C. (1995). Bisexual identities. In A. R. D'Augelli and C. Patterson, eds., *Lesbian, gay, and bisexual identities over the lifespan* (pp. 48–86). New York: Oxford University Press.

Freud, S. (1905/1962). *Three essays on the theory of sexuality,* J. Strachey, trans. New York: Basic Books.

Freund, K., and R. Blanchard. (1983). Is the distant relationship of fathers and homosexual sons related to the sons' erotic preference for male partners, or to the sons' atypical gender identity, or to both? *Journal of Homosexuality, 9*, 7–25.

Fuss, D. (1989). *Essentially speaking.* New York: Routledge.

Gagnon, J. H. (1990). Gender preference in erotic relations: The Kinsey scale and sexual scripts. In D. P. McWhirter, S. A. Sanders, and J. M. Reinisch, eds., *Homosexuality/heterosexuality: Concepts of sexual orientation* (pp. 177–207). New York: Oxford University Press.

Gagnon, J. H., and W. Simon. (1968). The social meaning of prison homosexuality. *Federal Probation, 32,* 28–29.

———. (1973). *Sexual conduct: The social sources of human sexuality.* Chicago: Aldine.

Galef, B. G., and H. C. Kaner. (1980). Establishment and maintenance of preference for natural and artificial olfactory stimuli in juvenile rats. *Journal of Comparative Physiology and Psychology, 4,* 588–595.

Garland, J. T., R. D. Morgan, and A. M. Beer. (2005). Impact of time in prison and security level on inmates' sexual attitude, behavior, and identity. *Psychological Services, 2,* 151–162.

Garofalo, R., R. C. Wolf, L. S. Wissow, E. R. Woods, and E. Goodman. (1999). Sexual orientation and risk of suicide attempts among a representative sample of youth. *Archives of Pediatrics and Adolescent Medicine, 153,* 487–493.

Gay, J. (1985). "Mummies and babies" and friends and lovers in Lesotho. Special Issue: Anthropology and homosexual behavior. *Journal of Homosexuality, 11,* 97–116.

Ghali, S. A., B. Gottlieb, R. Lumbroso, L. K. Beitel, Y. Elhaji, J. Wu, L. Pinsky, and M. A. Trifiro. (2003). The use of androgen receptor amino/carboxyl-terminal interaction assays to investigate androgen receptor gene mutations in subjects with varying degrees of androgen insensitivity. *Journal of Clinical Endocrinology and Metabolism, 88,* 2185–2193.

Gilden, D. L. (1991). On the origins of dynamical awareness. *Psychological Review, 98,* 554–568.

Gilligan, C. (1982). *In a different voice: Psychological theory and women's development.* Cambridge, MA: Harvard University Press.

Golden, C. (1987). Diversity and variability in women's sexual identities. In Boston Lesbian Psychologies Collective, ed., *Lesbian psychologies: Explorations and challenges* (pp. 19–34). Urbana: University of Illinois Press.

———. (1994). Our politics and choices: The feminist movement and sexual orientation. In B. Greene and G. M. Herek, eds., *Lesbian and gay psychology: Theory, research, and clinical applications* (pp. 54–70). Thousand Oaks, CA: Sage.

———. (1996). What's in a name? Sexual self-identification among women. In R. C. Savin-Williams and K. M. Cohen, eds., *The lives of lesbians, gays, and bisexuals: Children to adults* (pp. 229–249). Fort Worth, TX: Harcourt Brace.

Golombok, S., and F. Tasker. (1996). Do parents influence the sexual orientation of their children? Findings from a longitudinal study of lesbian families. *Developmental Psychology, 32*, 3–11.

Gomez, J., and B. Smith. (1990). Taking the home out of homophobia: Black lesbian health. In E. C. White, ed., *The black women's health book: Speaking for ourselves* (pp. 198–213). Seattle, WA: Seal.

Gonsiorek, J. C. (2004). Reflections from the conversion therapy battlefield. *Counseling Psychologist, 32*, 750–759.

Goode, E., and L. Haber. (1977). Sexual correlates of homosexual experience: An exploratory study of college women. *Journal of Sex Research, 13*, 12–21.

Gooren, L. (1990a). Biomedical theories of sexual orientation: A critical examination. In D. P. McWhirter, S. A. Sanders, and J. M. Reinisch, eds., *Homosexuality/heterosexuality: Concepts of sexual orientation* (pp. 71–87). New York: Oxford University Press.

———. (1990b). The endocrinology of transsexualism: A review and commentary. *Psychoneuroendocrinology, 15*, 3–14.

———. (2006). The biology of human psychosexual differentiation. *Hormones and Behavior, 50*, 589–601.

Gorzalka, B. B., and G. L. Lester. (1987). Oxytocin-induced facilitation of lordosis behaviour in rats is progesterone-dependent. *Neuropeptides, 10*, 55–65.

Gottschalk, L. (2003). Same-sex sexuality and childhood gender non-conformity: A spurious connection. *Journal of Gender Studies, 12*, 35–50.

Gould, S. J., and R. C. Lewontin. (1979). The spandrels of San Marco and the Panglossian paradigm: A critique of the adaptationist program. *Proceedings of the Royal Society of London*, B 205, 581–598.

Gould, S. J., and E. S. Vrba. (1982). Exaptation: A missing term in the science of form. *Paleobiology, 8*, 4–15.

Gramick, J. (1984). Developing a lesbian identity. In T. Darty and S. Potter, eds., *Women-identified women* (pp. 31–44). Palo Alto, CA: Mayfield.

Granic, I. (2005). Timing is everything: Developmental psychopathology from a dynamic systems perspective. *Developmental Review, 25*, 386–407.

Granic, I., and G. R. Patterson. (2006). Toward a comprehensive model of antisocial development: A dynamic systems approach. *Psychological Review, 113*, 101–131.

Graves, F. C., and M. B. Hennessy. (2000). Comparison of the effects of the mother and an unfamiliar adult female on cortisol and behavioral responses of pre and postweaning guinea pigs. *Developmental Psychobiology*, 36, 91–100.

Green, R. (1987). *The "sissy boy syndrome" and the development of homosexuality.* New Haven, CT: Yale University Press.

Greenberg, A. S., and J. M. Bailey. (1993). Do biological explanations of homosexuality have moral, legal, or policy implications? *Journal of Sex Research*, 30, 245–251.

Greene, B. (1986). When the therapist is white and the patient is black: Considerations for psychotherapy in the feminist heterosexual and lesbian communities. *Women and Therapy*, 5, 41–66.

Grellert, E. A., M. D. Newcomb, and P. M. Bentler. (1982). Childhood play activities of male and female homosexuals and heterosexuals. *Archives of Sexual Behavior*, 11, 451–478.

Griffith, M., and C. E. Walker. (1975). Menstrual cycle phases and personality variables as related to response to erotic stimuli. *Archives of Sexual Behavior*, 4, 599–603.

Groneman, C. (1994). Nymphomania: The historical construction of female sexuality. *Signs: Journal of Women in Culture and Society*, 19, 337–367.

Grosz, E. (1994). *Volatile bodies: Towards a corporeal feminism.* Bloomington, IN: Indiana University Press.

Haldeman, D. C. (1994). The practice and ethics of sexual orientation conversion therapy. *Journal of Consulting and Clinical Psychology*, 62, 221–227.

Hall, L. S., and C. T. Love. (2003). Finger-length ratios in female monozygotic twins discordant for sexual orientation. *Archives of Sexual Behavior*, 32, 23–28.

Halpern, C. T. (2003). Biological influences on adolescent romantic and sexual behavior. In P. Florsheim, ed., *Adolescent romantic relations and sexual behavior: Theory, research, and practical implications.* Mahwah, NJ: Lawrence Erlbaum.

Halpern, D. F., and M. G. Haviland. (1997). The correlates of left-handedness: Moderating variables in the epidemiology of left-handedness. *Annals of Epidemiology*, 7, 165–166.

Halpern, D. F., and S. Ikier. (2002). Causes, correlates, and caveats: Understanding the development of sex differences in cognition. In A. McGillicuddy-De Lisi and R. De Lisi, eds., *Biology, society, and be-*

havior: The development of sex differences in cognition (pp. 3–19). Ablex Publishing.

Halpert, S. C. (2000). "If it ain't broke, don't fix it": Ethical considerations regarding conversion therapies. *International Journal of Sexuality and Gender Studies, 5*, 19–35.

Halsam, N., and S. R. Levy. (2006). Essentialist beliefs about homosexuality: Structure and implications for prejudice. *Personality and Social Psychology Bulletin, 32*, 471–485.

Hamer, D. H., S. Hu, V. L. Magnuson, N. Hu, and A. M. L. Pattatuchi. (1993). A linkage between DNA markers on the X chromosome and male sexual orientation. *Science, 261*, 321–327.

Hamilton College and Zogby International. (2001). High school seniors liberal on gay issues. *USA Today*, 8D.

Hansen, K. V. (1992). "Our eyes behold each other": Masculinity and intimate friendship in antebellum New England. In P. Nardi, ed., *Men's friendships* (pp. 35–58). Newbury Park, CA: Sage.

Harding, S. (1991). *Whose science? Whose knowledge? Thinking from women's lives*. Ithaca, NY: Cornell University Press.

Hatfield, E. (1987). Passionate and companionate love. In R. J. Sternberg and M. L. Barnes, eds., *The psychology of love* (pp. 191–217). New Haven, CT: Yale University Press.

Hatfield, E., E. Schmitz, J. Cornelius, and R. L. Rapson. (1988). Passionate love: How early does it begin? *Journal of Psychology and Human Sexuality, 1*, 35–52.

Hazan, C., and L. M. Diamond. (2000). The place of attachment in human mating. *Review of General Psychology, 4*, 186–204.

Hazan, C., and P. R. Shaver. (1987). Romantic love conceptualized as an attachment process. *Journal of Personality and Social Psychology, 52*, 511–524.

———. (1994). Attachment as an organizational framework for research on close relationships. *Psychological Inquiry, 5*, 1–22.

Hedblom, J. H. (1973). Dimensions of lesbian sexual experience. *Archives of Sexual Behavior, 2*, 329–341.

Heiman, J. R. (1975). The physiology of erotica: Women's sexual arousal. *Psychology Today, 8*, 90–94.

Hencken, J. (1984). Conceptualizations of homosexual behavior which preclude homosexual self-labeling. *Journal of Homosexuality, 9*, 53–63.

Henry, J. P., and S. Wang. (1998). Effects of early stress on adult affiliative behavior. *Psychoneuroendocrinology, 23,* 863–875.

Hensley, C., and R. Tewksbury. (2002). Inmate-to-inmate prison sexuality: A review of empirical studies. *Trauma, Violence, and Abuse, 3,* 226–243.

Hensley, C., J. Wright, M. Koscheski, T. Castle, and R. Tewksbury. (2002). Examining the relationship between female inmate homosexual behavior and attitudes toward homosexuality and homosexuals. *International Journal of Sexuality and Gender Studies, 7,* 293–306.

Herdt, G. (1984). *Ritualized homosexuality in Melanesia.* Berkeley, CA: University of California Press.

Herdt, G., and A. M. Boxer. (1993). *Children of Horizons: How gay and lesbian teens are leading a new way out of the closet.* Boston: Beacon Press.

Herek, G. M. (1986). On heterosexual masculinity: Some psychical consequences of the social construction of gender and sexuality. *American Behavioral Scientist, 29,* 563–577.

Hershberger, S. L. (1997). A twin registry study of male and female sexual orientation. *Journal of Sex Research, 34,* 212–222.

Hidalgo, H. (1984). The Puerto Rican lesbian in the United States. In T. Darty and S. Potter, eds., *Women-Identified women* (pp. 105–150). Palo Alto, CA: Mayfield.

Hill, M. (1993). A matter of language. In E. D. Rothblum and A. D. Brehony, eds., *Boston marriages* (pp. 194–201). Amherst: University of Massachusetts Press.

Hiller, J. (2004). Speculations on the links between feelings, emotions and sexual behaviour: Are vasopressin and oxytocin involved? *Sexual and Relationship Therapy, 19,* 393–429.

Hines, M. (2004a). Androgen, estrogen, and gender: Contributions of the early hormone environment to gender-related behavior. In A. H. Eagly, A. E. Beall, and R. J. Sternberg, eds., *The psychology of gender,* 2nd ed. (pp. 9–37). New York: Guilford Press.

———. (2004b). *Brain gender.* New York: Oxford University Press.

Hines, M., S. F. Ahmed, and I. A. Hughes. (2003). Psychological outcomes and gender-related development in complete androgen insensitivity syndrome. *Archives of Sexual Behavior, 32,* 93–101.

Hines, M., and M. L. Collaer. (1993). Gonadal hormones and sexual differentiation of human behavior: Developments from research on endocrine syndromes and studies of brain structure. *Annual Review of Sex Research,* 4, 1–48.

Hofer, M. A. (1987). Early social relationships: A psychobiologist's view. *Child Development,* 58, 633–647.

Hoffman, K. A., S. P. Mendoza, M. B. Hennessy, and W. A. Mason. (1995). Responses of infant titi monkeys, Callicebus moloch, to removal of one or both parents: Evidence for paternal attachment. *Developmental Psychobiology,* 28, 399–407.

Hollander, G. (2000). Questioning youths: Challenges to working with youths forming identities. *School Psychology Review,* 29, 173–179.

Hrdy, S. B. (1987). The primate origins of human sexuality. In R. Bellig and G. Stevens, eds., *The evolution of sex* (pp. 101–132). San Francisco: Harper and Row.

Hu, S., A. M. L. Pattatucci, C. Patterson, L. Li, D. W. Fulker, S. S. Cherny, L. Kruglyak, and Dean H. Hamer. (1995). Linkage between sexual orientation and chromosome Xq28 in males but not in females. *Nature Genetics,* 11, 248–256.

Hunnisett, R. (1986). Developing phenomenological method for researching lesbian existence. *Canadian Journal of Counseling,* 20, 255–286.

Hyde, J. S. (2005). The genetics of sexual orientation. In J. S. Hyde, ed., *Biological substrates of human sexuality* (pp. 9–20). Washington, DC: American Psychological Association Press.

Hyde, J. S., and A. M. Durik. (2000). Gender differences in erotic plasticity—Evolutionary or sociocultural forces? Comment on Baumeister (2000). *Psychological Bulletin,* 126, 375–379.

Icard, L. (1986). Black gay men and conflicting social identities: Sexual orientation versus racial identity. *Journal of Social Work and Human Sexuality,* 4, 83–93.

Imperato-McGinley, J., R. E. Peterson, T. Gautier, and E. Sturla. (1980). Androgens and the evolution of male-gender identity among male pseudohermaphrodites with 5alpha-reductase deficiency. *Annual Progress in Child Psychiatry and Child Development,* 192–202.

Imperato-McGinley, J., R. E. Peterson, R. Stoller, and W. E. Goodwin. (1999). Gender role change with puberty. In S. J. Ceci and W. M. Williams, eds., *The nature-nurture debate: The essential readings* (pp. 76–80). Blackwell Publishing.

Insel, T. R. (1997). A neurobiological basis of social attachment. *American Journal of Psychiatry,* 154, 726–735.

Insel, T. R., and T. J. Hulihan. (1995). A gender-specific mechanism for pair bonding: Oxytocin and partner preference formation in monogamous voles. *Behavioral Neuroscience,* 109, 782–789.

Insel, T. R., and J. T. Winslow. (1998). Serotonin and neuropeptides in affiliative behaviors. *Biological Psychiatry,* 44, 207–219.

Isay, R. A. (1989). *Being homosexual: Gay men and their development.* New York: Farrar, Straus, and Giroux.

Izard, C. E., B. P. Ackerman, K. M. Schoff, and S. E. Fine. (2000). Self-organization of discrete emotions, emotion patterns, and emotion-cognition relations. In M. D. Lewis and I. Granic, eds., *Emotion, development, and self-organization: Dynamic systems approaches to emotional development* (pp. 15–36). New York: Cambridge University Press.

Jayakar, K. (1994). Women of the Indian subcontinent. In L. Comas-Diaz and B. Greene (Eds.), *Women of color: Integrating ethnic and gender identities in psychotherapy* (pp. 161–181). New York: Guilford.

Jensen, K. L. (1999). *Lesbian epiphanies: Women coming out in later life.* New York: Harrington Park Press.

Judd, H. L., and S. S. C. Yen. (1973). Serum androstenedione and testosterone levels during the menstrual cycle. *Journal of Clinical Endocrinology and Metabolism,* 36, 475–481.

Julien, D., C. Bouchard, M. Gagnon, and A. Pomerleau. (1992). Insiders' views of marital sex: A dyadic analysis. *Journal of Sex Research,* 29, 343–360.

Katz, J. (1976). *Gay American history.* New York: Crowell.

Kendler, K. S., M. C. Neale, L. M. Thornton, S. H. Aggen, S. E. Gilman, and R. C. Kessler. (2002). Cannabis use in the last year in a US national sample of twin and sibling pairs. *Psychological Medicine,* 32, 551–554.

Kendler, K. S., L. M. Thornton, S. E. Gilman, and R. C. Kessler, (2000). Sexual orientation in a U.S. national sample of twin and nontwin sibling pairs. *American Journal of Psychiatry,* 157, 1843–1846.

Kendler, K. S., L. M. Thornton, and N. L. Pedersen. (2000). Tobacco consumption in Swedish twins reared apart and reared together. *Archives of General Psychiatry,* 57, 886–892.

Keverne, E. B., C. M. Nevison, and F. L. Martel. (1999). Early learning and the social bond. In C. S. Carter, I. I. Lederhendler, and B. Kirkpatrick, eds., *The integrative neurobiology of affiliation* (pp. 263–274). Cambridge, MA: MIT Press.

Kinsey, A. C., W. B. Pomeroy, and C. E. Martin. (1948). *Sexual behavior in the human male.* Philadelphia: W. B. Saunders.

Kinsey, A. C., W. B. Pomeroy, C. E. Martin, and P. H. Gebhard. (1953). *Sexual behavior in the human female.* Philadelphia: W. B. Saunders.

Kirk, K. M., J. M. Bailey, M. P. Dunne, and N. G. Martin. (2000). Measurement models for sexual orientation in a community twin sample. *Behavior Genetics,* 30, 345–356.

Kirkpatrick, R. C. (2000). The evolution of human homosexual behavior. *Current Anthropology,* 41, 385–413.

Kirsch, P., C. Esslinger, Q. Chen, D. Mier, S. Lis, S. Siddhanti, H. Gruppe, V. S. Mattay, B. Gallhofer, and A. Meyer-Lindenberg. (2005). Oxytocin modulates neural circuitry for social cognition and fear in humans. *Journal of Neuroscience,* 25, 11489–11493.

Kitzinger, C. (1987). *The social construction of lesbianism.* London: Sage.

———. (1995). Social constructionism: Implications for lesbian and gay psychology. In A. R. D'Augelli and C. Patterson, eds., *Lesbian, gay, and bisexual identities over the lifespan* (pp. 136–161). New York: Oxford University Press.

Kitzinger, C., and S. Wilkinson. (1995). Transitions from heterosexuality to lesbianism: The discursive production of lesbian identities. *Developmental Psychology,* 31, 95–104.

Klein, F. (1993). *The bisexual option,* 2nd ed. New York: Harrington Park Press.

Knight, R. H. (2005). *Born or bred? Science does not support the claim that homosexuality is genetic.* Retrieved May 11, 2006, from http://www.cwfa.org/articledisplay.asp?id=5458anddepartment=CFIandcategoryid=papers.

Knoth, R., K. Boyd, and B. Singer. (1988). Empirical tests of sexual selection theory: Predictions of sex differences in onset, intensity, and time course of sexual arousal. *Journal of Sex Research,* 24, 73–89.

Knox, S. S., and K. Uvnäs-Moberg. (1998). Social isolation and cardiovascular disease: An atherosclerotic pathway? *Psychoneuroendocrinology,* 23, 877–890.

Kogan, L. (2006). Gayle and Oprah—Uncensored. *O, The Oprah Magazine,* August.

Kosfeld, M., M. Heinrichs, P. J. Zak, U. Fischbacher, and E. Fehr. (2005). Oxytocin increases trust in humans. *Nature,* 435, 673–676.

Krafft-Ebing, R. (1882). *Psychopathia sexualis,* M. E. Wedneck, trans. New York: Putnam's.

Kwan, M., W. J. Greenleaf, J. Mann, L. Crapo, and J. M. Davidson.

(1983). The nature of androgen action on male sexuality: A combined laboratory-self-report study on hypogonadal men. *Journal of Clinical Endocrinology and Metabolism, 57,* 557–562.

Kyrakanos, J. (1998). LUGgin' It. *InsideOUT Magazine, 9.*

Laan, E., J. Sonderman, and E. Janssen. (1995). *Straight and lesbian women's sexual responses to straight and lesbian erotica: No sexual orientation effects.* Paper presented at the twenty-first annual meeting of the International Academy of Sex Research, Provincetown, MA.

Lalumiere, M. L., R. Blanchard, and K. J. Zucker. (2000). Sexual orientation and handedness in men and women: A meta-analysis. *Psychological Bulletin, 126,* 575–592.

Laumann, E. O., J. H. Gagnon, R. T. Michael, and F. Michaels. (1994). *The social organization of sexuality: Sexual practices in the United States.* Chicago: University of Chicago Press.

Laumann, E. O., and J. Mahay. (2002). The social organization of women's sexuality. In G. M. Wingood and R. J. DiClemente, eds., *Handbook of women's sexual and reproductive health* (pp. 43–70). New York: Academic/Plenum.

Laumann, E. O., A. Paik, and R. C. Rosen. (1999). Sexual dysfunction in the United States: Prevalence and predictors. *Journal of the American Medical Association, 281,* 537–544.

Lee, J. A. (1977). Going public: A study in the sociology of homosexual liberation. *Journal of Homosexuality, 3,* 47–78.

Leiblum, S. R., and R. C. Rosen. (1988a). Introduction: Changing perspectives on sexual desire. In S. R. Leiblum and R. C. Rosen, eds., *Sexual desire disorders* (pp. 1–17). New York: Guilford.

———. (1988b). *Sexual desire disorders.* New York: Guilford Press.

———. (2000). Introduction: Sex therapy in the age of Viagra. In S. R. Leiblum and R. C. Rosen, eds., *Principles and practice of sex therapy,* 3rd ed. (pp. 1–13). New York: Guilford.

Leitenberg, H., and K. Henning. (1995). Sexual fantasy. *Psychological Bulletin, 117,* 469–496.

Leland, J. (July 17, 1995). Bisexuality. *Newsweek,* 44–50.

LeVay, S. (1991). A difference in hypothalamic structure between heterosexual and homosexual men. *Science, 253,* 1034–1037.

Lewis, M. D. (1995). Cognition-emotion feedback and the self-organization of developmental paths. *Human Development, 38,* 71–102.

———. (2000). The promise of dynamic systems approaches for an integrated account of human development. *Child Development,* 71, 36–43.

Lewis, M. D., S. Zimmerman, T. Hollenstein, and A. V. Lamey. (2004). Reorganization in coping behavior at one and one-half years: Dynamic systems and normative change. *Developmental Science,* 7, 56–73.

Light, K. C., K. M. Grewen, and J. A. Amico. (2005). More frequent partner hugs and higher oxytocin levels are linked to lower blood pressure and heart rate in premenopausal women. *Biological Psychology,* 69, 5–21.

Light, K. C., K. M. Grewen, J. A. Amico, M. Boccia, K. A. Brownley, and J. M. Johns. (2004). Deficits in plasma oxytocin responses and increased negative affect, stress, and blood pressure in mothers with cocaine exposure during pregnancy. *Addictive Behaviors,* 29, 1541–1564.

Light, K. C., T. E. Smith, J. M. Johns, K. A. Brownley, J. A. Hofheimer, and J. A. Amico. (2000). Oxytocin responsivity in mothers of infants: A preliminary study of relationships with blood pressure during laboratory stress and normal ambulatory activity. *Health Psychology,* 19, 560–567.

Lim, M. M., and L. J. Young. (2006). Neuropeptidergic regulation of affiliative behavior and social bonding in animals. *Hormones and Behavior,* 50, 506–517.

Lippa, R. A. (2000). Gender-related traits in gay men, lesbian women, and heterosexual men and women: The virtual identity of homosexual-heterosexual diagnosticity and gender diagnosticity. *Journal of Personality,* 68, 899–926.

———. (2003). Are 2D:4D finger-length ratios related to sexual orientation? Yes for men, no for women. *Journal of Personality and Social Psychology,* 85, 179–188.

———. (2006). Is high sex drive associated with increased sexual attraction to both sexes? It depends on whether you are male or female. *Psychological Science,* 17, 46–52.

Loewenstein, S. F. (1985). On the diversity of love object orientations among women. *Journal of Social Work and Human Sexuality,* 3, 7–24.

Loftus, J. (2001). America's liberalization in attitudes toward homosexuality. *American Sociological Review,* 66, 762–782.

Luisi, M., and F. Franchi. (1980). Double-blind group comparative study of testosterone undecanoate and mesterolone in hypogonadal male patients. *Journal of Endocrinological Investigation, 3*, 305–308.

MacDonald, A. P. (1981). Bisexuality: Some comments on research and theory. *Journal of Homosexuality, 6*, 21–35.

MacInnes, C. (1973). *Loving them both: A study of bisexuality and bisexuals.* London: Martin Brian and O'Keeffe.

Magai, C., and S. H. McFadden. (1995). *The role of emotions in social and personality development: History, theory, and research.* New York: Plenum Press.

Malinowski, B. C. (1929). *The sexual life of savages in northwestern Melanesia.* London: Routledge and Kegan Paul.

Manalansan, M. F. (1996). Double minorities: Latino, black, and Asian men who have sex with men. In R. C. Savin-Williams and K. M. Cohen, eds., *The lives of lesbians, gays, and bisexuals: Children to adults* (pp. 393–415). Fort Worth, TX: Harcourt Brace.

Manning, J. T., B. Fink, N. Neave, and N. Caswell. (2005). Photocopies yield lower digit ratios (2D:4D) than direct finger measurements. *Archives of Sexual Behavior, 34*, 329–333.

Martin, J. I., and D. R. Yonkin. (2006). Transgender identity. In D. F. Morrow and L. Messinger, eds., *Sexual orientation and gender expression in social work practice: Working with gay, lesbian, bisexual, and transgender people* (pp. 105–128). New York: Columbia University Press.

Mason, W. A., and S. P. Mendoza. (1998). Generic aspects of primate attachments: Parents, offspring and mates. *Psychoneuroendocrinology, 23*, 765–778.

Mays, V. M., and S. D. Cochran. (1988). The black women's relationships project: A national survey of black lesbians. In M. Shernoff and W. A. Scott, eds., *The sourcebook on lesbian/gay health care* (pp. 54–62). Washington, DC: National Lesbian and Gay Health Foundation.

Mays, V. M., S. D. Cochran, and S. Rhue. (1993). The impact of perceived discrimination on the intimate relationships of black lesbians. *Journal of Homosexuality, 25*, 1–14.

McCarthy, M. M., and M. Altemus. (1997). Central nervous system actions of oxytocin and modulation of behavior in humans. *Molecular Medicine Today, 3*, 269–275.

McCarthy, M. M., L. M. Kow, and D. W. Pfaff. (1992). Speculations concerning the physiological significance of central oxytocin in maternal behavior. *Annals of the New York Academy of Science,* 652, 70–82.

McClintock, M. K., and G. Herdt. (1996). Rethinking puberty: The development of sexual attraction. *Current Directions in Psychological Science,* 5, 178–183.

McFadden, D. (2002). Masculinization effects in the auditory system. *Archives of Sexual Behavior,* 31, 99–111.

McFadden, D., and C. A. Champlin. (2000). Comparison of auditory evoked potentials in heterosexual, homosexual, and bisexual males and females. *Journal of the Association for Research in Otolaryngology,* 1, 89–99.

McFadden, D., J. C. Loehlin, S. M. Breedlove, R. A. Lippa, J. T. Manning, and Q. Rahman. (2005). A reanalysis of five studies on sexual orientation and the relative length of the 2nd and 4th fingers (the 2D:4D ratio). *Archives of Sexual Behavior,* 34, 341–356.

McFadden, D., J. C. Loehlin, and E. G. Pasanen. (1996). Additional findings on heritability and prenatal masculinization of cochlear mechanisms: Click-evoked otoacoustic emissions. *Hearing Research,* 97, 102–119.

McFadden, D., and E. G. Pasanen. (1998). Comparison of the auditory systems of heterosexuals and homosexuals: Click-evoked otoacoustic emissions. *Proceedings of the National Academy of Sciences of the United States of America,* 95, 2709–2713.

———. (1999). Spontaneous otoacoustic emissions in heterosexuals, homosexuals, and bisexuals. *Journal of the Acoustical Society of America,* 105, 2403–2413.

McGillicuddy-De Lisi, A., and R. De Lisi. (2002). *Biology, society, and behavior: The development of sex differences in cognition.* Ablex Publishing.

McGue, M. (1999). The behavioral genetics of alcoholism. *Current Directions in Psychological Science,* 8, 109–115.

McIntosh, M. (1968). The homosexual role. *Social Problems,* 16, 182–192.

McIntyre, M. H. (2003). Digit ratios, childhood gender role behavior, and erotic role preferences of gay men. *Archives of Sexual Behavior,* 32, 495–497.

Mead, M. (1943). *Coming of age in Samoa: A psychological study of primitive youth.* New York: Penguin.

Mellen, S. L. W. (1982). *The evolution of love:* San Francisco: W. H. Freeman.

Meyer-Bahlburg, H. F. (1979). Sex hormones and female homosexuality: A critical examination. *Archives of Sexual Behavior,* 8, 101–119.

———. (1999). Gender assignment and reassignment in 46,XY pseudohermaphroditism and related conditions. *Journal of Clinical Endocrinology and Metabolism,* 84, 3455–3458.

———. (2005). Gender identity outcome in female-raised 46,XY persons with penile agenesis, cloacal exstrophy of the bladder, or penile ablation. *Archives of Sexual Behavior,* 34, 423–438.

Meyer-Bahlburg, H. F., A. A. Ehrhardt, L. R. Rosen, and R. S. Gruen. (1995). Prenatal estrogens and the development of homosexual orientation. *Developmental Psychology,* 31, 12–21.

Meyer-Bahlburg, H. F. L. (2002). Gender assignment and reassignment in intersexuality: Controversies, data, and guidelines for research. *Advances in Experimental Medicine and Biology,* 511, 199–223.

Migeon, C. J., and A. B. Wisniewski. (2000). Human sex differentiation: From transcription factors to gender. *Hormone Research,* 53, 111–119.

———. (2003). Human sex differentiation and its abnormalities. Best practice and research. *Clinical Obstetrics and Gynaecology,* 17, 1–18.

Minto, C. L., K. L.-M. Liao, G. S. Conway, and S. M. Creighton. (2003). Sexual function in women with complete androgen insensitivity syndrome. *Fertility and Sterility,* 80, 157–164.

Minton, H. L., and G. J. McDonald. (1983). Homosexual identity formation as a developmental process. *Journal of Homosexuality,* 9, 91–104.

Mohr, J., and R. Fassinger. (2000). Measuring dimensions of lesbian and gay male experience. *Measurement and Evaluation in Counseling and Development,* 33, 66–90.

Money, J. (1980). *Love and love sickness: The science of sex, gender differences, and pair-bonding.* Baltimore: Johns Hopkins University Press.

———. (1981). The development of sexuality and eroticism in humankind. *Quarterly Review of Biology,* 56, 379–404.

———. (1987). Sin, sickness, or status? Homosexual gender identity and Psychoneuroendocrinology. *American Psychologist,* 42, 384–399.

———. (1988). *Gay, straight, and in-between: The sexology of erotic orientation.* New York: Oxford University Press.

———. (1990). Agenda and credenda of the Kinsey scale. In D. P. McWhirter, S. A. Sanders, and J. M. Reinisch, eds., *Homosexuality/heterosexuality: Concepts of sexual orientation* (pp. 41–60). New York: Oxford University Press.

———. (2002). Amative orientation: The hormonal hypothesis examined. *Journal of Pediatric Endocrinology and Metabolism,* 15, 951–957.

Morales, E. (1992). Latino gays and Latina lesbians. In S. H. Dworkin and F. J. Gutierrez, eds., *Counseling gay men and lesbians: Journey to the end of the rainbow* (pp. 125–139). Alexandria, VA: American Association for Counseling and Development.

Morrow, S. L., and A. L. Beckstead. (2004). Conversion therapies for same-sex attracted clients in religious conflict: Context, predisposing factors, experiences, and implications for therapy. *Counseling Psychologist,* 32, 641–650.

Mosher, W. D., A. Chandra, and J. Jones. (2005). Sexual behavior and selected health measures: Men and women fifteen to forty-four years of age, United States, 2002. *Advance data from vital and health statistics,* no. 362. Hyattsville, MD: National Center for Health Statistics.

Murray, S. O. (2000). *Homosexualities.* Chicago: University of Chicago Press.

Mustanski, B. S., and J. M. Bailey. (2003). A therapist's guide to the genetics of human sexual orientation. *Sexual and Relationship Therapy,* 18, 429–436.

Mustanski, B. S., J. M. Bailey, and S. Kaspar. (2002). Dermatoglyphics, handedness, sex, and sexual orientation. *Archives of Sexual Behavior,* 31, 113–122.

Mustanski, B. S., M. L. Chivers, and J. M. Bailey. (2002). A critical review of recent biological research on human sexual orientation. *Annual Review of Sex Research,* 13, 89–140.

Mustanski, B. S., M. G. Dupree, C. M. Nievergelt, S. Bocklandt, N. J. Schork, and D. H. Hamer. (2005). A genomewide scan of male sexual orientation. *Human Genetics,* 114, 272–278.

Nardi, P. M. (1992). "Seamless souls": An introduction to men's friendships. In P. Nardi, ed., *Men's friendships* (pp. 1–14). Newbury Park, CA: Sage.

Nathanson, C. A. (1991). *Dangerous passage: The social control of sexuality in women's adolescence.* Philadelphia: Temple University Press.

National Gay, Lesbian, and Bisexual Task Force. (2000). *Legislating equality: A review of laws affecting gay, lesbian, bisexual, and transgendered people in the United States.* Washington, DC: National Gay, Lesbian, and Bisexual Task Force.

Near, H. (1991). *Fire in the rain, singer in the storm: An autobiography.* New York: Quill.

Nelson, E. E., and J. Panksepp. (1996). Oxytocin mediates acquisition of maternally associated odor preferences in preweanling rat pups. *Behavioral Neuroscience,* 110, 583–592.

———. (1998). Brain substrates of infant-mother attachment: Contributions of opioids, oxytocin, and norepinephrine. *Neuroscience and Biobehavioral Reviews,* 22, 437–452.

New, M. I., L. Ghizzoni, and P. W. Speiser. (1996). Update on congenital adrenal hyperplasia. In F. Lifshitz, ed., *Pediatric endocrinology,* vol. 3 (pp. 305–320). New York: Marcel Dekker.

Nichols, M. (1987). Lesbian sexuality: Issues and developing theory. In Boston Lesbian Psychologies Collective, ed., *Lesbian psychologies: Explorations and challenges* (pp. 97–125). Urbana: University of Illinois Press.

———. (1990). Lesbian relationships: Implications for the study of sexuality and gender. In J. C. Gonsiorek and J. D. Weinrich, eds., *Homosexuality: Research implications for public policy* (pp. 350–364). Newbury Park, CA: Sage.

Nicolosi, J., A. D. Byrd, and R. W. Potts. (2000). Retrospective self-reports of changes in homosexual orientation: A consumer survey of conversion therapy clients. *Psychological Reports,* 86, 1071–1088.

O'Carroll, R., C. Shapiro, and J. H. Bancroft. (1985). Androgens, behaviour and nocturnal erection in hypogonadal men: The effects of varying the replacement dose. *Clinical Endocrinology,* 23, 527–538.

O'Connor, P. (1992). *Friendships between women: A critical review.* New York: The Guilford Press.

Oliker, S. J. (1989). *Best friends and marriage: Exchange among women.* Berkeley: University of California Press.

O'Sullivan, L., and E. S. Byers. (1992). College students' incorporation of initiator and restrictor roles in sexual dating interactions. *Journal of Sex Research,* 29, 435–446.

Otis, M. D., and W. F. Skinner. (2004). An exploratory study of differences in views of factors affecting sexual orientation for a sample of lesbians and gay men. *Psychological Reports,* 94, 1173–1179.

Padgug, R. (1992). Sexual matters: On conceptualizing sexuality in history. In E. Stein, ed., *Forms of desire: Sexual orientation and the social constructionist controversy* (pp. 43–67). New York: Routledge.

Panksepp, J. (1998). *Affective neuroscience: The foundations of human and animal emotions.* New York: Cambridge University Press.

Panksepp, J., B. Knutson, and D. L. Pruitt. (1997). Toward a neuroscience of emotion: The epigenetic foundations of emotional development. In M. F. Mascolo and S. Griffin, eds., *What develops in emotional development? Emotions, personality, and psychotherapy* (pp. 53–84). New York: Plenum.

Parker, R. (1989). Youth, identity, and homosexuality: The changing shape of sexual life in contemporary Brazil. *Journal of Homosexuality,* 17, 269–289.

Parkman, F. (1969). *The Oregon Trail.* Madison: University of Wisconsin Press.

Partridge, T. (2005). Are genetically informed designs genetically informative? Comment on McGue, Elkins, Walden, and Iacono (2005) and quantitative behavioral genetics. *Developmental Psychology,* 41, 985–988.

Pattatucci, A. M. L., and D. H. Hamer. (1995). Development and familiality of sexual orientation in females. *Behavior Genetics,* 25, 407–420.

Patterson, C. J. (2003). Children of lesbian and gay parents. In L. D. Garnets and D. C. Kimmel, eds., *Psychological perspectives on lesbian, gay, and bisexual experiences,* 2nd ed. (pp. 497–548). New York: Columbia University Press.

Pedersen, C. A., L. Ahnert, G. Anzenberger, J. Belsky, P. Draper, A. S. Fleming, K. Grosmann, N. Sachser, S. Sommer, D. Tietze, and L. Young. (2005). Beyond infant attachment: The origins of bonding in later life. In C. S. Carter, L. Ahnert, K. E. Grossmann, S. B. Hrdy, M. E. Lamb, S. W. Porges, and N. Sachser, eds., *Attachment and bonding: A new synthesis* (pp. 385–427). Cambridge, MA: MIT Press.

Pedersen, C. A., J. D. Caldwell, C. Walker, and G. Ayers. (1994). Oxytocin activates the postpartum onset of rat maternal behavior in the ventral tegmental and medial preoptic areas. *Behavioral Neuroscience,* 108, 1163–1171.

Penelope, J., and S. J. Wolfe. (1989). *The original coming out stories.* Freedom, CA: Crossing Press.

Peplau, L. A. (2001). Rethinking women's sexual orientation: An interdisciplinary, relationship-focused approach. *Personal Relationships, 8,* 1–19.

Peplau, L. A., and S. D. Cochran. (1990). A relationship perspective on homosexuality. In D. P. McWhirter, S. A. Sanders, and J. M. Reinisch, eds., *Homosexuality/heterosexuality: The Kinsey scale and current research* (pp. 321–349). New York: Oxford University Press.

Peplau, L. A., and L. D. Garnets. (2000). A new paradigm for understanding women's sexuality and sexual orientation. *Journal of Social Issues, 56,* 329–350.

Peplau, L. A., and L. R. Spalding. (2000). The close relationships of lesbians, gay men, and bisexuals. In C. Hendrick and S. S. Hendrick, eds., *Close relationships: A sourcebook* (pp. 111–123). Thousand Oaks, CA: Sage.

Peplau, L. A., L. R. Spalding, T. D. Conley, and R. C. Veniegas. (1999). The development of sexual orientation in women. *Annual Review of Sex Research, 10,* 70–99.

Pew Research Center for the People and the Press. (2006). *Less opposition to gay marriage, adoption and military service.* Retrieved May 15, 2006, from http://people-press.org/reports/display.php3?ReportID= 273.

Phillips, G., and R. Over. (1992). Adult sexual orientation in relation to memories of childhood gender conforming and gender nonconforming behaviors. *Archives of Sexual Behavior, 21,* 543–558.
———. (1995). Differences between heterosexual, bisexual, and lesbian women in recalled childhood experiences. *Archives of Sexual Behavior, 24,* 1–20.

Pickering, T. G. (2003). Men are from Mars, women are from Venus: Stress, pets, and oxytocin. *Journal of Clinical Hypertension, 5,* 86–88.

Pillard, R. C. (1990). The Kinsey scale: Is it familial? In D. P. McWhirter, S. A. Sanders, and J. M. Reinisch, eds., *Homosexuality/heterosexuality: Concepts of sexual orientation* (pp. 88–100). New York: Oxford University Press.

Pleck, E., and J. Pleck. (1980). *The American man.* Englewood Cliffs, NJ: Prentice Hall.

Plummer, D. C. (2001). The quest for modern manhood: Masculine stereotypes, peer culture and the social significance of homophobia. *Journal of Adolescence, 24,* 15–23.

Plummer, K. (1975). *Sexual stigma: An interactionist account*. Boston: Routledge and Kegan Paul.

———. (1995). *Telling sexual stories*. New York: Routledge.

———, ed. (1981). *The making of the modern homosexual*. London: Hutchinson.

Ponse, B. (1978). *Identities in the lesbian world: The social construction of self*. Westport, CT: Greenwood Press.

———. (1984). The problematic meanings of "lesbian." In J. D. Douglas, ed., *The sociology of deviance* (pp. 25–33). Boston: Allyn and Bacon.

Popik, P., J. Vetulani, and J. M. van Ree. (1992). Low doses of oxytocin facilitate social recognition in rats. *Psychopharmacology, 106*, 71–74.

Pratt, M. B. (1995). *S/he*. Ithaca, NY: Firebrand Books.

Purcell, D. W., R. Blanchard, and K. J. Zucker. (2000). Birth order in a contemporary sample of gay men. *Archives of Sexual Behavior, 29*, 349–356.

Rahman, Q. (2005). Fluctuating asymmetry, second to fourth finger length ratios and human sexual orientation. *Psychoneuroendocrinology, 30*, 382–391.

Rahman, Q., and G. D. Wilson. (2003). Born gay? The psychobiology of human sexual orientation. *Personality and Individual Differences, 34*, 1337–1382.

Ramos, J., ed. (1994). *Companeras: Latina lesbians*. New York: Routledge.

Read, S. J., and L. C. Miller. (2002). Virtual personalities: A neural network model of personality. *Personality and Social Psychology Review, 6*, 357–369.

Redoute, J., S. Stoleru, M. C. Gregoire, N. Costes, L. Cinotti, F. Lavenne, D. Le Bars, M. G. Forest, and J.-F. Pujol. (2000). Brain processing of visual sexual stimuli in human males. *Human Brain Mapping, 11*, 162–177.

Regan, P. C., and E. Berscheid. (1995). Gender differences in beliefs about the causes of male and female sexual desire. *Personal Relationships, 2*, 345–358.

Reina, R. (1966). *The law of the saints: A Pokoman pueblo and its community culture*. Indianapolis, IN: Bobbs-Merrill.

Reiner, W. G., and J. P. Gearhart. (2004). Discordant sexual identity in some genetic males with cloacal exstrophy assigned to female sex at birth. *New England Journal of Medicine, 350*, 333–341.

Reinisch, J. M., and S. A. Sanders. (1992). Prenatal hormonal contributions to sex differences in human cognitive and personality development. In A. A. Gerall, H. Moltz, and I. L. Ward, eds., *Sexual differentiation* (pp. 221–243). New York: Plenum Press.

Reiss, I. L. (1986). A sociological journey into sexuality. *Journal of Marriage and the Family,* 48, 233–242.

Remafedi, G., M. Resnick, R. Blum, and L. Harris. (1992). Demography of sexual orientation in adolescents. *Pediatrics,* 89, 714–721.

Rice, G., C. Anderson, N. Risch, and G. Ebers. (1999). Male homosexuality: Absence of linkage to microsatellite markers at Xq28. *Science,* 284, 665–667.

Rich, A. (1979). It is the lesbian in us. In A. Rich, *On lies, secrets, and silence* (pp. 199–202). New York: Norton.

———. (1980). Compulsory heterosexuality and lesbian existence. *Signs: Journal of Women in Culture and Society,* 5, 631–660.

Richards, J. (1987). "Passing the love of women": Manly love and Victorian society. In J. A. Mangan and J. Walvin, eds., *Manliness and morality: Middle-class masculinity in Britain and America, 1800–1940* (pp. 92–122). Manchester, England: Manchester University Press.

Richardson, D. (1984). The dilemma of essentiality in homosexual theory. *Journal of Homosexuality,* 9, 79–90.

———. (1987). Recent challenges to traditional assumptions about homosexuality: Some implications for practice. *Journal of Homosexuality,* 13, 1–12.

Richardson, D., and J. Hart. (1981). The development and maintenance of a homosexual identity. In J. Hart and D. Richardson, eds., *The theory and practice of homosexuality.* London: Routledge and Kegan Paul.

Richgels, P. B. (1992). Hypoactive sexual desire in heterosexual women: A feminist analysis. *Women and Therapy,* 12, 123–135.

Rieger, G., J. M. Bailey, and M. L. Chivers. (2005). Sexual arousal patterns of bisexual men. *Psychological Science,* 16, 579–584.

Riley, A. J. (1988). Oxytocin and coitus. *Sexual and Marital Therapy,* 3, 29–36.

Rimer, S. (June 5, 1993). Campus lesbians step into unfamiliar light. *New York Times,* p. A2.

Risch, N., E. Squires-Wheeler, and B. J. Keats. (1993). Male sexual orientation and genetic evidence. *Science,* 262, 2063–2065.

Robinson, S. J., and J. T. Manning. (2000). The ratio of second to fourth digit length and male homosexuality. *Evolution and Human Behavior,* 21, 333–345.

Roen, K. (2002). "Either/or" and "both/neither": Discursive tensions in transgender politics. *Signs: Journal of Women in Culture and Society,* 27, 501–522.

Rosario, M., H. F. Meyer-Bahlburg, J. Hunter, T. M. Exner, M. Gwadz, and A. M. Keller. (1996). The psychosexual development of urban lesbian, gay, and bisexual youths. *Journal of Sex Research,* 33, 113–126.

Rosario, M., E. W. Schrimshaw, J. Hunter, and L. Braun. (2006). Sexual identity development among lesbian, gay, and bisexual youths: Consistency and change over time. *Journal of Sex Research,* 43, 46–58.

Rose, S., D. Zand, and M. A. Cimi. (1993). Lesbian courtship scripts. In E. D. Rothblum and K. A. Brehony, eds., *Boston marriages* (pp. 70–85). Amherst: University of Massachusetts Press.

Rosenbloom, S. (August 11, 2005). She's so cool, so smart, so beautiful: Must be a girl crush. *New York Times,* p. 1.

Ross, E., and R. Rapp. (1981). Sex and society: A research note from social history and anthropology. *Comparative Studies in Society and History,* 23, 51–72.

Ross, M. W., S.-A. Månsson, K. Daneback, and R. Tikkanen. (2005). Characteristics of men who have sex with men on the internet but identify as heterosexual, compared with heterosexually identified men who have sex with women. *CyberPsychology and Behavior,* 8, 131–139.

Ross, M. W., and J. P. Paul. (1992). Beyond gender: The basis of sexual attraction in bisexual men and women. *Psychological Reports,* 71, 1283–1290.

Rothblum, E. D. (1993). Early memories, current realities. In E. D. Rothblum and K. A. Brehony, eds., *Boston marriages* (pp. 14–18). Amherst, MA: University of Massachusetts Press.

Rotundo, E. A. (1989). Romantic friendships: Male intimacy and middle-class youth in the northern United States, 1800–1900. *Journal of Social History,* 23, 1–25.

Rubin, L. (1985). *Just friends: The role of friendship in our lives.* New York: Harper and Row.

Russell, S. T., and T. B. Consolacion. (2003). Adolescent romance and emotional health in the U.S.: Beyond binaries. *Journal of Clinical Child and Adolescent Psychology, 32,* 499–508.

Rust, P. C. R. (1992). The politics of sexual identity: Sexual attraction and behavior among lesbian and bisexual women. *Social Problems, 39,* 366–386.

———. (1993). Coming out in the age of social constructionism: Sexual identity formation among lesbians and bisexual women. *Gender and Society, 7,* 50–77.

———. (1995). *Bisexuality and the challenge to lesbian politics: Sex, loyalty, and revolution.* New York: New York University Press.

———. (2000a). Academic literature on situational homosexuality in the 1960s and 1970s. In P. C. R. Rust, ed., *Bisexuality in the United States: A reader and guide to the literature* (pp. 221–249). New York: Columbia University Press.

———. (2000b). Alternatives to binary sexuality: Modeling bisexuality. In P. C. R. Rust, ed., *Bisexuality in the United States: A reader and guide to the literature* (pp. 33–54). New York: Columbia University Press.

———. (2000c). The biology, psychology, sociology, and sexuality of bisexuality. In P. C. R. Rust, ed., *Bisexuality in the United States: A reader and guide to the literature* (pp. 471–497). New York: Columbia University Press.

———. (2000d). *Bisexuality in the United States: A reader and guide to the literature.* New York: Columbia University Press.

———. (2000e). Heterosexual gays, heterosexual lesbians, and homosexual straights. In P. C. R. Rust, ed., *Bisexuality in the United States: A reader and guide to the literature* (pp. 279–306). New York: Columbia University Press.

———. (2000f). Popular images and the growth of bisexual community and visibility. In P. C. R. Rust, ed., *Bisexuality in the United States: A reader and guide to the literature* (pp. 537–553). New York: Columbia University Press.

———. (2003). Finding a sexual identity and community: Therapeutic implications and cultural assumptions in scientific models of coming out. In L. D. Garnets and D. C. Kimmel, eds., *Psychological perspectives on lesbian, gay, and bisexual experiences,* 2nd ed. (pp. 227–269). New York: Columbia University Press.

———. (2006). Reparative science and social responsibility: The concept of a malleable core as theoretical challenge and psychological comfort. In J. Drescher and K. J. Zucker, eds., *Ex-gay research: Analyzing the Spitzer study and its relation to science, religion, politics, and culture* (pp. 171–177). Binghamton, NY: Haworth Press.

Ryan, G. W., and H. R. Bernard. (2003). Techniques to identify themes. *Field Methods,* 15, 85–109.

Safe Schools Coalition of Washington. (1999). *Selected findings of eight population-based studies as they pertain to anti-gay harassment and the safety and well-being of sexual minority students.* Retrieved May 15, 2006, from http://www.safeschoolscoalition.org/83000youth.pdf.

Saghir, M. T., and E. Robins. (1973). *Male and female homosexuality: A comprehensive investigation.* Baltimore, MD: Williams and Wilkins.

Sahli, N. (1979). Smashing: Women's relationships before the fall. *Chrysalis,* 8, 17–27.

Salmimies, P., G. Kockott, K. M. Pirke, H. J. Vogt, and W. B. Schill. (1982). Effects of testosterone replacement on sexual behavior in hypogonadal men. *Archives of Sexual Behavior,* 11, 345–353.

Salonia, A., R. E. Nappi, M. Pontillo, R. Daverio, A. Smeraldi, A. Briganti, F. Fabbri, G. Zanni, P. Rigatti, and F. Montorsi. (2005). Menstrual cycle–related changes in plasma oxytocin are relevant to normal sexual function in healthy women. *Hormones and Behavior,* 47, 164–169.

Sameroff, A. (1975). Transactional models in early social relations. *Human Development,* 18, 65–79.

San Francisco Department of Public Health (SFDPH). (1993). *Health behaviors among lesbian and bisexual women: A community-based women's health survey.* San Francisco, CA: SFDPH, Prevention Services Branch, AIDS Office.

Sarrel, P., B. Dobay, and B. Wiita. (1998). Estrogen and estrogen-androgen replacement in postmenopausal women dissatisfied with estrogen-only therapy: Sexual behavior and neuroendocrine responses. *Journal of Reproductive Medicine,* 43, 847–856.

Savin-Williams, R. C. (1990). *Gay and lesbian youth: Expressions of identity.* Washington, DC: Hemisphere.

———. (1996). Ethnic- and sexual-minority youth. In R. C. Savin-Williams and K. M. Cohen, eds., *The lives of lesbians, gays, and bisexuals: Children to adults* (pp. 152–165). Fort Worth, TX: Harcourt Brace.

———. (1998). *". . . and then I became gay": Young men's stories.* New York: Routledge.

———. (2005). *The new gay teenager.* Cambridge, MA: Harvard University Press.

Savin-Williams, R. C., and L. M. Diamond. (2000). Sexual identity trajectories among sexual-minority youths: Gender comparisons. *Archives of Sexual Behavior,* 29, 607–627.

———. (2004). Sex. In R. M. Lerner and L. Steinberg, eds., *Handbook of Adolescent Psychology* (pp. 189–231). New York: Wiley.

Schafer, S. (1977). Sociosexual behavior in male and female homosexuals. *Archives of Sexual Behavior,* 6, 355–364.

Schiavi, R. C., D. White, J. Mandeli, and A. C. Levine. (1997). Effect of testosterone administration on sexual behavior and mood in men with erectile dysfunction. *Archives of Sexual Behavior,* 26, 231–241.

Schlegel, A., and H. Barry III. (1991). *Adolescence: An anthropological inquiry.* New York: The Free Press.

Schroeder, M., and A. Shidlo. (2001). Ethical issues in sexual orientation conversion therapies: An empirical study of consumers. *Journal of Gay and Lesbian Psychotherapy,* 5, 131–166.

Schutte, A. R., and J. P. Spencer. (2002). Generalizing the dynamic field theory of the A-not-B error beyond infancy: Three-year-olds' delay- and experience-dependent location memory biases. *Child Development,* 73, 377–404.

Schwarzberg, H., G. L. Kovács, G. Szabó, and G. Telegdy. (1981). Intraventricular administration of vasopressin and oxytocin effects the steady-state levels of serotonin, dopamine and norepinephrine in rat brain. *Endocrinologia Experimentalis,* 15, 75–80.

Sears, J. T. (1989). The impact of gender and race on growing up lesbian and gay in the South. *National Women's Studies Association Journal,* 1, 422–457.

Sell, R. L., and C. Petrulio. (1996). Sampling homosexuals, bisexuals, gays, and lesbians for public health research: A review of the literature from 1990 to 1992. *Journal of Homosexuality,* 30, 31–47.

Shackelford, T. K., and A. T. Goetz. (2006). Comparative evolutionary psychology of sperm competition. *Journal of Comparative Psychology,* 120, 139–146.

Shackelford, T. K., and N. Pound, eds. (2005). *Sperm competition in humans: Classic and contemporary readings.* New York: Springer.

Shackelford, T. K., N. Pound, and A. T. Goetz. (2005). Psychological and physiological adaptations to sperm competition in humans. *Review of General Psychology,* 9, 228–248.

Sherwin, B. B., and M. M. Gelfand. (1987). The role of androgen in the maintenance of sexual functioning in oophorectomized women. *Psychosomatic Medicine*, 49, 397–409.

Sherwin, B. B., M. M. Gelfand, and W. Brender. (1985). Androgen enhances sexual motivation in females: A prospective, crossover study of sex steroid administration in the surgical menopause. *Psychosomatic Medicine*, 47, 339–351.

Shuster, R. (1987). Sexuality as a continuum: The bisexual identity. In Boston Lesbian Psychologies Collective, ed., *Lesbian psychologies: Explorations and challenges* (pp. 56–71). Urbana, IL: University of Illinois Press.

Silber, L. J. (1990). Negotiating sexual identity: Non-lesbians in a lesbian feminist community. *Journal of Sex Research*, 27, 131–139.

Skakkebaek, N. E., J. H. Bancroft, D. W. Davidson, and P. Warner. (1981). Androgen replacement with oral testosterone undecanoate in hypogonadal men: A double blind controlled study. *Clinical Endocrinology*, 14, 49–61.

Slob, A. K., M. Ernste, and J. J. van der Werff ten Bosch. (1991). Menstrual cycle phase and sexual arousability in women. *Archives of Sexual Behavior*, 20, 567–577.

Small, M. F. (1993). *Female choices: Sexual behavior of human primates.* Ithaca, NY: Cornell University Press.

Smith, A. (1997). Cultural diversity and the coming-out process: Implications for clinical practice. In B. Greene, ed., *Ethnic and cultural diversity among lesbians and gay men,* vols. 279–300. Thousand Oaks, CA: Sage.

Smith-Rosenberg, C. (1975). The female world of love and ritual: Relations between women in nineteenth century America. *Signs: Journal of Women in Culture and Society*, 1, 1–29.

Sophie, J. (1986). A critical examination of stage theories of lesbian identity development. *Journal of Homosexuality*, 12, 39–51.

Spitzer, R. L. (2003). Can some gay men and lesbians change their sexual orientation? Two hundred participants reporting a change from homosexual to heterosexual orientation. *Archives of Sexual Behavior*, 32, 403–417.

Stanislaw, H., and F. J. Rice. (1988). Correlation between sexual desire and menstrual cycle characteristics. *Archives of Sexual Behavior*, 17, 499–508.

Stanley, J. P., and S. J. Wolfe. (1980). *The coming out stories*. Watertown, MA: Persephone Press.

Steenbeek, H., and P. van Geert. (2005). A dynamic systems model of dyadic interaction during play of two children. *European Journal of Developmental Psychology*, 2, 105–145.

Stein, E. (1994). The relevance of scientific research about sexual orientation to lesbian and gay rights. *Journal of Homosexuality*, 27, 269–308.

Stein, T. S. (1996). A critique of approaches to changing sexual orientation. In R. P. Cabaj and T. S. Stein, eds., *Textbook of homosexuality and mental health* (pp. 525–537). Washington, DC: American Psychiatric Press.

Stokes, J. P., W. Damon, and D. J. McKirnan. (1997). Predictors of movement toward homosexuality: A longitudinal study of bisexual men. *Journal of Sex Research*, 34, 304–312.

Stokes, J. P., D. McKirnan, and R. Burzette. (1993). Sexual behavior, condom use, disclosure of sexuality, and stability of sexual orientation in bisexual men. *Journal of Sex Research*, 30, 203–213.

Stokes, J. P., R. L. Miller, and R. Mundhenk. (1998). Toward an understanding of behaviourally bisexual men: The influence of context and culture. *Canadian Journal of Human Sexuality*, 7, 101–113.

Stoller, R. J., and G. H. Herdt. (1985). Theories of origins of male homosexuality: A cross-cultural look. *Archives of General Psychiatry*, 42, 399–404.

Straub, K., and J. Epstein, eds. (1991). *Body guards: The cultural politics of gender ambiguity*. New York: Routledge.

Streitmatter, R., ed. (1998). *Empty without you: The intimate letters of Eleanor Roosevelt and Lorena Hickok*. New York: Simon and Schuster.

Suomi, S. J. (1999). Attachment in rhesus monkeys. In J. Cassidy and P. R. Shaver, eds., *Handbook of attachment: Theory, research, and clinical applications* (pp. 181–197). New York: Guilford.

Suppe, F. (1984). In defense of a multidimensional approach to sexual identity. *Journal of Homosexuality*, 10, 7–14.

Taylor, S. E., S. S. Dickerson, and L. C. Klein. (2002). Toward a biology of social support. In C. R. Snyder and S. J. Lopez, eds., *Handbook of positive psychology* (pp. 556–569). New York: Oxford University Press.

Taylor, S. E., L. C. Klein, B. P. Lewis, T. L. Gruenewald, R. A. R. Gurung, and J. A. Updegraff. (2000). Biobehavioral responses to stress in females: Tend-and-befriend, not fight-or-flight. *Psychological Review,* 107, 411–429.

Taywaditep, K. J., and J. P. Stokes. (1998). Male bisexualities: A cluster analysis of men with bisexual experience. *Journal of Psychology and Human Sexuality,* 10, 15–41.

Tennov, D. (1979). *Love and limerence: The experience of being in love.* New York: Stein and Day.

Thelen, E. (2005). Dynamic systems theory and the complexity of change. *Psychoanalytic Dialogues,* 15, 255–283.

Thelen, E., J. A. S. Kelso, and A. Fogel. (1987). Self-organizing systems and infant motor development. *Developmental Review,* 7, 39–65.

Thelen, E., and L. B. Smith. (1994). *A dynamic systems approach to the development of cognition and action.* Cambridge, MA: MIT Press.

Tiefer, L. (2001). The selling of "female sexual dysfunction." *Journal of Sex and Marital Therapy,* 27, 625–628.

Tiefer, L., M. Hall, and C. Tavris. (2002). Beyond dysfunction: A new view of women's sexual problems. *Journal of Sex and Marital Therapy,* 28, 225–232.

Tolman, D. L. (1991). Adolescent girls, women and sexuality: Discerning dilemmas of desire. *Women and Therapy,* 11, 55–69.

———. (2002). *Dilemma of desire: Teenage girls and sexuality.* Cambridge, MA: Harvard University Press.

Tolman, D. L., and L. M. Diamond. (2001). Desegregating sexuality research: Combining cultural and biological perspectives on gender and desire. *Annual Review of Sex Research,* 12, 33–74.

Tolman, D. L., M. I. Striepe, and T. Harmon. (2003). Gender matters: Constructing a model of adolescent sexual health. *Journal of Sex Research,* 40, 4–12.

Traub, J. (January 23, 2005). Lawrence Summers, provocateur. *New York Times,* p. 4.

Tremble, B., M. Schneider, and C. Appathurai. (1989). Growing up gay or lesbian in a multicultural context. *Journal of Homosexuality,* 17, 253–267.

Trivers, R. L. (1972). Parental investment and sexual selection. In B. Campbell, ed., *Sexual selection and the descent of man* (pp. 1136–1179). Chicago: Aldine.

Troiden, R. (1988). *Gay and lesbian identity: A sociological analysis.* Six Hills, NY: General Hall.

Troiden, R. R. (1979). Becoming homosexual: A model of gay identity acquisition. *Psychiatry,* 42, 362–373.

Tucker, J. S., J. C. Cullen, R. R. Sinclair, and W. W. Wakeland. (2005). Dynamic systems and organizational decision-making processes in nonprofits. *Journal of Applied Behavioral Science,* 41, 482–502.

Turner, R. A., M. Altemus, T. Enos, B. Cooper, and T. McGuinness. (1999). Preliminary research on plasma oxytocin in normal cycling women: Investigating emotion and interpersonal distress. *Psychiatry,* 62, 97–113.

Turner, R. A., M. Altemus, D. N. Yip, E. Kupferman, D. Fletcher, A. Bostrom, D. M. Lyons, and J. A. Amico. (2002). Effects of emotion on oxytocin, prolactin, and ACTH in women. *Stress: The International Journal on the Biology of Stress,* 5, 269–276.

Tygart, C. E. (2000). Genetic causation attribution and public support of gay rights. *International Journal of Public Opinion Research,* 12, 259–275.

Uckert, S., A. J. Becker, B. O. Ness, C. G. Stief, F. Scheller, W. H. Knapp, and U. Jonas. (2003). Oxytocin plasma levels in the systemic and cavernous blood of healthy males during different penile conditions. *World Journal of Urology,* 20, 323–326.

Udry, J. R. (1988). Biological predispositions and social control in adolescent sexual behavior. *American Sociological Review,* 53, 709–722.

———. (1990). Hormonal and social determinants of adolescent sexual initiation. In J. H. Bancroft and J. M. Reinisch, eds., *Adolescence and puberty* (pp. 70–87). New York: Oxford University Press.

———. (1993). The politics of sex research. *Journal of Sex Research,* 30, 103–110.

———. (1995). Sociology and biology: What biology do sociologists need to know? *Social Forces,* 73, 1267–1278.

Udry, J. R., and J. O. G. Billy. (1987). Initiation of coitus in early adolescence. *American Sociological Review,* 52, 841–855.

Udry, J. R., L. M. Talbert, and N. M. Morris. (1986). Biosocial foundations for adolescent female sexuality. *Demography,* 23, 217–230.

Ussher, J. M. (1993). The construction of female sexual problems: Regulating sex, regulating woman. In J. M. Ussher and C. D. Baker, eds., *Psychological perspectives on sexual problems: New directions in theory and practice* (pp. 9–40). New York: Routledge.

Ussher, J. M., and C. D. Baker, eds. (1993). *Psychological perspectives on sexual problems: New directions in theory and practice.* New York: Routledge.

Uvnäs-Moberg, K. (1994). Role of efferent and afferent vagal nerve activity during reproduction: Integrating function of oxytocin on metabolism and behavior. *Psychoneuroendocrinology, 19,* 687–695.

———. (1998). Oxytocin may mediate the benefits of positive social interaction and emotions. *Psychoneuroendocrinology, 23,* 819–835.

———. (2004). *The oxytocin factor: Tapping the hormone of calm, love, and healing,* R. W. Francis, trans. Cambridge, MA: Da Capo Press.

Uvnäs-Moberg, K., G. Bruzelius, P. Alster, and T. Lundeberg. (1993). The antinociceptive effect of non-noxious sensory stimulation is mediated partly through oxytocinergic mechanisms. *Acta Physiologica Scandinavica, 149,* 199–204.

Uvnäs-Moberg, K., and M. Eriksson. (1996). Breastfeeding: Physiological, endocrine and behavioural adaptations caused by oxytocin and local neurogenic activity in the nipple and mammary gland. *Acta Paediatrica, 85,* 525–530.

van Anders, S. M., and E. Hampson. (2005). Testing the prenatal androgen hypothesis: Measuring digit ratios, sexual orientation, and spatial abilities in adults. *Hormones and Behavior, 47,* 92–98.

Vance, B. K., and V. Green. (1984). Lesbian identities: An examination of sexual behavior and sex role acquisition as related to age of initial same-sex encounter. *Psychology of Women Quarterly, 8,* 293–307.

Vance, C. (1984). *Pleasure and danger: Exploring female sexuality.* Boston: Routledge and Kegan Paul.

van Geert, P., and H. Steenbeek. (2005). Explaining after by before: Basic aspects of a dynamic systems approach to the study of development. *Developmental Review, 25,* 408–442.

Vasquez, E. (1979). Homosexuality in the context of the Mexican American culture. In D. Kukel, ed., *Sexual issues in social work: Emerging concerns in education and practice* (pp. 131–147). Honolulu: University of Hawaii School of Social Work.

Veniegas, R. C., and T. D. Conley. (2000). Biological research on women's sexual orientations: Evaluating the scientific evidence. *Journal of Social Issues, 56,* 267–282.

Vetere, V. A. (1982). The role of friendship in the development and maintenance of lesbian love relationships. *Journal of Homosexuality, 8,* 51–65.

Von Sydow, K. (1995). Unconventional sexual relationships: Data about German women ages fifty to ninety-one years. *Archives of Sexual Behavior,* 24, 271–290.

Voracek, M., J. T. Manning, and I. Ponocny. (2005). Digit ratio (2D:4D) in homosexual and heterosexual men from Austria. *Archives of Sexual Behavior,* 34, 335–340.

Wallen, K. (1990). Desire and ability: Hormones and the regulation of female sexual behavior. *Neuroscience and Biobehavioral Review,* 14, 233–241.

———. (1995). The evolution of female sexual desire. In P. R. Abramson and S. D. Pinkerton, eds., *Sexual nature/sexual culture* (pp. 57–79). Chicago: University of Chicago Press.

Wallen, K., and W. A. Parsons. (1998). *Androgens may increase sexual motivation in ovariectomized estrogen-treated rhesus monkeys by increasing estrogen availability.* Paper presented at the Serono International Symposium on Biology of Menopause, Newport Beach, CA.

Wallen, K., and P. L. Tannenbaum. (1997). Hormonal modulation of sexual behavior and affiliation in rhesus monkeys. *Annals of the New York Academy of Sciences,* 807, 185–202.

Ward, D. A., and G. G. Kassebaum. (1965). *Women's prison: Sex and social structure.* Chicago: Aldine.

Weeks, J. (1986). *Sexuality.* New York: Tavistock Publications.

Weinberg, M. S., C. J. Williams, and D. W. Pryor. (1994). *Dual attraction: Understanding bisexuality.* New York: Oxford University Press.

West, D. J. (1977). *Homosexuality reexamined.* Minneapolis: University of Minnesota Press.

Whisman, V. (1993). Identity crisis: Who is a lesbian anyway? In A. Stein, ed., *Sisters, sexperts, queers: Beyond the lesbian nation* (pp. 47–60). New York: Penguin.

———. (1996). *Queer by choice: Lesbians, gay men, and the politics of identity.* New York: Routledge.

Whitam, F. L., and R. M. Mathy. (1986). *Male homosexuality in four societies: Brazil, Guatemala, the Philippines, and the United States.* New York: Praeger.

Williams, J. R., T. R. Insel, C. R. Harbaugh, and C. S. Carter. (1994). Oxytocin administered centrally facilitates formation of a partner preference in female prairie voles (Microtus ochrogaster). *Journal of Neuroendocrinology,* 6, 247–250.

Williams, T. J., M. E. Pepitone, S. E. Christensen, B. M. Cooke, A. D.

Huberman, N. J. Breedlove, T. J. Breedlove, C. L. Jordan, and S. M. Breedlove. (2000). Finger length patterns and human sexual orientation. *Nature,* 404, 455–456.

Williams, W. L. (1992). The relationship between male-male friendship and male-female marriage. In P. Nardi, ed., *Men's friendships* (pp. 187–200). Newbury Park, CA: Sage.

Wilson, E. (1998). *Neural geographies: Feminism and the microstructure of cognition.* New York: Routledge.

Wisniewski, A. B., and C. J. Migeon. (2002). Long-term perspectives for 46,XY patients affected by complete androgen insensitivity syndrome or congenital micropenis. *Seminars in Reproductive Medicine,* 20, 297–304.

Witt, D. M., J. T. Winslow, and T. R. Insel. (1992). Enhanced social interactions in rats following chronic, centrally infused oxytocin. *Pharmacology, Biochemistry and Behavior,* 43, 855–861.

Wooden, W. S., H. Kawasaki, and R. Mayeda. (1983). Lifestyles and identity maintenance among gay Japanese-American males. *Alternative Lifestyles,* 5, 236–243.

Wrangham, R. W. (1980). An ecological model of female-bonded primate groups. *Behavior,* 75, 262–300.

Young, L. J., and Wang, Z. (2004). The neurobiology of pair bonding. *Nature Neuroscience,* 7, 1048–1054.

Young, R. M., and I. H. Meyer. (2005). The trouble with "MSM" and "WSW": Erasure of the sexual-minority person in public health discourse. *American Journal of Public Health,* 95, 1144–1149.

Zinik, G. (1985). Identity conflict or adaptive flexibility? Bisexuality reconsidered. *Journal of Homosexuality,* 11, 7–19.

Zucker, K. J., R. Blanchard, and M. Siegelman. (2003). Birth order among homosexual men. *Psychological Reports,* 92, 117–118.

Zucker, K. J., and S. J. Bradley. (1995). *Gender identity disorder and psychosexual problems in children and adolescents.* New York: The Guilford Press.

Zucker, K. J., S. J. Bradley, G. Oliver, and J. Blake. (1996). Psychosexual development of women with congenital adrenal hyperplasia. *Hormones and Behavior,* 30, 300–318.

Notes

1. Will the Real Lesbians Please Stand Up?

1. Reviewed in Diamond, 2003b.
2. Reviewed in Mustanski, Chivers, and Bailey, 2002. Also see Black-wood and Wieringa, 2003, for an anthropological perspective on the invisibility of female same-sex sexuality.
3. Rahman and Wilson, 2003, p. 1371.
4. Kitzinger and Wilkinson, 1995, p. 95.
5. Rust, 2000e, p. 279.
6. Goode and Haber, 1977.
7. Blumstein and Schwartz, 1977, p. 173.
8. Sophie, 1986.
9. Klein, 1993.
10. Herdt, 1984.
11. Blackwood, 1985; Foucault, 1980; Kitzinger, 1987; Plummer, 1975; Richardson, 1984; Richardson and Hart, 1981.
12. Rich, 1980.
13. Weinberg, Williams, and Pryor, 1994, pp. 163, 164.
14. Elise, 1997, 1998; Freud, 1905/1962; Money, 1987, 1990; Zinik, 1985.
15. Golden, 1987, 1994, 1996.
16. Golden, 1996, p. 240. See also Cass, 1990.
17. Kitzinger and Wilkinson, 1995, p. 96.
18. Rust, 1992, 1993.
19. Shuster, 1987, pp. 61, 62.
20. Cass, 1990, p. 261.

21. Whisman, 1996. More recently, see also Otis and Skinner, 2004.
22. Baumeister, 2000.
23. Chivers et al., 2005; Laan, Sonderman, and Janssen, 1995.
24. Hyde and Durik, 2000.
25. Blumstein and Schwartz, 1990, p. 307.
26. Baumeister and Twenge, 2002; Laumann and Mahay, 2002; Nathanson, 1991; Tolman, Striepe, and Harmon, 2003; Vance, 1984.
27. Reviewed in Fine, 1988; Tolman and Diamond, 2001; Ussher, 1993.
28. Diamond, 2003a; Golden, 1996; Loewenstein, 1985.
29. Diamond, 1998, 2000a, 2000b, 2002, 2003a, 2005a, 2005b, 2005c.
30. For perspectives on these issues see Brookey, 2000; Gonsiorek, 2004; Stein, 1994; Tygart, 2000.
31. Drescher, 2002.
32. Bancroft, 1989; Cass, 1990; Money, 1988.
33. Gagnon and Simon, 1968; Garland, Morgan, and Beer, 2005; Herdt, 1984; Laumann et al., 1994; Murray, 2000.
34. Baumeister, 2000; Rosario et al., 2006.
35. See Diamond, 2003a, 2005c; Hollander, 2000; Rust, 2003.
36. Pratt, 1995, p. 11.

2. Gender Differences in Same-Sex Sexuality

1. Bogaert, 2005; Mustanski, Bailey, and Kaspar, 2002; Mustanski, Chivers, and Bailey, 2002; Rahman and Wilson, 2003.
2. M. Diamond, 1995; Fausto-Sterling, 2000; C. T. Halpern, 2003; Tolman and Diamond, 2001; Udry, 1990; Udry, Talbert, and Morris, 1986.
3. Greenberg and Bailey, 1993.
4. Mustanski, Bailey, and Kaspar, 2002, p. 127.
5. Hyde, 2005, p. 16; Bailey, Dunne, and Martin, 2000; Peplau, 2001; Peplau and Garnets, 2000; Peplau et al., 1999.
6. Mustanski, Bailey, and Kaspar, 2002.
7. Blumstein and Schwartz, 1977; Epstein, 1987; Richardson and Hart, 1981; Rust, 1993.
8. Butler, 1990; Foucault, 1980; Murray, 2000; K. Plummer, 1981; Richardson, 1987; Weeks, 1986.
9. D'Emilio, 1983; Foucault, 1980; Padgug, 1992.
10. Boswell, 1990a, 1990b; Katz, 1976; Whitam and Mathy, 1986.

11. Baumeister, Catanese, and Vohs, 2001.
12. Buss and Schmitt, 1993; Trivers, 1972.
13. Shackelford and Goetz, 2006; Shackelford and Pound, 2005; Shackelford, Pound, and Goetz, 2005; Small, 1993; Wallen, 1995.
14. Foucault, 1980.
15. Baumeister and Twenge, 2002; Coontz and Henderson, 1986; Fine, 1988; Groneman, 1994; Nathanson, 1991; Tolman, 2002; C. Vance, 1984.
16. Fine, 1988; Tolman and Diamond, 2001.
17. Heiman, 1975; Laumann, Paik, and Rosen, 1999. For feminist perspectives on this issue see Tiefer, 2001; Ussher, 1993.
18. Blackwood, 2000; Gagnon and Simon, 1973; Laumann and Mahay, 2002; Tolman and Diamond, 2001.
19. On this topic, see the eloquent writings of the feminist biologist Anne Fausto-Sterling, 2000.
20. Ehrhardt, 2000; Fausto-Sterling, 2000; Fuss, 1989; McClintock and Herdt, 1996; Tolman and Diamond, 2001; Udry, 1993, 1995; Wilson, 1998.
21. Grosz, 1994.
22. Money, 1990.
23. Bem, 1996; Fausto-Sterling, 2000, p. 20.
24. Dick et al., 2001; McGue, 1999.
25. Dick et al., 2001; Mustanski and Bailey, 2003.
26. Block, 1909; Forel, 1908; Krafft-Ebing, 1882.
27. Kinsey, Pomeroy, and Martin, 1948, p. 639.
28. Pattatucci and Hamer, 1995; Phillips and Over, 1995.
29. Mustanski, Chivers, and Bailey, 2002.
30. Mustanski, Chivers, and Bailey, 2002; Sell and Petrulio, 1996.
31. For examples, see Burr, 1996.
32. Bailey, Dunne, and Martin, 2000; Garofalo et al., 1999; Laumann et al., 1994.
33. For example, M. W. Ross et al., 2005; Young and Meyer, 2005.
34. Carballo-Dieguez and Dolezal, 1994; Laumann et al., 1994; Manalansan, 1996.
35. Savin-Williams and Diamond, 2000.
36. Hamer et al., 1993.
37. Hu et al., 1995.
38. See reviews of this research in Bailey, 1995; Rice et al., 1999.

39. Mustanski et al., 2005.
40. For reviews, see Bailey, 1995; Bailey and Pillard, 1995; Hyde, 2005; Mustanski et al., 2002; Rahman and Wilson, 2003; Risch, Squires-Wheeler, and Keats, 1993.
41. Bailey and Bell, 1993; Bailey and Benishay, 1993; Bailey and Pillard, 1991, 1995; Bailey et al., 1993.
42. Bailey et al., 2000; Kendler et al., 2000.
43. Reviewed in Hyde, 2005; Mustanski et al., 2002.
44. Bailey, 2003.
45. Bailey et al., 2000; Hershberger, 1997; Kendler et al., 2000; Kirk et al., 2000.
46. Kendler, Thornton, and Pedersen, 2000; Kendler et al., 2002; McGue, 1999.
47. Bell, Weinberg, and Hammersmith, 1981; M. Diamond, 1995; Downey and Friedman, 1998; Freund and Blanchard, 1983.
48. Bailey and Darwood, 1998; Green, 1987.
49. Golombok and Tasker, 1996.
50. Cohen-Bendahan, van de Beek, and Berenbaum, 2005; Colapinto, 2000; Imperato-McGinley et al., 1980; Imperato-McGinley et al., 1999; Meyer-Bahlburg, 2005; Reiner and Gearhart, 2004.
51. Herdt, 1984; Stoller and Herdt, 1985.
52. M. Diamond, 1993.
53. M. Diamond, 1995; Mustanski, Chivers, and Bailey, 2002.
54. Ehrhardt, 1985; L. Ellis and Ames, 1987; L. Ellis and Cole-Harding, 2001; Meyer-Bahlburg, 1979; Meyer-Bahlburg et al., 1995; Mustanski, Chivers, and Bailey, 2002; van Anders and Hampson, 2005.
55. Gooren, 1990a; Meyer-Bahlburg, 1979; Veniegas and Conley, 2000.
56. Reviewed in Baum, 2006; Gooren, 2006.
57. Caplan et al., 1997; D. F. Halpern and Ikier, 2002; Hines, 2004b; McGillicuddy-De Lisi and De Lisi, 2002.
58. Finder, Healy, and Zernike, 2006; Traub, 2005. For more discussion of this issue see Hines, 2004b.
59. McGillicuddy-De Lisi and De Lisi, 2002.
60. Baum, 2006; Collaer and Hines, 1995; Gooren, 2006; Hines, 2004a; Hines and Collaer, 1993; Reinisch and Sanders, 1992.
61. Reviewed in Baum, 2006; Gooren, 2006.
62. Ehrhardt, 1985; L. Ellis, 1996; L. Ellis and Cole-Harding, 2001;

Meyer-Bahlburg, 1979; Meyer-Bahlburg et al., 1995; Mustanski, Chivers, and Bailey, 2002; van Anders and Hampson, 2005.

63. Gooren, 1990b; Meyer-Bahlburg, 2002; Migeon and Wisniewski, 2000, 2003; Money, 1981; Money, 2002; Baum, 2006, p. 580.

64. Reviewed in Gooren, 2006; Mustanski, Chivers, and Bailey, 2002.

65. Reviewed in Baum, 2006.

66. Block, 1909; H. Ellis, 1933/1978; Forel, 1908; Krafft-Ebing, 1882.

67. Bailey, 2003; L. Ellis, 1996; Mustanski, Chivers, and Bailey, 2002; Rahman and Wilson, 2003.

68. New, Ghizzoni, and Speiser, 1996.

69. Berenbaum and Hines, 1992; Berenbaum and Resnick, 1997; Cohen-Bendahan, van de Beek, and Berenbaum, 2005.

70. Dittmann, 1997; Zucker et al., 1996.

71. As reviewed in Veniegas and Conley, 2000.

72. Ehrhardt, 1985; Ehrhardt et al., 1989; Meyer-Bahlburg et al., 1995.

73. Ghali et al., 2003; Hines, Ahmed, and Hughes, 2003; Meyer-Bahlburg, 1999; Minto et al., 2003; Wisniewski and Migeon, 2002.

74. Bailey, Willerman, and Parks, 1991; L. Ellis and Cole-Harding, 2001; Mustanski, Chivers, and Bailey, 2002.

75. Blanchard, 2001; Blanchard and Ellis, 2001; Purcell, Blanchard, and Zucker, 2000; Zucker, Blanchard, and Siegelman, 2003.

76. Blanchard, 1997; Blanchard and Ellis, 2001; Blanchard et al., 2002.

77. Bradley and Zucker, 1990; D. F. Halpern and Haviland, 1997; Lalumiere, Blanchard, and Zucker, 2000; Zucker et al., 1996.

78. LeVay, 1991.

79. Reviewed in Mustanski, Chivers, and Bailey, 2002.

80. Dörner, 1976.

81. Breedlove, Cooke, and Jordan, 1999; W. M. Brown, Hines, Fane, and Breedlove, 2002.

82. W. M. Brown, Finn, Cooke, and Breedlove, 2002; Hall and Love, 2003; Lippa, 2003; Manning et al., 2005; McFadden et al., 2005; McIntyre, 2003; Rahman, 2005; Robinson and Manning, 2000; Voracek, Manning, and Ponocny, 2005; T. J. Williams et al., 2000.

83. Reviewed in McFadden, 2002.

84. McFadden, Loehlin, and Pasanen, 1996; McFadden and Pasanen, 1998, 1999.

85. McFadden and Champlin, 2000.

86. H. Ellis, 1933/1978; Krafft-Ebing, 1882.

87. Bailey, 1996; Bailey et al., 2000; Bailey, Nothnagel, and Wolfe, 1995; Bailey and Oberschneider, 1997; Bailey and Zucker, 1995; Lippa, 2000.

88. Gottschalk, 2003; Herek, 1986; D. C. Plummer, 2001.

89. Bailey, 1995, 1996; Green, 1987; Zucker and Bradley, 1995.

90. Bailey, 1996; Bradley and Zucker, 1997; Corbett, 1998, 1999; Grellert, Newcomb, and Bentler, 1982; Phillips and Over, 1992, 1995.

91. West, 1977.

92. Peplau and Spalding, 2000.

93. Blanchard et al., 2002.

94. E. Ross and Rapp, 1981, p. 51.

95. Curtis, 1988; Penelope and Wolfe, 1989; Stanley and Wolfe, 1980.

96. Charbonneau and Lander, 1991; L. M. Diamond, 1998; L. M. Diamond and Savin-Williams, 2000; Dixon, 1984; Golden, 1987; Kitzinger and Wilkinson, 1995; Savin-Williams, 1998.

97. Chan, 1992; Collins, 1990; Espin, 1984; Hidalgo, 1984; Icard, 1986; Morales, 1992.

98. Espin, 1997; Savin-Williams, 1996.

99. Amaro, 1978; Chan, 1992; Espin, 1984, 1987; Hidalgo, 1984; Jayakar, 1994; Smith, 1997; Tremble, Schneider, and Appathurai, 1989; Vasquez, 1979; Wooden, Kawasaki, and Mayeda, 1983.

100. Carrier, 1989; Parker, 1989; Ramos, 1994.

101. Clarke, 1983; Collins, 1990; De Monteflores, 1986; Gomez and Smith, 1990; Greene, 1986; Icard, 1986; Mays and Cochran, 1988.

102. Carballo-Dieguez, 1989; Carballo-Dieguez and Dolezal, 1994; Clarke, 1983; De Monteflores, 1986; Gomez and Smith, 1990; Icard, 1986; Mays and Cochran, 1988; Mays, Cochran, and Rhue, 1993; Vasquez, 1979.

103. Bailey, 1996; Bailey and Zucker, 1995; Bell and Weinberg, 1978; Chapman and Brannock, 1987; L. M. Diamond, 1998; Herdt and Boxer, 1993; Isay, 1989; Savin-Williams, 1990, 1998; Sears, 1989; Troiden, 1988; Weinberg, Williams, and Pryor, 1994.

104. Blumstein and Schwartz, 1990; L. M. Diamond, 2000a, 2002, 2006; Gramick, 1984; Hedblom, 1973; Ponse, 1978; Rose, Zand, and Cimi, 1993; Schafer, 1977; B. K. Vance and Green, 1984; Vetere, 1982; Weinberg, Williams, and Pryor, 1994.

105. Blumstein and Schwartz, 1990; Cass, 1990; Cooper, 1990; Esterberg,

1994; Nichols, 1990; Ponse, 1984; Rust, 1993, 1995; Sears, 1989; Silber, 1990.

106. Bell and Weinberg, 1978; Chapman and Brannock, 1987; Dixon, 1984, 1985; Esterberg, 1994; Golden, 1987, 1994, 1996; Hencken, 1984; Hunnisett, 1986; Rust, 1992; Sophie, 1986; Weinberg, Williams, and Pryor, 1994; Whisman, 1996.
107. Kitzinger and Wilkinson, 1995.
108. Fine, 1988; Kitzinger and Wilkinson, 1995; Rust, 1993; Tolman and Diamond, 2001.
109. Blumstein and Schwartz, 1990; Boxer and Cohler, 1989; K. Plummer, 1995.
110. Bergler, 1954; Defries, 1976; Goode and Haber, 1977; Whisman, 1993.

3. Sexual Fluidity in Action

1. Blumstein and Schwartz, 1977; Pattatucci and Hamer, 1995; Stokes, Damon, and McKirnan, 1997; Stokes, McKirnan, and Burzette, 1993; Weinberg, Williams, and Pryor, 1994.
2. I analyzed the qualitative portions of the interview using a technique called thematic analysis, in which transcripts are read for core, recurring themes; the themes are narrowed down according to the aims of the research question; and independent raters are trained to code the transcripts for the occurrence of these themes. For more detail on this process, see Ryan and Bernard, 2003.
3. The methodologically inclined will be interested to know that my percentage measure proved to have excellent test-retest reliability. This means that when individuals are given this measure at different testing sessions, around two weeks apart, they give the same responses both times. This is important because it means that when individuals do give notably *different* responses over longer periods, we can safely conclude that it is not a measurement "fluke," and that some sort of change has occurred.
4. Rust, 1992.
5. Firestein, 1996; Rust, 1995, 2000d.
6. Fox, 1995; Rust, 1993.
7. Carey, 2005; Leland, 1995.
8. McIntosh, 1968.

9. For more examples see Weinberg, Williams, and Pryor, 1994.

10. Rust, 1993.

11. Rosario et al., 1996; Savin-Williams, 1998; Savin-Williams and Diamond, 2000.

12. Bell, Weinberg, and Hammersmith, 1981; Bergler, 1954; Burch, 1993; Ettore, 1980; Money, 1988; Ponse, 1978.

13. Bell, Weinberg, and Hammersmith, 1981, pp. 200–201.

14. Burch, 1993; Rust, 1995.

15. Bell, Weinberg, and Hammersmith, 1981; Fox, 1995; Pattatucci and Hamer, 1995; Phillips and Over, 1992, 1995; Rust, 1992; Weinberg, Williams, and Pryor, 1994.

16. Kirkpatrick, 2000.

17. Cass, 1979; Coleman, 1981/1982; Lee, 1977; Minton and McDonald, 1983; Mohr and Fassinger, 2000; Troiden, 1979.

18. Hollander, 2000; Savin-Williams, 2005.

19. Weinberg, Williams, and Pryor, 1994, p. 292.

20. Davis, 1999; Kyrakanos, 1998; Rimer, 1993.

4. Nonexclusive Attractions and Behaviors

1. For the most comprehensive overview of the diverse range of current and historical views of bisexuality, see Paula Rodriguez Rust's landmark anthology, *Bisexuality in the United States* (2000d), which contains both reprinted articles by a variety of scholars as well as Rust's own integrative commentaries.

2. Rust, 1995.

3. Rust, 2000f.

4. Savin-Williams, 2005.

5. Rust, 1995.

6. Reviewed in Rust, 1995.

7. Laumann et al., 1994.

8. Garofalo et al., 1999; Kirk et al., 2000; Mosher, Chandra, and Jones, 2005; Remafedi et al., 1992.

9. Rich, 1980.

10. Chivers et al., 2005.

11. Heiman, 1975.

12. Laan, Sonderman, and Janssen, 1995.

13. Rieger, Bailey, and Chivers, 2005.

14. Lippa, 2006.
15. For example, Dickerson and Kemeny, 2004.
16. Fine, 1988; Tolman, 2002; Tolman and Diamond, 2001; Udry, Talbert, and Morris, 1986.
17. Laumann et al., 1994.
18. Cassingham and O'Neil, 1993; Charbonneau and Lander, 1991; Kitzinger and Wilkinson, 1995.
19. Rust, 1992.
20. Cochran and Mays, 1988; San Francisco Department of Public Health (SFDPH), 1993.
21. Gagnon, 1990; Pillard, 1990.
22. Rust, 1992.
23. Rust, 1992, p. 380.
24. Clausen, 1999; Near, 1991.
25. Cass, 1990; Kinsey et al., 1953.
26. Blumstein and Schwartz, 1990; Klein, 1993; Rust, 1993, 2000b, 2000c.
27. For example, see Bode, 1976; Coons, 1972; MacInnes, 1973; Ross and Paul, 1992; Weinberg, Williams, and Pryor, 1994.
28. With some exceptions, such as Tolman, 2002.
29. Jacobellis v. Ohio, 378 U.S. 184, 197 (1964).
30. Laumann and Mahay, 2002, p. 44.
31. Money, 1980, 1987.
32. Blumstein and Schwartz, 1977; Diamond, 1998; Klein, 1993; MacDonald, 1981; Stokes, Miller, and Mundhenk, 1998; Taywaditep and Stokes, 1998; Weinberg, Williams, and Pryor, 1994.
33. Ross and Paul, 1992; Rust, 2000b; Weinberg, Williams, and Pryor, 1994.
34. Klein, 1993; Zinik, 1985.
35. Elise, 1997, 1998; Freud (1905/1962); Money, 1987, 1990; Zinik, 1985.
36. Baumeister, 2000; Chivers et al., 2005; Lippa, 2006.

5. Change in Sexual Attractions

1. See the discussions of this topic on the website for Concerned Women for America: http://www.cultureandfamily.org/articledisplay.asp?id=5458anddepartment=CFIandcategoryid=papers.

2. A view endorsed by the American Psychological Association: http://www.apa.org/topics/orientation.html.

3. See http://www.nickyee.com/ponder/gaygene.html.

4. For a radical view on these issues, see www.queerbychoice.com/.

5. See Beckett et al., 1992; Drescher, 2002; Drescher and Zucker, 2006; Gonsiorek, 2004; Haldeman, 1994; Halpert, 2000; Morrow and Beckstead, 2004; Nicolosi, Byrd, and Potts, 2000; Stein, 1996.

6. See http://www.psychologymatters.org/hooker.html.

7. See http://www.psych.org/psych_pract/copptherapyaddendum83100.cfm; Bright, 2004; Drescher and Zucker, 2006.

8. As in Drescher and Zucker, 2006.

9. Schroeder and Shidlo, 2001.

10. Baumeister, 2000; Baumeister, Catanese, and Vohs, 2001; Cass, 1990.

11. Laumann, Paik, and Rosen, 1999.

12. Tiefer, Hall, and Tavris, 2002; Ussher, 1993; Leiblum and Rosen, 1988b, 2000.

13. Udry, 1990; Wallen, 1990, 1995.

14. Chivers et al., 2005; Rieger, Bailey, and Chivers, 2005.

15. Baumeister, 2000.

16. Kinsey, Pomeroy, and Martin, 1948; Money, 1988.

17. Blumstein and Schwartz, 1977; Cassingham and O'Neil, 1993; Charbonneau and Lander, 1991; Kitzinger and Wilkinson, 1995; Loewenstein, 1985; Saghir and Robins, 1973.

18. Saghir and Robins, 1973.

19. Loewenstein, 1985, p. 122.

20. Kitzinger, 1995, p. 100.

21. Golden, 1987, 1994, 1996.

22. Weinberg, Williams, and Pryor, 1994.

23. Stokes, Damon, and McKirnan, 1997; Stokes, McKirnan, and Burzette, 1993.

24. Pattatucci and Hamer, 1995.

25. Weinberg, Williams, and Pryor, 1994.

6. Attractions to "the Person, Not the Gender"

1. Buss, 1989.

2. Reviewed in Hazan and Diamond, 2000.

3. Blumstein and Schwartz, 1990; Cass, 1990; Cassingham and O'Neil, 1993; Golden, 1996; Whisman, 1996.
4. Blumstein and Schwartz, 1990, p. 346.
5. Blumstein and Schwartz, 1990, p. 348.
6. Weinberg, Williams, and Pryor, 1994.
7. Jensen, 1999; Stanley and Wolfe, 1980.
8. Reviewed in Rust, 2000b.
9. Ross and Paul, 1992, advanced a similar notion specifically with respect to bisexual individuals.
10. Savin-Williams, 2005.
11. Brown, 1995.
12. Kinsey, Pomeroy, and Martin, 1948.
13. Gagnon, 1990, p. 199.
14. Bailey, 1996; Diamond, 2002; Gottschalk, 2003; Money, 1987.
15. Bornstein, 1994; Cole et al., 2000; Feinberg, 1996; Martin and Yonkin, 2006; Roen, 2002; Straub and Epstein, 1991.
16. Reviewed in Bailey, 1996.

7. How Does Fluidity Work?

1. Regan and Berscheid, 1995, p. 346.
2. Beach, 1976; Hrdy, 1987; Wallen, 1995.
3. Bancroft, 1989; Baumeister, 2000; Fisher, 1998; Wallen, 1995.
4. Beach, 1976.
5. See reviews in Bancroft, 1978; Udry, 1988.
6. Alexander and Sherwin, 1993; Arver et al., 1996; Davidson, Camargo, and Smith, 1979; Kwan et al., 1983; Luisi and Franchi, 1980; O'Carroll, Shapiro, and Bancroft, 1985; Salmimies et al., 1982; Sarrel, Dobay, and Wiita, 1998; Schiavi et al., 1997; Sherwin and Gelfand, 1987; Sherwin, Gelfand, and Brender, 1985; Skakkebaek et al., 1981.
7. Adams, Gold, and Burt, 1978; Judd and Yen, 1973; Stanislaw and Rice, 1988.
8. Abramson, Repczynski, and Merrill, 1976; Griffith and Walker, 1975; Slob, Ernste, and van der Werff ten Bosch, 1991.
9. Bancroft et al., 1974; Kwan et al., 1983.
10. Beck, Bozman, and Qualtrough, 1991; Blumstein and Schwartz,

1983; Byers and Heinlein, 1989; Ellis and Symons, 1990; Julien et al., 1992; Knoth, Boyd, and Singer, 1988; Laumann et al., 1994; Leitenberg and Henning, 1995; O'Sullivan and Byers, 1992.

11. Baumeister, Catanese, and Vohs, 2001.

12. Reviewed in Wallen, 1995.

13. Fine, 1988; Gagnon and Simon, 1973; Reiss, 1986; Richgels, 1992; Tolman, 1991, 2002; Tolman and Diamond, 2001.

14. Baumeister, 2000.

15. Reviewed by Schlegel and Barry, 1991.

16. Herdt, 1984; Murray, 2000.

17. Bell, Weinberg, and Hammersmith, 1981; Gagnon and Simon, 1968; Garland, Morgan, and Beer, 2005; Hensley and Tewksbury, 2002; Hensley et al., 2002; Money, 1988; Rust, 2000a; Ward and Kassebaum, 1965.

18. L. M. Diamond, 2003a; Diamond, 2005; Rust, 1992.

19. Bergler, 1954.

20. Cass, 1990; Money, 1988.

21. Kinsey, Pomeroy, and Martin, 1948; Pattatucci and Hamer, 1995; Russell and Consolacion, 2003; Sell and Petrulio, 1996.

22. Fisher, 1998; Hatfield, 1987; Tennov, 1979.

23. Tennov, 1979.

24. Hatfield et al., 1988.

25. Udry, 1990; Udry and Billy, 1987; Udry, Talbert, and Morris, 1986.

26. Reviewed in Curtis and Wang, 2003; Emanuele et al., 2006.

27. Bartels and Zeki, 2000.

28. A. Aron et al., 2005.

29. Arnow et al., 2002; Redoute et al., 2000.

30. Blackwood, 1985; Faderman, 1981; Gay, 1985; Hansen, 1992; Nardi, 1992; Sahli, 1979; Smith-Rosenberg, 1975; W. L. Williams, 1992.

31. Parkman, 1969; W. L. Williams, 1992.

32. Brain, 1976; Firth, 1967; Malinowski, 1929; Mead, 1943; Reina, 1966.

33. Brain, 1976, pp. 39–40.

34. Streitmatter, 1998.

35. Streitmatter, 1998, p. 19.

36. Kogan, 2006.

37. Hill, 1993; O'Connor, 1992.

38. D'Emilio and Freedman, 1988; Faderman, 1981; Nardi, 1992.

39. Faderman, 1981.

40. Faderman, 1993; Smith-Rosenberg, 1975.
41. Sahli, 1979, p. 22.
42. Faderman, 1993, p. 35.
43. O'Connor, 1992.
44. Diamond, 2000; Rothblum, 1993; Von Sydow, 1995.
45. Crumpacker and Vander Haegen, 1993; Diamond, 2000.
46. Rubin, 1985; Oliker, 1989, p. 5.
47. Von Sydow, 1995, p. 288.
48. Espin, 1993, p. 207.
49. Rosenbloom, 2005.
50. Nardi, 1992; W. L. Williams, 1992.
51. Derlega et al., 1989.
52. See Mellen, 1982.
53. Bowlby, 1958, 1973a, 1973b, 1973c, 1979, 1980, 1982.
54. Hazan and Shaver, 1987, 1994.
55. Bowlby, 1958, 1973b, 1979, 1980, 1982.
56. Ainsworth et al., 1978.
57. Graves and Hennessy, 2000; Hofer, 1987; Hoffman et al., 1995; Suomi, 1999.
58. Gould and Vrba, 1982.
59. Panksepp, 1998.
60. Gould and Lewontin, 1979; Gould and Vrba, 1982.
61. Lim and Young, 2006.
62. Carter, 1998.
63. Carter, Lederhendler, and Kirkpatrick, 1999; E. E. Nelson and Panksepp, 1996; C. A. Pedersen et al., 1994; Uvnäs-Moberg, 1994.
64. Insel, 1997.
65. E. E. Nelson and Panksepp, 1996; E. E. Nelson and Panksepp, 1998; Popik, Vetulani, and van Ree, 1992; Uvnäs-Moberg, 1998; J. R. Williams et al., 1994.
66. Reviewed in Bartz and Hollander, 2006; Carter and Altemus, 1997; Carter and DeVries, 1999; Knox and Uvnäs-Moberg, 1998; Lim and Young, 2006; Taylor, Dickerson, and Klein, 2002; Taylor et al., 2000; Uvnäs-Moberg, 1998.
67. Henry and Wang, 1998; Knox and Uvnäs-Moberg, 1998; Light, Grewen, and Amico, 2005; Taylor et al., 2002; Uvnäs-Moberg, 1998, 2004.
68. Carter et al., 1999; Galef and Kaner, 1980; E. E. Nelson and Panksepp, 1996; E. E. Nelson and Panksepp, 1998.

69. Field, 1998; Knox and Uvnäs-Moberg, 1998; Uvnäs-Moberg et al., 1993; Witt, Winslow, and Insel, 1992.
70. Reviewed in Pedersen et al., 2005.
71. Cho et al., 1999; Insel and Hulihan, 1995; J. R. Williams et al., 1994.
72. Kirsch et al., 2005; Kosfeld et al., 2005; Light et al., 2005; R. A. Turner et al., 1999; R. A. Turner et al., 2002.
73. Young and Wang, 2004.
74. Anderson-Hunt and Dennerstein, 1995; Carmichael et al., 1994; K. C. Light et al., 2000; K. C. Light et al., 2004; M. M. McCarthy and Altemus, 1997; Pickering, 2003; Salonia et al., 2005; R. A. Turner et al., 1999; R. A. Turner et al., 2002; Uckert et al., 2003; Uvnäs-Moberg and Eriksson, 1996.
75. Bagdy and Arato, 1998; Depue and Morrone-Strupinsky, 2005; Insel and Winslow, 1998; Panksepp, 1998; Panksepp, Knutson, and Pruitt, 1997; Schwarzberg et al., 1981.
76. A. P. Aron et al., 1989; Hazan and Diamond, 2000.
77. Gay, 1985; Hansen, 1992; Katz, 1976; Richards, 1987; Rotundo, 1989; Sahli, 1979; Smith-Rosenberg, 1975.
78. D'Emilio and Freedman, 1988; Pleck and Pleck, 1980; Richards, 1987; Smith-Rosenberg, 1975.
79. Von Sydow, 1995, p. 288.
80. Carter and Keverne, 2002; S. E. Taylor et al., 2000; Wallen and Tannenbaum, 1997; Wrangham, 1980.
81. Baldwin, 1985; Dunbar, 1996; Wallen and Tannenbaum, 1997.
82. Keverne, Nevison, and Martel, 1999.
83. DeVries, Johnson, and Carter, 1997.
84. DeVries and Carter, 1999.
85. Mason and Mendoza, 1998.
86. Argiolas et al., 1987; Arletti and Bertolini, 1985; Caldwell, 2002; Caldwell, Prange, and Pedersen, 1986; Carmichael et al., 1994; Floody, Cooper, and Albers, 1998; Gorzalka and Lester, 1987; Riley, 1988.
87. Gagnon and Simon, 1973; Hyde and Durik, 2000.
88. Hyde and Durik, 2000; Leiblum and Rosen, 1988.
89. Caldwell et al., 1994; Carter, 1992; Hiller, 2004; M. M. McCarthy, Kow, and Pfaff, 1992.
90. De Wied, Diamant, and Fodor, 1993; Panksepp, 1998.

91. Blackwood, 1985, 2000; Fine, 1988; Tolman, 2002; Tolman and Diamond, 2001; Ussher and Baker, 1993; C. Vance, 1984.
92. Similar to arguments made by Hiller, 2004.

8. Implications of Female Sexual Fluidity

1. D. Carter, 2005; D'Emilio, 1983.
2. For example Faderman, 1991.
3. Loftus, 2001.
4. National Gay, Lesbian, and Bisexual Task Force, 2000.
5. Blumstein and Schwartz, 1990; Cass, 1990; DeCecco and Shively, 1984; Golden, 1987; Kitzinger, 1987; Kitzinger and Wilkinson, 1995; Peplau and Cochran, 1990; Peplau and Garnets, 2000; Peplau et al., 1999; Rust, 1993.
6. Fogel, 1993; Fogel and Thelen, 1987; Thelen, Kelso, and Fogel, 1987; Thelen and Smith, 1994.
7. Reviewed in Fausto-Sterling, 2000.
8. Christman, 2002; Elman, 1995; Fogel et al., 1992; Fogel and Thelen, 1987; Gilden, 1991; Granic and Patterson, 2006; Izard et al., 2000; Lewis, 2000; Lewis et al., 2004; Magai and McFadden, 1995; Read and Miller, 2002; Steenbeek and van Geert, 2005; Thelen and Smith, 1994; Tucker et al., 2005.
9. Fausto-Sterling, 2000.
10. Savin-Williams and Diamond, 2004; Tolman and Diamond, 2001; Udry, 1990.
11. See Granic, 2005; Partridge, 2005; Tolman and Diamond, 2001.
12. Coleman and Watson, 2000; Lewis, 1995, 2000; Sameroff, 1975.
13. Thelen, 2005, pp. 259–260.
14. Fogel, 1993.
15. Erlhagen and Schöner, 2002; Schutte and Spencer, 2002; van Geert and Steenbeek, 2005.
16. Pew Research Center for the People and the Press, 2006.
17. Reviewed in Patterson, 2003.
18. Federal Bureau of Investigation, 2004; Safe Schools Coalition of Washington, 1999.
19. Knight, 2005.
20. Byrd, 2006.
21. Drescher, 2002.

22. Spitzer, 2003.
23. Beckstead, 2006, p. 79.
24. Murray, 2000.
25. Savin-Williams, 2005.
26. Kinsey, Pomeroy, and Martin, 1948, p. 639.
27. Rust, 2006.
28. Halsam and Levy, 2006.
29. Bem, 1993; Gilligan, 1982; Harding, 1991.
30. Hamilton College and Zogby International, 2001.
31. *In Style* magazine, December 2006, p. 141.
32. Savin-Williams, 2005, p. 1.

Acknowledgments

Ritch Savin-Williams has been by my side as a trusted mentor, colleague, and friend from the very first day I decided that I wanted to interview a whole bunch of women and follow them for as long as possible. He must have known that it would be pointless to try to talk me out of it, and so instead he became my most steadfast and stalwart supporter, as he remains to this day. I have learned so much from him and cannot thank him enough.

I am also deeply grateful to a number of senior colleagues who have been generous with their support and guidance, and who consistently reassured me that this project was worthwhile: Cindy Hazan, Carla Golden, Deb Tolman, and Anne Peplau.

I have been blessed by a loyal army of transcribers over the years, all of them undergraduates at the University of Utah, who have plowed through hundreds of hours of audiotape, faithfully representing each woman's story in perfect detail. I'm also grateful to the Society for the Scientific Study of Sexuality and the Society for the Psychological Study of Social Issues for providing grants to support this effort.

Elizabeth Knoll, my editor at Harvard, shared my vision for this book from the very beginning of the process, and her guidance was pitch-perfect.

Mom, Dad, Nicole, Bob, Aidan, and Chloe: I don't know very many people with a family as extraordinarily loving as mine. Your love and support have made all my successes possible and all my setbacks easier to bear. And a special thanks goes to Marshall, with whom I talked through many of the ideas in this book during long summer runs in the hills above Griffith Park.

Most important, I thank my partner, soulmate, and wife, Judi. There is no way I could have done this without you.

Index